W9-AJU-975

URSULA BUCHAN
GARDENING
for *PLEASURE*

URSULA BUCHAN

GARDENING for PLEASURE

A Practical Guide to the Essential Skills

CONRAN OCTOPUS

This book is dedicated to the memory of Barbara Buchan, my mother,
a fine gardener who first taught me the point of it all.

First published in 1996 by Conran Octopus Limited, 37 Shelton Street, London
WC2H 9HN

Text copyright © 1996 Ursula Buchan
Design and layout copyright © 1996 Conran Octopus Limited

The right of Ursula Buchan to be identified as the Author of this Work has been
asserted by her in accordance with the Copyright, Designs and Patents Act 1988.

All rights reserved. No part of this book may be reproduced, stored in a retrieval
system, or transmitted in any form or by means, electronic, electrostatic, magnetic
tape, mechanical, photocopying, recording or otherwise, without the prior
permission in writing of the Publisher.

COMMISSIONING EDITOR Sarah Pearce
PROJECT EDITOR Helen Ridge
COPY EDITOR Caroline Taylor
ART EDITOR Sue Storey
PICTURE RESEARCH Julia Pashley
PRODUCTION Julia Golding
VISUALIZER Lesley Craig
ILLUSTRATOR Vanessa Luff

ISBN 1-85029-775-4

Printed in Hong Kong

CONTENTS

INTRODUCTION 7

INTRODUCTION

The theory and practice of gardening must be learned. Severed as most of us are from ancient oral tradition, and usually oblivious to the practical and aesthetic dimensions of the garden in childhood, gardening has to be consciously learned rather than unconsciously absorbed. This should not distress us unduly, for most keen gardeners would maintain that hopeful travelling is quite as good as arriving. It is in an attempt to satisfy the desire for essential practical knowledge on the part of all hopeful, would-be gardeners, without filling their breasts either with alarm or despondency, that I have written this book.

My purpose is to explain why and how certain jobs are done, but to reduce the litany of garden tasks to a manageable selection that will be helpful to people who wish to do their very best for their gardens but who, because of the ties of work or children, cannot commit themselves to daily care. These are the people for whom all those lovely little perfectionist jobs, like rigging up protective newspaper shelters around seedlings to shield them from the sun's rays, are just not possible. This book is for the potentially passionate gardener, always short of time yet keen to pursue her interest with energy and dedication, who wishes to know how to grow plants well. (And when I say 'her', I do, of course, mean 'his' as well.) For such people, this book will act as an informative and, I hope, readable introduction.

But it is also for those who like the idea of gardening, but may not yet have done a great deal, like the person who is well-disposed towards the Church, but whose activities have so far been restricted to buying raffle tickets for the church bazaar. This book is intended to

This effect may look sophisticated, but its success is based on simple gardening principles. Nothing here is difficult to grow or put together; all that is needed is a certain vigilance and a pair of stout gloves!

coax these people out of their agnosticism and give them faith. Most important, it is intended to encourage people to have confidence in themselves, for the most powerful brake on enthusiasm is the feeling that you cannot do it and that you are left out of the magic circle of *cognoscenti*, whose overheard conversation is all but incomprehensible to you.

This book is a highly personal account, and it would be astonishing if my experiences always accorded with those of other gardeners. It is, after all, perfectly possible for diametrically opposite but still valid points of view to be held (usually vehemently) on almost every gardening subject. Nor is this, nor is it intended to be, a comprehensive reference book.

Paradoxically, I do not wish to compromise with excellence. I am not interested in gardening as housework out-of-doors, an activity designed merely to keep the garden acceptably tidy. The garden is not for me a place primarily to lounge, sunbathe, play or cook gristly bits of meat on sticks. Gardening is not for me a 'leisure' pursuit like lawn badminton, but a solace, a respite from an often alarming world, and an activity with profound and (usually) satisfying consequences. Gardening, especially the growing of plants, is my passion, so this book is written for other gardeners, and for potential converts, not for non-gardeners who happen to own gardens. If you wish for a way of avoiding work or involvement, this book is not for you.

To succeed as a gardener does not depend solely on reading sufficient information on the subject. You must also establish honestly your own capabilities, limitations and, most important, tolerances. It is no good pretending that the inevitably untidy 'romantic' garden is for you if you become apoplectic when your children leave their toys lying about in the house, and suicidal if anyone puts odd scraps of paper on your beautifully clear desk. If you are tidy-minded, you will want a tidy garden, and that

means spending much time cutting the edges, trimming back the shrubs, and hoeing, hoeing, hoeing. If, on the other hand, you are naturally scruffy, however much you may be anxious to impress on your neighbours how orderly you are, the state of your tool shed (if you are foolish enough to let them inside) is bound to give the game away. Do not fight your instincts too hard for, unfortunately, gardens, like houses, become the physical manifestations of personality, so that you will be unable for long to disguise your inclinations.

Be honest about what you want out of the garden, and about how much time you have. This is a great deal easier said than done, for although you may fool yourself that you have one full day a week to devote to it, in reality that precious 'hard space' will probably either be

This is the kind of spring garden we all like to see; with a little practical knowledge, it is perfectly easy to achieve.

nibbled into by the exigent demands of family or work, or scotched by the weather. It is wiser to work out a schedule and halve it; you will be better pleased with yourself for achieving the modest score you aimed at, than if, in your ambition, you miss the target altogether.

Don't forget to include the 'nostalgia factor'. This is very important for all those (about half the population, including myself) who wish to return to the good old days when the potatoes tasted better, the garden was full of the double sweet rocket, Father only used one spray, mixed up in a bucket, for the roses, and the sun seemed always to be shining.... If you are one of these, take into account that this will mean using only a weedkiller like sodium chlorate, which will creep sideways from the path into the flower beds and kill your plants, trimming your hedges with shears, and mowing your lawn with a hand mower. You may, on second thoughts, find the information contained in this book about newer equipment and more modern means of weed and pest control useful, even if you condescend to follow the advice only under protest.

Try also to be relaxed about your achievements, or lack of them. Gardening may sometimes appear to be a nightmare running race in which everyone else disappears out of sight, leaving you rooted to the spot with legs too heavy to move, but it is not in fact a competition. More than anything, gardening is to be enjoyed, not viewed as a self-inflicted but necessary hardship to be endured for one's ultimate benefit, like going on a diet or plucking one's eyebrows.

Finally, on no account be intimidated by experts. Your experience is just as valid as theirs, and you will get to know your garden and its vagaries better than anyone else. Experts can be very withering and god-like in their judgements, but so don't let them get away with it. If their experience does not accord with yours, back your judgement against theirs. And that goes for anything I say, too.

The point of gardening is not a competition with your friends or neighbours, nor is it to build up your character. It is for your own enjoyment, and so, in the end, you should suit yourself.

1

THE FIRST STEPS

THE FIRST EXPERIENCE OF GARDENING THAT MOST OF US HAVE IS WHEN WE MOVE INTO OUR FIRST HOUSE. FEW OF US ARE CONSCIOUS OF ANYTHING HORTICULTURAL (APART FROM THE NEGATIVE AWARENESS AS CHILDREN THAT GARDENING IS AN OCCUPATION THAT DISTRACTS PARENTS' ATTENTION FROM THE ALL-IMPORTANT SUBJECT OF OURSELVES) UNTIL WE BUY A HOUSE AND THE GARDEN THAT, WILLY-NILLY, GOES WITH IT.

WHAT WE ARE TOLD, WHAT WE READ, AND WHAT WE SEE, ESPECIALLY IN THE FIRST FEW FORMATIVE MONTHS, WILL DETERMINE WHAT SORT OF GARDENER WE BECOME, OR EVEN IF WE BECOME ONE AT ALL. BUT BEFORE WE DEVELOP A CLOSE ATTACHMENT TO EPIPHYTIC ORCHIDS, OR ATTEMPT TO GROW GIANT ONIONS, THERE WILL INEVITABLY BE SOME GENERAL THINGS THAT WE WILL NEED TO DO TO OUR GARDEN, AND FIRST AMONG THESE IS TO DRAW UP SOME KIND OF PLAN.

This is the kind of garden to which, I would guess, most people would aspire. It is well laid out, being a good balance of simple but effective 'hard' and 'soft' features, and full of flower and foliage, but there is also space for people. Yet, with a little care and thought, this garden is easily attainable, even by those who have little previous experience.

New gardens

If you move into a newly built house you will, in all probability, have virtually no garden. There may be an old apple tree left marooned in a sea of mud by a more than usually thoughtful builder, but that is likely to be all. At least you do not have the problem of working your plan around existing plants or what gardeners call 'hard landscaping', or having to move plants when, like people, they are too old to do so without complaint. You have a fresh slate on which to draw a picture.

I suggest you first take plenty of photographs of the house and 'garden'. On these you will be able to scribble with a felt pen the shapes of shrubs and trees you would like to introduce. Many people find this easier than to imagine the result from a two-dimensional ground plan, although a plan is essential for

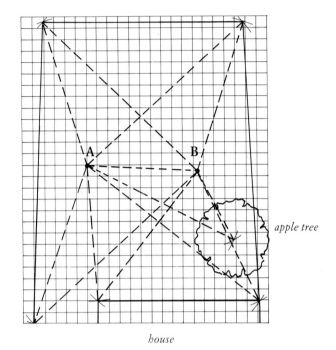

apple tree

house

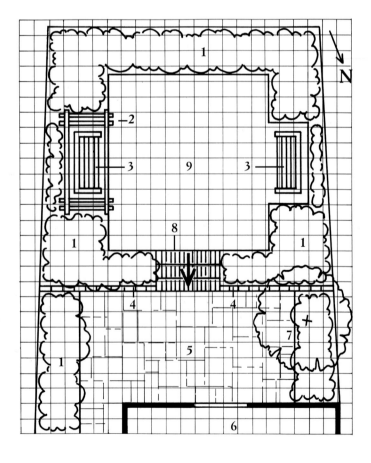

The easiest way to measure your garden accurately is to select two fixed points – A and B (see above). Measure from A to one corner of the garden and then from B to the same corner. Repeat for the remaining corners and for any existing features, such as 'apple tree' and 'house' as well as window positions, sight lines and aspect (i.e. which way is North). Using a scale ruler, make a simple 'triangulation' by marking down points A and B on tracing paper, then, with a pair of compasses, make an arc of the appropriate radius from both points to one corner of the garden. Where the arcs intersect is the position of the corner. Repeat this for all the corners and features in the garden. Transfer the plan onto graph paper and rough out your design ideas on tracing paper laid on top (see left).

1 Border
2 Pergola
3 Bench
4 Brick wall
5 Paved area

6 House
7 Apple tree
8 Steps
9 Raised lawn

Here is an obviously carefully planned garden. Although the shrubs against the fence pronounce it as quite new, it already looks well established.

plotting the shape of borders and marking out major features, as well as for working out how many plants are required.

To create a plan, you must first measure your garden and then draw up the plan to scale. To do this, borrow or buy a 30m (100ft) measuring tape and measure the garden (back and front separately) in different directions from two fixed points to which you can always refer (A and B in the diagram, left) – these could be bamboo canes stuck in the ground, for example, or the corners of the house. However square your garden looks, it is unlikely to be so.

Next, draw the shape of the garden on an A3 or A2 sheet of tracing paper, using a pair of compasses to measure and mark the distance from the fixed points, and a scale ruler with 1:100 and 1:50 measurements on it. 1:100 is the right scale for the outline of borders and features, and 1:50 for planting plans. Finally, transfer this ground plan onto graph paper and use tracing paper for roughing out ideas on top.

It is not within the scope of this book to tell you how to design your garden, but it is important to consider how you and your family will want to use the garden, both now and in the future, before you settle on the final plan.

There are then some basic things to do. If your garden needs some shelter, which gardens nearly always do, you should, at the first appropriate moment, fence it in or plant a hedge or build some walls. If you have less than 30cm (12in) of top-soil, you should order some from a reliable source, and spread it evenly over the garden. You will need much more than you think: about a tonne (ton) for every 8sq m (10sq yd) if you have no top-soil at all. You should then mark out what garden designers call 'the hard landscape', that is, paving, paths, steps, walls, ornamental ponds and fountains. Next, decide where the borders and lawn are to be; you can mark these out with canes and string. New borders will need to be well-dug and manured (see page 66); if you have any reason to suspect that there are perennial weeds in the soil, wait until the spring and 'weedkill' it at least twice, when the weeds are growing vigorously, using glyphosate (see page 179).

Existing gardens

If there is already an established garden attached to your newly acquired house it is *most* unlikely to be in immaculate condition. For one thing, there will have been a hiatus between the house being put up for sale, and your moving in, and it is a rare person who will continue to work energetically in a garden that no longer properly belongs to her.

Even if they are still visible amongst the weeds, you will be a fortunate (or tolerant, or lazy) gardener if you can live with all your predecessors' plants and flower beds. It is far more likely that your tastes will differ – how could they honestly have expected you to buy *those* carpets and curtains?

But there are many gardens that have been neglected for a sufficiently long time for all those lines to have become blurred. You may, for example, be the first occupant of a renovated nineteenth-century terraced house, and the garden will consist entirely of leaning long grass, an overgrown apple tree and a few spindly rose bushes, with a large clump of nettles where the bonfire heap once was. It looks extremely unpromising but, curiously, this is an easier situation to deal with than the established garden that is, in your opinion, completely wrong.

I shall discuss renovating neglected apple trees in chapter 12, roses in chapter 9, and lawns in chapter 3, but in the meantime wait until late spring and take the rotary mower to the grass, avoiding obvious clumps of anything more interesting as you do it. The perennial weeds you must deal with, however, for they will otherwise confound your plans for ever. They will poke their way up through the cracks of the newly laid paving stones, creep out of the crumbling walls, and soon overtake the new and struggling occupants of your borders. You have two alternatives: you can either dig up the entire border, removing every piece of weed root you can find, and throwing away the worst infested perennials, or you can paint or spray the weeds, especially those coming through the walls, with systemic weedkiller (see page 179).

The most successful solution is to do first the one and then the other. Then you can begin to improve the soil (chapter 2), replan the borders and, finally, plant them up.

Just as for a new garden, mark out the dimensions of your garden on a scale plan, and use tracing paper on top of the graph paper to indicate what you want to retain, and to experiment with new ideas. It is impossible to compute exactly how much this minor discipline will save you in time and labour in later years, but it will certainly be considerable. Then gradually begin altering the shapes of beds you are not happy with. If there are plants in the way, heel them in in a sheltered empty place. (Gardeners do alterations in the autumn or early spring, because that is the best time to move bare-rooted plants.) Otherwise, try to leave the planted areas more or less alone (apart from a holding weeding operation) for a year, to establish what is growing already. It is tempting to fill apparent gaps with new plants immediately – unless, of course, work on the house precludes such activity by filling the flower beds with scaffolding and hiding the lawn with stacks of tiles.

Mark major existing features on your master-plan, and make particular note of good plants; for example: 'purple crocus patch (early autumn)', 'red plants about 60cm (2ft) high (mid-summer)'. You may not know what all the plants are, but there are excellent illustrated dictionaries of plants available and, with a bit of perseverance, you will eventually get to know what you have. Gardening relations, when they come to see what is being done to the house, can make themselves very useful: 'And today we have naming of plants.' As you note what is growing, put a cane, with a label attached to it, next to the plant or clump, giving all the details that you have gleaned about it. This is especially helpful for hardy perennials and bulbs, which die down so completely that you have little hope of finding them if you wish to move them in the dormant season.

Above all, resist the temptation to buy masses of unfamiliar plants even if the borders are empty. Go to the garden centre or nursery by all

FAR LEFT: A common sight to greet a new house owner! Neglected and overgrown, there is only an apple tree and lilac to recommend this garden. But the situation is far from hopeless.
LEFT: The following spring, the owners rotovate the 'lawn', to get a level surface, and resow.
ABOVE: The finished result. The existing tree and lilac have been retained but there is now a velvet lawn and the far fence is invisible.

means, and note down anything that is flowering or fruiting that attracts you. When you get home, look them up in the dictionary of plants. Play a waiting game, and be slow to commit yourself until you have learned a little more about them, and about your garden. I say this because I know well that the most depressing aspect of gardening (with the exception of weeding ground elder) is removing plants that you have managed to establish, because they turn out to be unsuitable.

Choosing plants

Deciding what to plant should be the fun part. Dismiss your feelings of inadequacy, your impression that just beyond your present knowledge are the perfect plants (perfect for beauty, ease of cultivation, and suitability), and that there are far too many plants available for any realistic choice ever to be made, and instead enjoy the search. Take account of colour, not just of flowers (which are often transient) but of foliage as well, when you plan; read, note, visit flower shows and nurseries, and, most important of all, put out of your

mind all ideas of immediate perfection; the making of your garden may well be a long process, stretching over years, and one that should never be hurried. You may, as like as not, be so seduced by the illustrations in your dictionary of plants, that you find the planting plan for the first border you ever design consists entirely of plants beginning with the first letters of the alphabet (*Acanthus, Achillea, Aquilegia, Borago*, and so on).

When designing your garden, I implore you not to fall into the trap of sneering at what is common. Common plants are not necessarily common because they are beautiful, as some would have us believe, but too lofty an attitude

will undoubtedly impoverish your garden. After all, no two gardens using identical plants will look quite the same, because of all the considerations that go into the placing of them. Your decision to exclude *Prunus* 'Kanzan', for example, should be guided less by the fact that it grows in every suburban street, than by the negative effect on you of its unnaturally stiff branches and bronze leaves clashing with the sickly pink double flowers.

'Instant gardening' is a relatively new phenomenon, much deprecated by professional gardeners, but very popular with amateurs. It has been made possible by the widespread availability of container-grown nursery stock (see page 19), which can be planted at all seasons. People who buy shrubs in flower that catch their eye, and take them home to plant them, have committed the offence of 'instant gardening'. What galls the working gardener is that, despite the learner having by-passed the three years of patient labour which the pro requires to rear such plants, the results can be very successful. By buying plants in flower the learner takes no chances with her colour schemes, and, provided she reads the labels and keeps her plants well-watered, she can in this way 'make' a garden in a season.

Experienced gardeners are proud of their 'something for nothing' mentality, engendered by the vegetable world's easy capacity for reproduction; they derive immense satisfaction from being self-reliant and never darkening the doors of a garden centre. I do sometimes feel sorry for the new recruit to gardening, easily flattened by an unduly superior boot. She may, after all, have no knowledge of propagation; may have little time to watch young plants grow; may feel the breath of mortality on her cheek; or may suspect that her employers will shortly move their offices to a distant location.

Asking for or accepting interesting plants from friends is a good idea, of course. For one thing, gardens, like houses, are receptacles for

memories. The pleasure I derive each autumn from the prodigious flowering of an enormous corm of *Cyclamen hederifolium* is sharpened by the fact that I was first shown it by my grandmother, from whom I later inherited it. When I am escorted around the gardens of well-known gardeners who pepper their commentary with remarks like, 'Margery Fish gave me this, the last time I saw her, and I have managed to keep it all these years', there is an agreeable sensation of continuity. Gardens are not solely places where we work, year in and year out, striving to make pretty pictures and ensure our charges' happiness; they also acquire accretions of experience (happy and otherwise) which help to

FAR LEFT: It is possible to plant your garden in an afternoon using plants bought at the garden centre. Here, hardy perennials are to be used to give summer colour. There is little guesswork involved because many of them are already in flower.
ABOVE: The antithesis of instant gardening! This lovely stand of the autumn-flowering Cyclamen hederifolium *and the white form* album *will have taken several years to build up from a few corms.*

make the whole business worthwhile. This experience will range from the awful winter night when the beech tree blew down, to that wonderful autumn when the leaves of the cherries turned to the colour of garnets. The exchange of plants adds substantially to the feeling that we have for our gardens.

Once your garden is established, buying plants is not often necessary, anyway. For example, it is perfectly quick and easy to divide hardy perennials in the autumn or spring (see pages 92-3); to take cuttings of rock plants (see pages 90-1) and nurse them in a cold frame, setting them out behind large labels until established; to sow annuals and perennials each year (see pages 88-9). However, I have finally

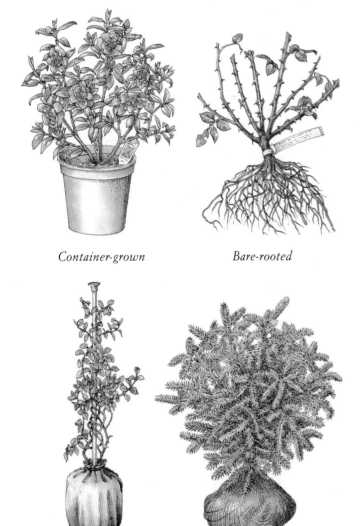

Container-grown

Bare-rooted

Polythene-wrapped

Hessian-wrapped

learned the foolishness of planting minute, home-reared shrubs and trees.

Some years ago, I planted a rooted cutting of the holly 'Golden King'. I bought it for next to nothing, which pleased me greatly. It was 8cm (3in) high, and, instead of planting it in the vegetable garden to 'grow on' for years and years, I planted it straight out into what we called, rather grandly, the Wild Garden. I had always been taught that small plants 'caught up' on large plants. Well, they probably do (or sufficiently anyway to give an intellectual basis to this deep-rooted parsimony), but my plant grew only 2.5cm (1in) in a year. Hidden amongst the long grasses, until they were mown at mid-summer, it was accidentally but regularly trodden on. What I should have done in this instance, with a shrub that is known to grow slowly, was to buy a plant five times the size for three times the price.

If I am honest, I have to admit that I wish my garden to look mature fairly quickly, rather than stuck for years in an awkward adolescence. That is why I now unashamedly buy and plant hardy and fast growing trees and shrubs to form the structure of the garden, while others, reared from rooted cuttings, are left to grow on in nursery rows.

You cannot ignore nurseries and garden centres, or expect to plant your entire garden with the generous gifts (or, as often, cast-offs) of others. For one thing, those kind people who arrive for Sunday lunch with an interesting plastic bag have not designed your garden for you, so are unlikely to bring you just the shade of astrantia that your colour scheme requires. The plant may be well grown, true to name, luxuriating in the right-sized pot, and in a good compost; if it is not, you will, of course, be far too polite to make any comment.

However, if you are paying for a plant, your critical judgement should not be suspended in the same way. I am loath to disillusion anyone (for illusions are amongst our most cherished possessions) but I have to say that as plants are alive, they differ from each other, any ill-treatment will affect them adversely, and there is always the possibility that they may be defective. Many plants on sale, even in reputable nurseries, will depart from the ideal.

Some nursery-grown plants, especially fruit trees and bushes, as well as roses, are sold with bare roots. They will have been grown in soil, usually out in a field, so they will be sturdy and the roots will have had the opportunity to branch. But in the process of lifting for sale, the roots of such plants are sometimes damaged or allowed to dry out.

Container-grown stock (the norm with garden centres and many nurseries these days) can also present problems. Plants are often kept too long in the same container, so that the roots start hurtling round the pot like a motor-cyclist on the Wall of Death. This can be serious with a tree or large, upright shrub for, if the roots are unable to take firm hold by spreading outwards in the soil after planting, the chances of the plant being rocked over in a gale are much greater than normal. If you have ever (and who has not?) decided to dig up a plant a year after planting to put it somewhere else, you may well have found that the root ball was very much the same shape as it was when first you planted it.

Conversely, container plants may also be sold before the root system has had a chance to establish itself; they may be diseased, damaged, malnourished, or be suffering from drought.

I am not at all averse to buying container plants, provided I can have a good look at them first. I look closely at the top of the pot to see how much weed and moss growth has had time to establish itself, pick up the pot to see how much root is growing out of the bottom, and sometimes, when I feel very brave, even knock a plant out of its pot if I suspect it of being tightly pot-bound.

Steer clear of neglected plants such as this, pot-bound and covered with weeds.

It is folly to buy trees or shrubs with large amounts of obviously dead wood. I know this is easier to tell with a rose which has green live wood, and brown dead wood, than it is with dormant woody shrubs, but if you suspect that half the plant is dead, because the wood looks wrinkled or dull, run your thumbnail down a little piece of stem. If it is green under the bark, the plant is all right – or has only recently died! Do not buy plants with damaged shoots, or ones with spots on their leaves, or ones that are obviously yellow (except in autumn, of course). If you can, buy a shrub with a well-balanced framework of branches, not one with just a stem in one corner of the pot. If you suspect an alpine plant of rotting, pull it gently to see if it is firm.

Whether bare-rooted or containerized, if you are buying grafted plants you will wish to check that the union between 'scion' and 'stock' is secure (see page 55). Look, as well, for diseased

The hellebore on the left is a healthy plant, fairly recently potted, yet with a well-developed root system. The one on the right is a poor specimen.

and dead growths and, in the case of blackcurrant bushes, abnormally big buds which mean the presence of a destructive mite. Try to get certified virus-free stock of blackcurrants, raspberries and cultivated blackberries, otherwise virus may substantially cut fruit yields.

The garden centre has a firm and unshakable place now in our gardening lives. It is convenient to be able to go there on a Saturday afternoon to buy lawn fertilizer, bird seed, a houseplant for your aunt's birthday, and honey for tea, all in the same place. You can see the plants on offer, and the better sort of garden centre has people on hand to give advice. If you are not very experienced, the anonymity is comforting. In the same way that the supermarkets have opened a new world for the wine novice, garden centres have widened the horizons of new gardeners.

It is only as you become more experienced that you begin to see their limitations. This realization usually coincides with the moment when you first attend a large flower show and discover a whole new range of exciting plants

that you did not know existed. You bring home catalogues which you have bought there: nursery lists of large mail-order firms as well as those of smaller concerns which specialize in anything from insectivorous plants to violas. You will begin to spend summer evenings bent over order forms, estimating carriage costs and tutting over the expense of it all (quite wrongly, for plants are expensive to rear and nurserymen make no fortunes).

However, although some nurseries are very much more efficient than others at the business of mail order, there are inherent problems – crops fail, stock is exhausted, plants arrive damaged – and many nurseries (bulb nurseries excepted) are now abandoning mail order, and asking for all plants to be collected.

If you do buy by mail order, you can do something to protect yourself by buying from firms recommended to you, and never from advertisements in newspapers which promise very cheap plants. In this business you get what you pay for. When ordering plants from a catalogue, you will be overwhelmed by how many plants

there are to choose from, and how meagre the descriptions are. Catalogues may tell you (not always accurately) what colour the plant is, and extol the virtues of the seed heads in winter with the low sun behind them, but may omit to tell you that it only thrives in an acid bog (which in your case you have not got). You will need an illustrated dictionary of plants at your elbow, to give you additional information, when ordering or planning.

The shortcomings of some garden centres, where a restricted selection of plants is offered, which are usually grown elsewhere and shifted quickly before any harm can come to them, has detonated an explosion of new, small, and often specialist businesses. These are often run by gardeners who wish to extend their interest in old-fashioned roses, say, or auriculas, by propagating and selling what were once just surplus plants. These nurseries are now often the repositories of rare plants, and though they may need to be searched out down pot-holed farm lanes,

FAR LEFT AND ABOVE: Two views of the same garden, in spring and early autumn, show clearly how plants and simple structures can change the atmosphere. Clever use has been made of trellis, both to draw the eye on in the spring, and to provide support for climbers as the season progresses. It also shows how useful bulbs are in borders because they disappear so completely shortly after flowering.

they do provide very pleasant afternoons for the enthusiast. Not only can the plants be seen flowering in the gardens that often adjoin these nurseries, but the owners are usually prepared to stand around for ages patiently explaining the difference between *Clematis orientalis* and *C. tangutica*.

If you do not know where to find these nurseries, look at the small advertisements in gardening magazines, scan the entries in garden gazeteers, or refer to *The Plant Finder* which lists plants available in nurseries all over the country and is updated annually.

2

DOWN TO
EARTH

IT IS COMMONLY BELIEVED THAT GARDENERS ARE ETERNAL OPTIMISTS; WHY ELSE WOULD THEY BOTHER WITH AN OCCUPATION SO FULL OF PROMISE WHICH OFTEN REMAINS UNFULFILLED? WELL, I WONDER. NEARLY EVERY GARDENER I HAVE MET HAS THOUGHT HERSELF UNIQUELY UNFORTUNATE, AND NOWHERE DOES SHE SEEM TO FEEL THIS MORE STRONGLY THAN IN THE MATTER OF THE SOIL THAT FATE HAS DOLED OUT AS HER PORTION. THERE ARE AS MANY GARDENERS WHO ADMIT TO GARDENING ON A FERTILE, FREE-DRAINING YET MOIST, SLIGHTLY ACID, MEDIUM LOAM, ALWAYS WORKABLE YET NEVER DRYING OUT COMPLETELY, AS THERE ARE NIGHTINGALES PREPARED TO SING IN BERKELEY SQUARE.

The answer, as they say, lies in the soil! The exuberant growth and generous flowering of the roses in this garden are only possible because time and trouble have been taken to ensure that the soil is both suitable and well-fed.

Soil

When I gardened on a sandy loam whose only fault was a tendency to dry to dust in the summer, I was hardly gracious about its virtues, and was loud in my complaints about the copious watering necessary in time of drought.

I was inclined to preach to my more unfortunate friends that dealing with an inhospitable (that is, to humans) soil was character-forming. And so it is. How you manage says a lot about your personality. I have known people who have opted out of buying a house – perfect in every other way – after digging their toe-caps into the soil in the garden. This is an extreme reaction and certainly unnecessary, for it is possible to improve to some extent even the most difficult soil. Like the old man who seems heavy weather at first but who, with patient coaxing, can be persuaded to tell his fund of funny stories, so the heavy soil is worth the effort of concentrated cultivation. The struggle itself, even setting aside its character-building aspects, can bring satisfaction, in the same way as the first flowering of a rare alpine or the winning of a prize for enormous leeks.

Soil is as important to plants as the air that we breathe is to us. For the plant roots, it provides anchorage, oxygen, water and food, and because these last two can only be absorbed by the roots from the soil water, gardeners go to immense lengths to prevent the soil drying out.

Soils differ in texture, that is to say in the proportion of their three main constituent parts (besides organic materials and humus): namely, sand, silt and clay. You will remember, from school science classes, that when soil was put into a glass tube filled with water, the sand (being the largest particles) sank to the bottom, the silt descended more slowly to form a discrete layer, and the tiny clay particles remained in suspension in the water. Gravel, which is a large sand constituent of many soils, can be 2mm ($\frac{1}{16}$in) or more in diameter, whereas clay particles are less than one hundredth of that dimension. Along the continuum between gravel and clay there are many intermediate particle sizes, so it is hardly surprising that soils differ so markedly from each other.

The ideal soil, which, as we have already established, virtually no one has, is a medium loam, but there are sandy loams which are lighter, and loamy sands which are lighter still. There are also silt loams, and clay loams, and sandy clays, and, as if that were not enough, there are chalk soils, peaty soils, and stony soils which may be 'light' if they have a great deal of sand in them, or very heavy if mixed with clay.

A stony soil can seem like a curse to the new gardener, but do not assume that you can, or should, remove every stone by raking. Where necessary, it is best to dig with a fork rather than a spade.

However, what you really need to know from a gardening point of view is whether your soil is light or heavy (easy or difficult to dig); whether it will dry out quickly or slowly in summer; whether it has a large proportion of clay in it; whether it is rich in humus. If in doubt about what you have, try asking your neighbour.

Much can be learned about your soil by look and feel. If the soil, when lightly raked, reveals stones, or they are apparent as knobbly bumps on the surface, then you have a stony soil; if the subsoil is white and not far below the dark brown surface layer, then it is chalky; if the soil is spongy in quality and dark in colour, you have a peaty soil; if your soil readily forms a ball, looks shiny when rubbed between the fingers, and, if wetted, becomes very sticky, you have a clay soil; if the soil will not easily cohere to form a ball in your hand, even when wet, you have a very sandy soil.

Soils contain, to a greater or lesser extent, organic material and humus. Organic material consists of a mixture of rotted, or rotting, compost or farmyard manure, as well as the decaying remains of fungi, leaves and animals. The decaying process is continued in the soil by worms, bacteria and fungi, which break it down still further into 'humus' (a black, structureless, nutrient-rich substance). A soil rich in humus is usually dark brown. Humus itself is not only rich in nutrients which are readily available for the plant to take up in the soil water; it also binds particles together to form crumbs, thus leaving bigger air spaces and improving the soil structure, especially of heavy clay soils. It also helps sandy soils to retain moisture, preventing nutrients from being washed away.

All these soils mentioned are top-soils, but it is not absolutely unheard of, especially for a new garden attached to a new house, to have no top-soil at all, but only subsoil (easily recognized by its yellowish or whitish appearance). Builders are as well known for carting away top-soil, as they are for accidentally burying it; so if either is the case, you will have to buy some top-soil that has been removed from some other beggar's new garden.

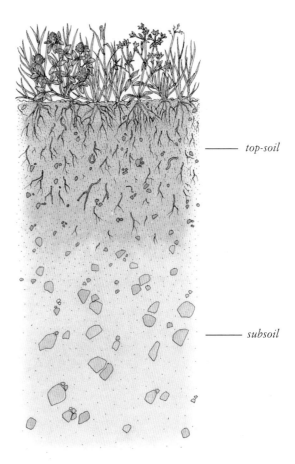

top-soil

subsoil

This soil profile shows how different in appearance and constituents are top-soil and subsoil.

Soils are acid, they are alkaline, or they are neutral – what the layman vaguely calls 'sour' or 'sweet' – and what they are will determine to some extent what you can grow. You can test what is called the 'pH level' of your soil (its acidity or alkalinity) by using a small and readily available kit or meter. Your soil will be somewhere from about 3.5 (very acid) to 8.0 (very alkaline); 'neutral' is 7.0. Even within a very small garden there can be differences in soil pH, depending on cultivation and land use, or even on quirks of geological formation.

This matters because some plants are most particular about what medium they grow in. The best known lime-hating (calcifuge) plant is the rhododendron in the *Ericaceae* family. Some acid-loving plants do just as well on alkaline soils as on acid, but none has such a decided preference for acid soil as the *Ericaceae*. In general, calcifuge plants are more adamant about

their needs than calcicoles (lime-loving plants like *Clematis*). Raspberries like it a little acid, brassicas slightly alkaline.

Some people feel the need to study soil so closely that they elevate it to the status of a hobby, nurturing their soil with as much care and interest as the plants that grow in it. I think that it is not as interesting a subject as the plants, but what may seem like barren theory nevertheless has perfectly practical applications, and you do need to know both about soil type, and how water and air are held in the soil.

Gravel can be used as an attractive mulch, to lessen the need for watering in the summer. Most of the plants here (even the hosta on the right) are reasonably drought-tolerant.

In a light soil, where the particles are large, there will be large holes between those particles. That means that water will pass through quickly, and there will be plenty of oxygen available for the plants' roots. However, the free-draining nature of the soil also means that the nutrients, which are dissolved in the soil water, are easily 'leached' or drained out. This is the reason why light soils must be fed regularly; they need plenty of humus to help retain essential moisture.

In heavy clay soil, the particles are tiny, therefore the spaces between those particles are tiny, and the water does not drain freely. However, as a result, nutrients remain in the soil, so clay soil is, in nearly all instances, a fertile one. (Life is rarely all bad.) However, if you walk on a clay soil when it is wet, you will compact the particles and squeeze out the air – which in turn may lead to suffocation and starvation of plant roots. That is why so much fuss is made about the importance of not walking on heavy soils if the soil is wet enough to stick to your boots; if you do, and this damaging compaction occurs, you will have to dig the soil to aerate it again. When clay soil finally does dry out, the particles are drawn so close together that the soil shrinks and the characteristic cracks in the ground appear.

Soil texture refers to the proportions of the constituent parts of sand, silt, clay and organic matter in the soil. Soil structure, on the other hand, means the way those particles are aggregated into 'crumbs'. A so-called 'friable' soil is one where the crumb structure is such that the soil is easy to work into a 'tilth' for seed-sowing. A soil with good structure has large crumbs so that there are wide pores for oxygen and water to pass through, but enough organic matter to retain some moisture and ensure fertility.

Going on at such length can only be justified if it facilitates the understanding of how one may improve an unsatisfactory soil in order to grow plants better. 'Unsatisfactory' is, of course, a subjective term, for plants have differing requirements. It is vain optimism to suppose that a soil can be radically and permanently altered, but most can be improved: clay soils can be ameliorated by a dressing of gypsum, which encourages the clay particles to 'flocculate' or form into crumbs (lime will do the same, but its application is hardly sensible if you already have an alkaline soil); a light, sandy soil can be improved by the incorporation of

quantities of rotted organic material like leaf mould, mushroom compost, garden compost or farmyard manure, which help to conserve moisture in the soil; and a heavy soil may be helped by digging in sand, grit or ashes, which will, by their presence, enlarge the air spaces, or organic material, which will add the much-needed humus. The situation is by no means hopeless, although it will cost a little money and not a little time.

It is possible to live in reasonable harmony with a stony soil, provided that a light one is enriched. Root crops are, admittedly, not very

Rhododendrons and azaleas are resolute lime-haters, which will only grow well in a soil with a pH below 6. Here are Rhododendron *'Charlotte de Rothschild' and* Azalea *'Palestrina'.*

successful, but everything else will grow satisfactorily if the soil's droughty leanings are taken into account. Dig this soil only shallowly, and use a garden fork; it is much easier than a spade. Likewise, a thin top-soil over chalk is tolerable, even though you may have to take a crowbar to make a large enough hole to plant a tree, and water furiously until the roots get established. Chalky soils are generally very free-draining, so a great deal of humus should be dug into the top-soil. They are also usually very alkaline, which will please many rock plants, pinks and irises. Peaty soils are acid and therefore fine for the *Ericaceae*, and usually suitable for bog plants. The application of lime (calcium carbonate) will raise the pH, but only temporarily. Peaty soils can be slow to drain, so it helps to dig in some grit for plants that resent even temporary waterlogging.

Most of these measures will result in a temporary improvement, but in the end you may have to grow those plants that will consent to thrive in the soil allotted to you, and, like the blighted heroine of a Russian novel, find consolation in the small pleasures of life, while trying not to weep too bitterly for what might have been.

If you are cursed with no top-soil at all, action is required because subsoils have little or no humus in them and are infertile. You have no alternative but to buy in top-soil, but do not plant in it until any weeds have been treated with glyphosate (see page 179).

If you find your soil does not drain well, it may be that there is an impermeable layer or 'pan' some 45-60cm (1½-2ft) below the surface. This is caused either by the compaction of heavy machinery or, in acid soils, by the filtering down of iron or manganese salts; it can be identified because there are bluish or brown streaks in the subsoil, and the surface easily becomes waterlogged. This 'pan' should be broken up with a cultivator so that the water can drain freely once more.

This attractive collection of lime-tolerant plants includes the evergreen shrub Daphne laureola, *often mistaken for a lime-hating rhododendron.*

Nutrients & fertilizers

The mention of iron and manganese brings us on to one of the most important, yet mysterious, subjects with which the gardener must contend: the matter of plant nutrients and fertilizers. This is a subject that the novice hates, for it looks, on the face of it, infinitely complicated, and as pregnant with hidden obstacles as a computer game. However, worrying about the subject will not increase the height of your shrubs, but feeding them properly will, so this is something you would be wise to know a bit about.

Plants need food, as we do. In nature, they absorb it, dissolved in water, through their roots; if sprayed with liquid fertilizer, they will also take it up through their leaves. Gardens are artificial environments where plants grow in fierce competition, depleting faster than they are replaced by the process of decay the three major nutrients: nitrogen (N), phosphorus (P) in the shape of phosphates, and potassium (K) in the form of potash. So far so good. There are also other elements, which are needed in much smaller quantities, called intermediate elements: carbon, sulphur and magnesium; and several 'trace' elements, which are required in tiny quantities and not usually deficient, such as boron, molybdenum, zinc and copper, as well as iron and manganese. These last two can become deficient in limy soil because calcium has the unfortunate effect of 'locking them up' or making them insoluble so that they cannot be absorbed by plants. Do not worry about deficiencies in the soil; it is possible to do something about them all. The symptoms of deficiency, and the remedies, can be found in the chart on page 33.

Now let us concern ourselves with how to achieve optimum growth from plants – something that is very different from merely ensuring their survival.

Most plants that are smaller than large trees (which seem to manage quite well for themselves) will benefit from a feed of some description at least once a year. This is, generally speaking, the 'bottom line', but there are considerable variations in what is required and how much.

Any roll call of plant foods has to begin with the organic foods such as farmyard manure and compost, which are used both as soil conditioners and as sources of nutrients. Farmyard manure has surprisingly low percentages of major elements, probably because the bulk is so large, there being only about $1/2$% N, $1/4$% P, $1/2$% K in manure ($3/4$% N, $1/4$% P, $1/2$% K in stable manure) whereas there are $1^1/2$% N, 2% P, $1/2$% K in garden compost. Of the manures, horse manure is the richest, followed by pig and cow. Strawy horse manure is particularly helpful in lightening heavy clay soils, while cow manure will give substance to light, sandy soils.

All these manures are still possible to come by in the country, or in towns near riding stables, but not everyone likes to use them; they are not always well rotted, and are heavy and awkward to move about in the garden. More concentrated forms of farmyard manure – usually poultry litter – are now available in bags, which, though expensive, are the answer for town dwellers who want a good organic soil-conditioning fertilizer.

Compost, if you can make enough, is wonderful stuff (see page 37). It is well worth the trouble, not only because it is cheap, but because it is an excellent soil improver and rich in nutrients. Added to this, it is always there, waiting like a discreet manservant on your convenience. I also recommend spent mushroom compost; its only disadvantage is a high pH, which means that it is anathema to the ericaceous family.

There are also green manures. Green-manuring is the widely advocated practice of sowing a quick-growing crop like mustard and, after a few weeks, digging it in to provide the soil with a supply of slow-release nitrogen. It is especially popular with energetic 'organic' gardeners.

It would be unrealistic to suggest that the whole of your garden will be treated to liberal amounts of dung each year, and in any event, some plants, like alpines, resent that kind of Good Life. However, it is to be hoped that at least part of the vegetable garden will have some 'manure' dug into or put onto it each year, and that some nutritious stuff will be laid on the ordinary flower borders at least every three years (this may be even more frequent if you use compost or manure as a mulch – see

Quick-germinating mustard is dug into the soil as an ecologically sound 'green manure', to provide a slow-release form of nitrogen.

page 35). Organic matter should certainly be dug in every time a new bed is made.

Whichever organic materials you choose to use, they may need to be supplemented by fertilizers, if you wish to achieve optimum growth, but we must be clear from the start that fertilizers are supplements, not substitutes, for bulky organic materials because they do not improve soil structure.

Some fertilizers are fast-acting, which means that they dissolve easily and quickly, and are immediately available to the plant, but soon exhausted; some, like bonemeal, are slow-

release, which means they take time to dissolve and become available; some are steady-release and, as their name suggests, release nutrients steadily over a long period of time into the soil.

Fertilizers contain some of the most picturesque names in horticulture: bonemeal, hoof and horn (I remember reading of a man who used to pare his fingernails out of the bathroom window onto a favourite rose to give it hoof and horn), dried blood, fishmeal, seaweed and poultry manure. Their active ingredients (our old friends N, P and K) are always displayed on the bag in that order.

Fertilizers come as granules; as dry or wettable powders; in highly concentrated liquid form which needs to be diluted; or, in the case of pot plant fertilizers, even in sticks. They can be single chemicals, called 'straights', or compounds. Non-liquid fertilizer can be applied as a 'base dressing', that is, raked or watered into the soil before sowing or planting, or as a 'top-dressing', which means scattered around the plant while it is growing. Spring 'base' dressings are applied a few days before planting or sowing so that the fertilizer has a chance to start to dissolve. Liquid fertilizers are diluted and watered onto growing plants.

The granules or powders are sprinkled, the liquids watered on from a watering can, and foliar feeds, which feed plants through the pores in their leaves, are usually sprayed from a sprayer or hose diluter. Foliar feeds are particularly useful in times of drought, when the roots cannot take up food because there is insufficient soil water, or if immediate and rapid growth is desired. There are some combined pesticide and fungicide preparations which include a foliar feed, on the sensible assumption that plants attacked need a feed to stimulate them into healthy growth once more.

As is apparent, in the matter of fertilizers there is *embarras de richesses*. What should you use? I am afraid that this is a case of horses for courses and that different ones (fertilizers, I mean, not horses) are needed at different times of year. It is, however, helpful to know what the various nutrients do (see page 33).

It is possible, for the sake of simplicity, to establish general rules about what to feed, and when, and my preferred regime is a simple one. I try to put a spring fertilizer of nitrogen on all growing plants (including the grass of the lawn) to replace what has been washed out of the top-soil during the winter, and an organic mulch on the borders; a mid-summer fertilizer for greedy feeders, such as roses, which will appreciate it for their fruiting or second flower development; and an autumn fertilizer on lawns (not compulsory) and newly planted plants. I dig organic material like manure into the vegetable garden in the autumn, lay it around fruit trees and bushes, and dig it into flower beds about to be planted up. Foliar feeds I use during droughts, and steady-release fertilizers for plants in containers. Liquid fertilizers I find helpful for giving a fillip to vegetables.

If you are short of time and money, limit the pharmacopoeia in your shed to a bag of blood, bone and fishmeal, a bag of sterilized bone-meal, a general liquid fertilizer, a specific liquid feed for tomatoes, which can be used for the flowers of a range of greedy feeders like roses, and a foliar feed.

How much of these supplements you need depends very much on the soil, both on its constituents and its pH, but the recommended dosages of fertilizers (as with other chemicals) are critical. If you were to add a little more manure to your soil than is strictly required (anyway it is impossible to say *exactly* what that requirement is) no harm will be done, but overdoing it with fertilizers, especially with those trace elements that react in particular soils, can be wasteful as they are easily leached out of the top-soil.

Some fertilizers are sold with scoops; if not, it may be helpful to weigh out 25g (1oz), 50g (2oz) and 100g (4oz) into a yoghurt pot or one of those cartons you get in washing powder boxes, and mark out the levels on the outside with a felt-tip pen, using a different pot for each type of fertilizer. Whatever you do, establish a quick way of measuring these amounts; not doing so may add up to just that amount of

disincentive that prevents you from doing the job at all. If you cannot measure out liquid feeds using the cap, or find, like me, that it is a sure way of spilling it, buy some plastic measuring cups or use more marked yoghurt pots.

Fertilizers of the solid variety need to be scattered. There cannot be many people who can measure a square metre or yard in their head, and translate it onto the ground, so it is worthwhile measuring it out once a season with string and bamboo, so that you have a good notion of what the area looks like. Leaf-scorching is especially likely on grass that has accidentally had a double dose of nitrogen in the spring.

I always wear gloves, not because I am a sissy but because, like a large proportion of the population, I find fertilizer powders and liquids act as irritants on my fair skin.

If granular fertilizers are an irritant to us, they are not popular in concentrated and undissolved form with plants either. Some, like sulphate of ammonia, will cause scorching (browning) on leaves if left to lie on them, or if they are hoed into dry soil, where there is not sufficient moisture for them to dissolve properly. All granular fertilizers, incidentally, should be applied to damp ground; if necessary, water the ground first.

Hoe in granular fertilizers around the stems of small plants, so that they are within reach of their roots, and, in the case of large plants, sprinkle the fertilizer in a circle on an imaginary line level with the outer edge of the leaf-cover, for that is where the young roots will be. It is only at the ends of the youngest roots that these dissolved nutrients can be absorbed.

Some people find, in the case of trees and large shrubs, that it is worth making a circle of holes in the soil or grass, and dropping fertilizer in so that the roots may have readier access to it. In my experience, it is rare that you need to feed a large tree, except when it is obvious that the roots are taking a great deal out of a flower bed and affecting the performance of the flowers therein. Though even then it is probably easier to feed the border plants than the tree. I certainly grant that there is a point in feeding fruit

Nutrients & fertilizers

The following nutrients and fertilizers are essential for healthy plant growth.

NUTRIENTS	WHAT THEY DO	DEFICIENCY SYMPTOMS	REMEDIES
Nitrogen (N)	Helps manufacture chlorophyll, which is essential for healthy leaf growth. Needed particularly by lawns and leafy vegetables such as brassicas, and especially in spring	Yellowing or reddening of leaves, especially in spring. Stunted growth. Least likely to be deficient in light soils	High-nitrogen fertilizer, e.g. dried blood or sulphate of ammonia
Phosphorus (P)	Helps with root development	Lack of vigorous growth. Dark green, purplish leaves. Least likely to be deficient in light soils	Bonemeal high in phosphates
Potassium (K)	Helps with fruit and flower development. Hardens up tender wood before winter	Small fruits and leaves with scorched margins which brown before autumn. Leaf discoloration. Least likely to be deficient in light soils	Sulphate of potash, or proprietary rose or tomato fertilizer
Calcium	Helps with cell and growing point formation	Curled leaf tips. Internal browning of Brussels sprouts. Bitter pit of apples. Deficient only in acid soil	Add lime (calcium carbonate). Do not lime and manure at the same time
Sulphur	Important for healthy cell growth	Yellow leaves. Thin, woody growth. Sulphur is often present in polluted air	Fertilizers containing sulphates
Magnesium	Constituent of chlorophyll	Yellow patches between green veins on leaves on acid soils or where there are high potash levels. Occurs most readily in alkaline soils; also in sandy soils with too much potash	Dissolved Epsom salts or seaweed fertilizer
Manganese	Helps formation of chlorophyll	Yellowing of leaf margins and between veins. Affects particularly acid-lovers in alkaline soils. Also occurs on acid soils with too much iron	Spray with manganese sulphate
Iron	Helps formation of chlorophyll	Yellowing young leaves	Chelated iron

trees, although I do not always get round to the late winter sprinkle of sulphate of potash for better, healthier fruit, and never to feeding the grass beneath with nitrogen in order that it will not compete for the tree's supply.

Store all solid fertilizers in plastic bags where they will not become damp. Fertilizers usually soak up moisture very readily, and after drying out become as hard as an ungrateful heart. I try to remember to throw fertilizers out after a couple of seasons but, in practice, I have usually

The plants here are obviously reaching their full potential. Nutrients, which can be introduced either in organic mulches, dry fertilizers or liquid feeds, are vital to maintain this growth, especially as there are hungry hedge plants and shrubs in the background.

forgotten when I bought them, and I refuse to make lists of bought items to go with all the other garden lists I am so adept at losing. Fertilizers do not go bad; they just lose their efficacy after a season or two.

Mulches

In the seventeenth century, mulch meant soft, or beginning to decay. It has changed its meaning over the years; we now tend to put decayed rather than decaying matter on the soil because we know that the bacteria that ferment decaying matter use nitrogen in the process and so deplete the soil's store.

A mulch is a layer of material laid on the ground in spring for the purposes of feeding, or preventing weed growth, or conserving moisture or, in many instances, all three. If an organic mulch is to be effective as a weed suppressant, it will need to be *at least* 5cm (2in) thick, so that little or no light can filter through to encourage leaf growth. Garden compost is the ideal all-purpose mulch, but the goodly fellowship of mulches also includes spent

It can be kept for that part of your garden where you want to simulate the right conditions for woodland plants, like rhododendrons. Leaf mould does break down quite quickly once it is in the soil, and is therefore less effective as a mulch than compost, but it lightens heavy soils well. There are fewer nutrients in it than in garden compost.

Other plant food mulches include seaweed, which must be composted before it is spread if you do not want your seaside garden to look as if it is reeling from the shock of a great sea storm. The use of seaweed is one of the few perks for those who own coastal gardens and are forced to smell it rotting on their beaches. Spent mushroom compost, which is usually high in calcium carbonate, is helpful if you also

Although not especially appealing, bark chippings make an excellent, clean and long-lasting mulch.

Cocoa shell, which smells deliciously of chocolate at first, adds nutrients to the soil and deters slugs.

mushroom compost, spent hops, leaf mould, seaweed, coarse or composted bark, and even gravel and black polythene. Well-rotted manure is all right, but it is inclined to sprout its own weeds.

Leaf mould is a good mulch, but you will need a great deal of it. It is best made separately from compost as it takes longer to rot down.

wish temporarily to neutralize your acid soil.

The most fashionable of all mulches these days is bark. It comes pulverized, shredded, and even composted, and is now a constituent of some potting composts. It is a by-product of the forestry industry and is relatively expensive. It is popular because it is clean to handle, breaks down only very slowly, and it pleases our

Straw, if you can find a supply, is the traditional way of protecting strawberries from mud-splash.

Grit and gravel are ideal for keeping the necks of alpine plants dry in winter, so preventing rot.

tidy minds. However, I think it lends a rather municipal look to the garden (perhaps by association because it has found its way into adventure playgrounds) and it is a nuisance if you like seedlings to establish themselves around small plants. It has its uses, but I think only in the shrub border or amongst large established plants. The cover will need 'topping up' every couple of years, for it is sometimes scattered by birds. In the process of slow decomposition, it uses up some nitrogen, although expert opinion is divided about exactly how much. It is probably wise in the spring to sprinkle some sulphate of ammonia on top to counteract that effect. If you do use it, you will need to scatter artificial fertilizers twice a year (unless the bed is very well dug and manured before planting), for it contains practically no nutrient. It may acidify the soil a little as it is usually derived from conifers.

Peat is no longer considered suitable as a mulch or soil conditioner by many gardeners, because it is a non-renewable resource. There are, however, several 'peat substitutes', such as coir (a waste product of the coconut matting industry) and mixes of wood and paper waste, which can be used instead.

More than a hundred years ago, William Robinson, author of *The English Flower Garden*, advocated 'Mulching with Life'. He particularly recommended pansies for planting round the stems of rose bushes, presumably because they looked pretty and did not take up as much moisture from the soil as they conserved by their green leaf-cover. Ground-cover of all sorts is suitable as a mulch but rampant plants, especially low shrubs, will take nutrients from the soil as well as moisture, and add nothing to it; nothing, that is, except a few leaves in the autumn if they are deciduous, in which case they are not so effective as a mulch in any event. Initial preparation of the soil must be very good, because their presence will make the putting down of nutritious plant food well-nigh impossible.

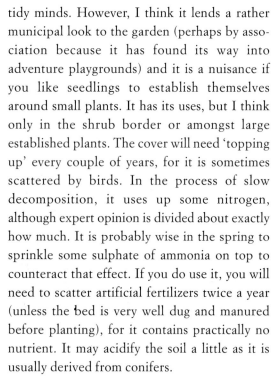

When applying a mulch, such as cocoa shell, make sure you do not cover the stems but leave a space so that water can penetrate the soil.

Other sterile mulches include 5mm ($^1/_4$in) gravel or grit, which is very popular with alpine plant enthusiasts because it conserves moisture well, while at the same time protecting the plant's neck against water which will rot it.

Black polythene is an efficient mulch, being particularly effective at suppressing perennial weeds, provided, that is, it is used on level ground and not punctured, except, of course, where plants are growing. It is not, however, a fit inhabitant for the garden (and I mean the vegetable garden as well) unless it is covered with bark or gravel.

There are extremely effective mulching products now on the market, called, generically, 'geotextiles'. These are permeable woven polypropylenes, which allow water through, but discourage weeds, particularly if bark chippings or something similar is put on top. If cut to size, these materials can be laid on an empty border and holes cut where plants are to go in. They will take several years to deteriorate. Although not cheap, their durability and effectiveness mean they will be used increasingly in the future by weed-conscious gardeners. It is obvious that neither grit, polythene or geotextile material will have any nutritional value.

There is little argument about the efficacy of mulching, or about when to do it. This is another job that really will save you time in the long run; indeed, in many larger gardens the weeds would be unstoppable without it. Even with a good 5cm (2in) layer, some weeds will emerge, but they will prove much easier to pull out. Mulch in the early spring, when the ground is damp, and before the weeds really get going.

Compost

The use of rotted-down kitchen and garden perishable waste to enrich the soil in order to grow plants which can in turn be used on compost heaps to rot down, and so on, is plainly a good thing. It reduces pressure on landfill sites and appeals very strongly to our desire to get something useful on the cheap. What is more, it can become an absorbing hobby, quite independently of gardening. Compost-making requires just the right amount of time and absorption to be attractive to very busy people, leaving them with no time for actual gardening. It is physically tiring, although not overmuch; there is a satisfactory scientific aspect to it, the facts of which are not difficult to grasp but are sufficiently mysterious to convince the intellectual that it is worth doing; it affords a golden opportunity for self-righteously bawling out younger members of the family for putting milk-bottle-tops in the compost bucket; there is some skill (although not much) in erecting a compost bin, which appeals to the householder's regrettable weakness for 'do-it-yourself'; there are several ways of doing it, all of them arguably the best, so there is considerable scope for slightly bad-tempered discussion and difference of opinion; it also costs nothing. I do not think you can ask more of a hobby than that. I commend it to all who have a garden, but are not keen on gardening.

How is it that if you dump a quantity of potato peelings, lawn clippings, crushed egg shells, torn-up newspapers and wine corks, add a little soil and sulphate of ammonia to the heap and cover it, there will be, in six months' time, a dark brown decomposed mound, full of little red worms and wine corks, which has completely lost its smell and which we may call 'compost'? It is because millions of bacteria work to break down the vegetable matter, a process accelerated by the sulphate of ammonia which the bacteria need. This bacterial activity is so intense in such a closed environment that the heap will heat up considerably – sufficient to germinate the avocado stones and to feel quite hot to the hand. The heat is very

This well-built compost bin has wooden sides and an old carpet to insulate, yet still has generous ventilation. The bottom plank is removable.

important; it is both proof, and accelerator, of frenzied microbial activity, and it may kill annual weed seeds (but do not depend on that). A compost heap is not supposed to be truly successful unless these weed seeds are killed, but this strikes me as being one of those sacred tenets of gardening, hallowed by tradition and handed down from generation to generation throughout all ages, unburdened by hard evidence. As we all know, there are so many millions of weed seeds in the soil already, and more coming in on the air all the time, that, in a sense, such an achievement is pointless. *By all means*, however, keep out perennial weeds; they will spread fast and relentlessly, and should not be encouraged.

Why should we be so keen on compost? Because, with the possible exception of well-rotted farmyard manure, compost is the best general bulky organic soil conditioner. The reason why rotted compost is a dark brown colour is because it has a high proportion of humus in it, and we know now what that does

to a soil. It is also often very fibrous, which helps water-retention in light soils.

Clearly, compost-making is a worthwhile way of spending time, and there seems no point in the business of decomposition taking any longer than it need. That means constructing a container which aids both air circulation and heat and moisture retention at one and the same time.

Whatever sort of home-made arrangement you make, you will ideally need two heaps, one finished and one being made. This is because (with the exception of bought plastic bins from which you can remove vertical slats) it is not easy to extract the rotted compost from the bottom while still adding to the top. After all, the time when you may need most compost, in the autumn, is also the time when you are adding to the heap most with swept leaves.

One method is to dig two shallow pits, about 1.2m (4ft) square. When one is full and covered, the other can be in the process of being filled. This works quite well but, because air circulation is minimal, you will have to turn the heap over every so often – a thoroughly enjoyable job, I might add, on a cold day, though not one for those with bad backs.

If you have somewhere shady and out of the way, yet reasonably accessible in awful weather (for you make just as much kitchen rubbish in

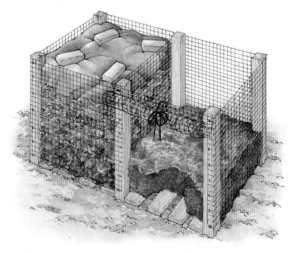

The chicken wire at the front of this compost bin can be rolled up and secured so that the rotted compost can be shovelled out easily.

the winter as in summer), you could hide a chicken-wire structure (see illustration below left). However, I must admit that they have a way of sagging in the middle, like a woman who has let herself go. They also fail to provide the necessary insulation to make a fast decomposing and hot heap, unless you line the inside of the wire with ugly polythene. Although I do not consider these enclosures wholly successful – certainly no more so than my two pits which use the earth for insulation – they are easy to erect, requiring only four short, say, 1.2m (4ft), stakes, painted with preservative (one for each corner), with the chicken wire stretched as tightly as possible and attached to the posts with U-staples. They should be about 1.2m (4ft) square. Make sure that you can roll back the front portion and fix it so that the compost is accessible.

If you wish to make the Rolls-Royce of compost bins (see illustration below), use breeze blocks or old bricks to build a double three-sided structure with walls about 90cm (3ft) or 1.2m (4ft) high and removable wooden slats slotted into the open front. Each section should again be about 1.2m (4ft) square. A few bricks left without mortar between the lower courses will ensure some air circulation. Find some kind of covering (such as black polythene, or even an old carpet, secured with bricks) to stop

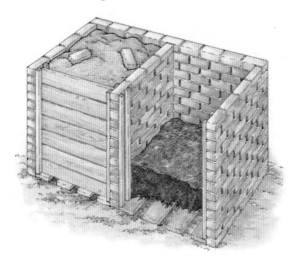

This is the ideal compost bin: air can enter from the bottom and sides, yet the bricks retain heat; the front planks are removable for easy shovelling.

the heap losing moisture and heat; the bacteria will not work properly in a cold, dry heap. Site the heap on a hard base if you can so that the compost is easy to shovel out.

It is also possible to buy an array of plastic compost bins: the larger and sturdier the better. Their main problem is lack of insulation, so it is hard to retain the heat in them.

There is little argument about what should go into compost: leaves, grass mowings (unless recently treated with weedkiller), straw, sawdust, manure of any kind such as that made by poultry, vegetable waste, tea leaves, coffee grounds, eggshells, annual weeds, non-woody and 'clean' (not diseased) and shredded prunings, cut down stems of herbaceous plants, wood ash and torn-up newspaper, or even old woollen jerseys cut up into pieces. There should be no animal fat: no breakfast toast and butter, no milk, no chop bones. As I discovered when certain foreign bodies found their way into my compost when I was not paying attention, these things encourage rats.

It is important to have a good mix of ingredients in your compost for maximum activity by the microbes. If you have a great deal of straw on it but no green weeds, add some sulphate of ammonia or a commercial accelerator which is nitrogen rich. If you put on about 15cm (6in) of compost ingredients (I usually stamp on it to drop the level), then a thin layer of soil (which contains the all-important bacteria), and repeat, covering the heap well with an impermeable material when it is as high as you wish it to be, you should have some good compost in about four months in the summer. Rotting will take longer in the autumn and winter because temperatures are lower and bacterial activity proportionately slower.

If you find your compost is not degrading as quickly as you would like, it may be that it is too dry, in which case water with a hose until it is moist. Or it may be that there is not enough air circulation for the bacteria to work efficiently, in which case a crowbar or stout pointed stick should be stabbed into the heap and pulled to-and-fro.

3

THE GREEN SWARD

I F ONE SETS ONESELF UP AS A PUNDIT, ONE MUST EXPECT TO BE ASKED FOR GARDENING ADVICE WHEN-EVER ONE GOES OUT TO A PARTY. IT WOULD BE CHURLISH TO COMPLAIN ABOUT SUCH A STATE OF AFFAIRS (EVEN THOUGH ONE WOULD OCCASIONALLY LIKE AN EVENING OFF TO TALK SERIOUSLY OF CRICKET OR TRIVIALLY OF PROUST) FOR THE QUESTION IS AS OFTEN A CONVERSA-TIONAL GAMBIT ON THE PART OF A SOCIABLE PERSON AS A DESIRE FOR FREE INFORMATION. HOUSEPLANTS ARE THE FAVOURITE TOPIC (FORTUNATELY, NOT IN MY PROVINCE), FOLLOWED CLOSELY BY LAWNS. I DO NOT FIND THE LAWN A VERY INTERESTING SUBJECT; NOT, THAT IS, UNLESS YOU ELEVATE ITS CARE TO THE STATUS OF AN ALL-ABSORBING HOBBY WHICH WILL RELIEVE YOU OF ANY RESPONSIBILITY FOR THE REST OF THE GARDEN.

Most gardeners feel that an expanse of green lawn is an asset in a garden. It sets plants off well, as can be seen here, and makes the cheapest, if not the most durable, surface for walking on. Achieving a 'bowling-green' effect requires dedication, as much work as the average border, and stern control of the younger members of the family. Fortunately, a much more practical sward can be achieved with relative ease.

The achievement of the bowling-green ideal will require a determined mixture of ingenuity, continuous effort and an unquenchable hope. My talk, if I am cornered at a party, is all of 'thatch' removal, and weedkilling, fertilizing and rolling, sweeping off worm casts and discouraging leatherjackets but, even if my interlocutor is foolish enough to take all the advice offered, the work will not repay in full the hours of unexciting labour. A really fine lawn needs as much, if not more work, than the average flower border, but no one except the gardener will properly appreciate the effort that has been put in.

If you do not wish to dedicate your life (or, at the least, your spare hours) to a stretch of green sward, then it is possible to provide a not unattractive surface for French cricket and novel-reading, that also acts as an effective green foil for the colourful flower borders, by following the advice I diffidently offer.

You will, I feel confident, have considered doing away with the lawn altogether in moments of intense exasperation with a non-starting petrol engine. I would not advise that, unless the grass is in deep shade and growing very badly, or the ground is so poorly drained that the water lies on it after rain and you have a sinking feeling that you will have to put in land-drains. In the first situation evergreen ground-covers will answer better than grass (even that grown from special shade mixtures), and in the second, paving or gravel may save you effort. These solutions are initially expensive but not when set in the context of a lifetime of annual mower servicing.

Most people, however, would like a lawn, and that being the case, you must first decide whether you want a 'fine grass' lawn or a more hard-wearing 'utility' lawn. The former will be more uniform in colour and texture and can be closely mown, while a utility lawn will be harder wearing and therefore useful for family activities. Fine lawns contain a high proportion of fine-leaved bent and fescue grasses, while utility lawns contain dwarf perennial rye grasses as well as smooth-stalked meadow grass, red fescue and browntop.

Mowing

An inevitable cause of concern to the inexperienced gardener is what kind of mower to buy (see also page 78). They are expensive items, and it is certainly important to consider the alternatives carefully before buying one.

There are two main types: the cylinder-action mower, and the rotary mower, which has a blade underneath revolving at very high speed. Cylinder mowers can be powered either by a petrol or an electric engine (or, rarely, a battery); they can also be hand mowers, which are less noisy but depend on the strength and determination of the operator.

Rotary mowers are always powered, either by petrol or electricity, although some have only the blades powered and not the wheels. Some rotary mowers are hover mowers, which glide over the grass on a cushion of air. Rotary mowers are noisier than cylinder types, but mowing is quicker and easier.

Cylinder mowers are preferable because they cut more cleanly (rotary blades tear the tips of the grass slightly which can cause them to brown), and because those with back rollers create the nostalgic striped effect that is so deeply satisfying to many people. Cylinder mowers will cut as low as 1cm (^{1}/2in), which is the only way that a fine-grassed lawn can be maintained (coarser grasses are discouraged at that height, as are many broad-leaved weeds), and also have better grass-collecting boxes than rotary mowers. Why, then, are a third of all mowers sold rotary mowers? Because rotary mowers allow for imperfections in terrain, as

well as for human error, and are cheaper to maintain. A cylinder mower is less than ideal on bumpy, uneven ground, because it scalps bumps, which allows weed-colonization, is *much* more easily damaged, and needs more, and more expensive, maintenance. Only a rotary mower can deal with the kind of long grass that will grow where wild flowers or bulbs are naturalized, and hover mowers can, with care, be used to cut sloping banks. Some large rotary mowers also have back rollers to achieve the desired striped effect. All mowers, hover, rotary or cylinder, should be treated with cir-cumspection, because accidents do happen with them. Make sure you wear stout, non-slip boots when mowing, and keep children away from the operation. It is now possible to buy small rotary mowers with plastic blades, as a safety feature. 'Deadman's handles' and blade brakes are also fitted to many machines.

Ordinary lawns (which most of us possess) are not fussy about what kind of mower you use; either kind will do the job. These should not be cut too short – to no less than 2.5cm

Very popular these days are wild-flower 'meadows', where the grass is left uncut until mid-summer, with simple paths mown for walking.

(1in), the height for which the rotary mower is ideally suited, but the important thing is to mow the lawn frequently: once a week from early spring onwards, and twice a week in the early summer. (If grasses are left to grow too long they will yellow at the base, which weakens them.) If the lawn is mown in this way, there is no need to put a box onto the machine. Short grass clippings will not normally be tracked into the house by dogs or children; much needed nutrient will over time be returned to the soil; a healthy lawn will be maintained, with grasses able to colonize quickly when moss and weeds are removed, and, provided some scari-fying is done each autumn (see page 44), be less vulnerable to fungal disease.

Of course, lawns are not mown the whole year round; the usual season is from mid-spring until late autumn, with the grass not left too long for the winter.

Feeding & weeding

A lawn really has to be fed and weeded at least once a year, in the spring. The spring work is important because, by the time the temperatures rise and the grass and weeds begin to grow, much of the nutrient will have been washed down by winter rains to below the top

drainage or no bad drainage, although its presence can be limited by regular 'spiking' (see illustration below left) in the autumn and the use of lawn sand or mosskiller. Once the moss has blackened as a result, it should really be scarified (raked out) with a spring-tined rake

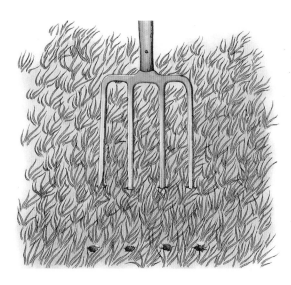

Spiking a lawn, to a depth of 15cm (6in) every 10cm (4in), is an excellent means of introducing air and moisture to grass roots on compacted lawns.

Scarifying with a rake removes moss, after it has been killed, but also dead grass ('thatch') which builds up and hinders rain getting to the roots.

15cm (6in) where the grass roots can make use of them. A high-nitrogen feed will green up the grass almost overnight, and make the grass healthier and stronger-growing. (You may think that that is a mixed blessing but the lawn really should be fed well enough to grow properly and healthily and be a rich colour.) 'Lawn sand' is a good spring feed for the average lawn. It contains nitrogen in the form of sulphate of ammonia, as well as ferrous sulphate which will kill the moss (without which few lawns are complete) and the top growth of many broad-leaved weeds (although not plantains, clover or buttercups). If your soil has a low pH, however, use a special mosskiller rather than lawn sand, because ferrous sulphate and sulphate of ammonia are both acid.

Moss is a fact of life in most lawns, bad

(see illustration above), to give the grasses a good chance of recolonizing the bare soil.

A lawn feed combined with a selective weed-killer is also available for mid-spring or early summer use. This comes in both granular and liquid forms, and is suitable for lawns without moss, or can be applied after a decent interval has elapsed after the lawn sand or mosskiller.

Granules are best spread with a lawn spreader, which is a little hopper attached to a long handle and balanced on two wheels. It appears expensive because of the small amount of use it gets in the year, however, so most people broadcast the granules by hand (gloved, of course). That requires laying canes 90cm (3ft) apart to ensure that the granules are spread evenly. This is a nuisance, and the granules will still not be spread really evenly. Uneven spreading will result either in a double application (which may cause scorching), or none at all (which will give the lawn a patchy look). I do, therefore, come down in favour of the granular fertilizer spreader; not only can you see where you have been, but it is calibrated so that, however fast or slow you push it, the right amount emerges from the bottom.

The liquid fertilizer and weedkiller needs to be diluted and applied either with a watering can and dribble bar, or by the use of a dilutor attached to the hosepipe. Dribble bars are often very short (though ones with extensions do exist), so that there is a great deal of walking up and down even on quite small lawns to ensure that the application is evenly applied. You will also have to calculate how fast you should walk to achieve the magic formula 'at the rate of x litres (gallons) per y sq metres (sq yards)'. (I feel it my duty to point out the potential difficulties in applying these substances, even if the result is a gloomy recital of which Eeyore could justifiably be proud.)

An additional autumn feed is a refinement, but, for the sake of completeness, I will tell you that autumn fertilizers contain a high proportion of phosphates and potash to strengthen the grass and encourage root growth during the winter. They are low in nitrogen, so that the grass is not encouraged to make sappy growth, which would become easy prey for fungal diseases during the winter.

My own feeling about weeds and moss is that I would rather feed, spike and scarify the lawn to grow strong, healthy grass as a match for them, and dig out the odd plantain which does appear, than use too many weedkillers. Having made the decision to use a rotary mower, it is rather fatuous to expect a fine lawn, so a few weeds are neither here nor there. However, moss, as we have seen, is best attacked in the spring with lawn sand or specialized mosskiller, and lawn weeds (which often look their worst in mid-summer) should be identified and eliminated with an appropriate selective weedkiller. In a small area, a kitchen knife is as effective, and ecologically more sound.

Proprietary lawn weedkillers that contain 2, 4-D and/or MCPA will kill the majority of broad-leaved weeds (with the exceptions of clover and speedwell); those that include dicamba or mecoprop should solve the problem of clover, pearlwort, self-heal and yarrow. I like speedwell in the lawn anyway, but it can be attacked with tar oil if you are desperate, though that will brown the grass as well. Many lawn weedkillers also include a lawn fertilizer. Whatever you use, you will need at least two applications, stretching over two springs, to rid the lawn of weeds. Grass clippings that have been subjected to selective weedkillers should not be placed on the compost heap for at least a month after the application, or you may adversely affect the growth of plants mulched with the compost.

I write of lawn pests elsewhere (see page 181), but diseases are rarely a serious problem on the ordinary lawn, provided that snow does not lie too long, the grass is not left to grow too tall or become waterlogged, and the soil is occasionally spiked to aerate it.

Lawn-care calendar

Spring
Start to mow with blades high at first, then progressively lower • Clip edges • Sow or turf new lawns • Lightly scarify lawn with a rake • Apply lawn sand if moss is a problem • Rake up moss when it has turned black, otherwise apply combined spring lawn 'weed and feed' • Reseed bare patches and repair damaged edges

Summer
Feed with lawn fertilizer (optional) • Use lawn weedkiller or dig out troublesome weeds by hand • Water only after a long dry spell • Mow regularly, less in times of drought

Autumn
Sow or turf new lawns • Rake up fallen leaves • Scarify to rid lawn of 'thatch' (optional) • Spike lawn and brush in top-dressing (optional) • Use autumn lawn feed (optional) • Apply mosskiller and fungicide (optional)

Winter
Stop mowing • Service tools and machinery

Edging

As a child, keen to be helpful in the garden, I was almost always detailed to cut the lawn edges. I suppose the idea was that I could hardly do any damage cutting edges, either to myself or to the garden, and I grew quite fond of my appointed job. I knew the edges, their bumps and idiosyncrasies, better than I knew the flowers. Nothing much changed when I grew up. There are 60 kilometres (40 miles) of lawn edges at the Royal Botanic Gardens, Kew, so they say, and I must have cut them all at one time or another. Although edge-cutting is a job I do not resent, if you do have great lengths to cut, I advise you to buy a battery- or mains-operated lawn edger.

You may need to straighten uneven lawn edges out first with a half-moon edging iron, but a lawn edger will save you both time and energy. An alternative is to pave right up to the grass, or lay bricks on edge, so that the mower can be taken right to the edge of the lawn. Grass will eventually grow over this edging, but an occasional skilful slice with the half-moon between paving and grass will solve that problem.

Mowing, feeding, edging – these seem unavoidable tasks, but there are others associated with lawn-cultivation that can be safely kept to a minimum. This is particularly true of those jobs recommended for early autumn (see chart, page 45). Autumn, however, will bring leaves onto the lawn and, if these fall in quantity, do rake them off, because a blanket of leaves makes yellow patches in time; it is also a very agreeable activity on a sunny autumn day. I find a rubber rake the best tool for the job.

Mowing is easier if there is a paved or brick edge onto which so many arching plants can flop, as here, otherwise the edges need regular clipping with edging shears to retain the sharp definition.

Restoration

What happens if you inherit a grassy wilderness? In the old days you would have dug it up and started again, but, with the advent of the rotary mower, it is now possible, in time, to rescue it without such a desperate remedy – unless the underlying soil is waterlogged or suffers from other problems, when rotovating and reseeding will be a better option.

First, remove any old bedsteads, car batteries, lumps of concrete, and other detritus from this jungle; then, in spring, with the blades on the highest setting, carefully cut the lawn. The sward (if such a grand term can be applied) will be very weedy, but with consistent mowing and the use of selective weedkillers, you will soon rid yourself of the worst. Weed grasses such as Yorkshire fog and creeping meadow grass will no doubt be present, as will couch, but the last cannot stand regular mowing, and the first two do not care for it very much either; the *coup de*

If you look closely at the lawn in this very well-kept garden, you will see some clover and moss. These are hard to eradicate completely, and it is doubtful whether a lot of effort to do so is justified.

grâce can be administered by cutting them with a knife before mowing. Spike and top-dress the 'lawn' during the first autumn. If your new lawn is very bumpy and uneven, take the half-moon and cut a line through the middle of the bump or hollow, make two cuts at right angles to that cut at each end, then roll back the turf both ways and remove, or add, some soil until the ground is flat when the turf is replaced. Finally, tread down the turf. (I would, however, be failing in my duty if I pretended that to do this successfully was as easy as writing about it.)

Sometimes, making a new lawn is unavoidable. This is never a job that I view with much pleasure, for there are so many stages to it that the weather rarely remains on your side. You should first decide whether you want, or can afford, to lay turf, by measuring the area and obtaining estimates from firms listed in the telephone book. If you decide to lay turf, try to view what is to be supplied, because turf varies enormously in quality. Some comes from old meadowland, with all the pests and weeds that naturally inhabit it; some (more expensive) is good 'parkland' turf which has been sprayed against weeds; and some (the most expensive) is seeded turf. Because it is seeded you can, in theory at least, acquire turf that contains the mixture of grasses that will make the sort of lawn you require.

A cheaper option is to sow grass seed (see illustrations below), but in either case you will need to prepare the site. You must first rake or take off all rubbish, and dig out any tree stumps. If you do this in spring, you can then spray the emerging weeds with glyphosate – ideally twice, at an interval of a few weeks. You can then level the soil more or less as you want it, by importing top-soil if necessary. If the soil is very heavy and very badly drained (that is, if

water lies on it after rain), you should consider removing the top-soil and spreading a layer of small stones or grit on top of the subsoil, before replacing the top-soil. (This form of drainage is, in reality, rarely necessary.) More often, the soil can be dug over, and sand or very small grit added if the land is very clayey, or a small quantity of peat or peat-substitute if it is very light. The first will aid drainage, the second will help water retention. Do not be tempted, in an excess of zeal, to add bulky organic material when digging, for the lawn will subside as the material rots down. The digging is done more to aerate the soil than to give an opportunity for feeding; after the digging, the broken-up soil can be roughly trodden down.

The next stage is important, whether you are turfing or seeding: namely raking the soil level. Raking is a deceptive activity; you will think the ground is level, until you stoop down almost to ground level and discover that it decidedly is not. A bump removed here somehow appears over there, but do not become disheartened; everyone finds raking difficult, if they are honest. After this initial raking, tread down the soil

Sowing grass seed

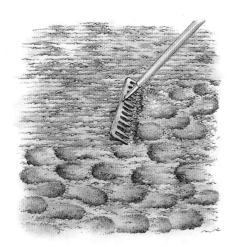

Before sowing lawn seed, it is important to rake the soil to create a fine tilth and then tread it down evenly to make a firm and level base. Rake the soil again, smoothly and gently, ready for sowing.

The ideal, but not essential, way to sow a lawn evenly is to use bamboo canes and string to mark out metre (yard) squares. Sow the seed at 45g per square metre (1½ oz per square yard).

After sowing, rake the soil very lightly to cover some of the seed. Water gently in dry weather to encourage the seed to germinate, and, if practicable, erect netting to protect it from birds.

evenly and carefully by taking little shuffling steps, with the weight on your heels, like an old gentleman in carpet slippers. If you have time, leave the proto-lawn for a while, to allow the annual weeds to germinate; then knock them over with a burst of contact herbicide, which is de-activated on contact with the soil. Once that is done, you must wait until very late summer before sowing, or early autumn before turfing.

Let us first take seed-sowing. I marginally prefer late summer or early autumn to spring as a time to sow grass seed, because the autumn rains should do the watering. Rake the soil smoothly and gently to achieve a tilth; then sow the mixture you want. For an ideal hard-wearing, acceptable lawn you will want a 'utility grade' mixture, which contains one or more of the newish dwarf rye grasses which do not grow tall enough to leave stalks behind by the mower. A suitable mixture might include creeping red fescue, smooth meadow grass, common bent, and a dwarf perennial rye grass. There are also 'shade' mixtures which make quite good (though hardly refined) lawns, and are drought-resistant. Do not expect, however, that they will grow well in deep shade. Cut the new lawn lightly when the seedling grass is 5cm (2in) tall.

Turfing (see illustrations below) is best done in early autumn, when the soil is moist but still quite warm, or in the early spring. It is possible to lay turf at any time from autumn until late spring, but conditions are rarely satisfactory in winter. That is the good news; the bad is that, once the turf arrives, it has to be laid within a few days or the grass, rolled up in Swiss rolls, will be in danger of dying. If you cannot manage that, undo the rolls and leave the turves face up in a shady place until you can lay them.

The turves will overlap the edges of your 'lawn', and will need to be cut to shape. Use a half-moon, accompanied by a plank for a straight edge, or a garden hose, laid to the appropriate shape, if the edge is to follow a more 'natural' curve. If the weather is dry, water before the turves start drying out, cracking and shrinking away from each other. A turf lawn need not be treated so carefully as a newly sown lawn, but can be mown more or less as you would a mature one. It will, however, dry out easily until well established.

Laying turf

Turf is fun to lay once you have achieved a level surface by raking the soil on which to put the turves. Lay the turves in courses, like bricks, so that long cracks cannot develop.

Using a wooden plank as a straight edge, work a half-moon edging tool along the plank to cut the turves. By standing on the plank, you avoid damaging the turves with your feet.

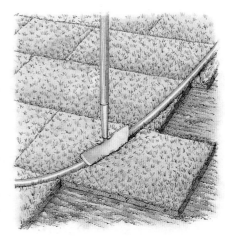

If you want a curved edge to the lawn, use a length of garden hose, secured firmly at both ends, as a guide. Water turves after laying in dry weather, or they will shrink away from each other.

4

CRACKING THE CODE

TODAY, MOST OF US ARE CUT OFF FROM OUR RURAL ROOTS AND HAVE NOT LEARNED GARDENING SKILLS AT OUR GRANDFATHER'S ELBOW IN THE GARDEN. NOT ONLY DO WE NOT KNOW HOW TO CARRY OUT COMPLIC-ATED OPERATIONS LIKE PRUNING, BUT WE ARE NONE TOO CLEAR EVEN HOW TO RAKE OR HOE PROPERLY. THIS SHOULD, HOWEVER, BE A CAUSE NOT FOR PRESENT SHAME BUT RATHER FOR FUTURE RESOLUTION. FORTUNATELY, I CAN THINK OF NO HORTICULTURAL TASK THAT MAY NOT EASILY BE MASTERED WITH A LITTLE PRACTICE. ON NO ACCOUNT LET YOURSELF BE PUT OFF BY ANY MYSTERIOUS WORD THAT YOU MAY ENCOUNTER. PROFESSIONALS LIKE USING OBSCURE TERMS LIKE 'HAULM' AND 'DICOT', 'PLEACH' AND 'SCANDENT', BUT I HOPE THAT, ONCE YOU HAVE READ THIS CHAPTER, YOU WILL HAVE A WORKING KNOWLEDGE OF THE WORDS YOU NEED AND THE CONFI-DENCE NOT TO WORRY ABOUT THE REST.

The satisfaction that comes from making a garden depends partly on confidence about your ability to carry out the practicalities. This garden, with its neatly pruned fruit trees, mulched border, weed-free planting bed and healthy, labelled sweet pea seedlings, is the work of a confident, competent gardener, but there is nothing here that need frighten the reader of this book.

Planting

One task that you must learn to do properly, if you are not to spend a great deal of time and money in vain, is planting. There is no avoiding this: you will need to plant, not only when a new garden is acquired but throughout the whole period of your stewardship; it is within everyone's capability to do well with practice; it is also a most enjoyable occupation.

Much emphasis is given in the literature on preparing the soil well beforehand: digging the ground, and incorporating some nutritious mixture, especially if the soil looks poor or does not have a good structure. It is certainly best to incorporate bulky organic material, especially on light soils, a few days or weeks before you plant, so that the rain can dissolve some of the nutrients into the soil water, and the soil level can settle (see page 66). However, if the choice lies between planting in unsuitable conditions and waiting impatiently on a friendly weather forecast, you can always prepare the ground and plant at the same time. In my experience, newly prepared soil does not settle as much as you might imagine it will, so take care not to plant too shallowly.

Avoid planting container-grown plants after late autumn if you can, and especially if you garden on a heavy clay soil; the soil will be cooling rapidly, and container-grown stock is often more vulnerable to frost damage because it is grown in peat-type composts which are more liable to freeze than soil-based composts, and has been reared in the protection of polythene tunnels by the growers. All in all, it is safest to leave the nurserymen to look after their plants through the winter, and buy them in spring as the soil begins to warm once more. If you do purchase a container-grown plant in the autumn, however, do not hesitate to put it in the ground rather than condemning it to sit outside in its pot all winter, where the roots will be frozen and thawed by turns. Even bone-hardy plants take a very dim view of such hostile conditions.

Mid- to late spring in temperate zones, or early summer in harsher climates, is the best time to plant slightly tender plants like cistus, which come to no harm in a summer drought, as well as evergreens, including conifers. Completely frost-tender plants must be planted when frost is no longer expected, which can vary enormously according to locality, but is usually early summer.

It is possible to plant container-grown shrubs and alpines in the height of summer, but it makes me unhappy to do so, as I am usually away when they are most likely to suffer from water-stress and possibly sun-scorch. However, provided that you can give them the water (and shade as well, in the case of evergreens) that they require, you can nurse new plants through the average summer.

Bare-rooted deciduous plants and those, like the divisions of herbaceous plants, which are dug with some soil attached to the roots, are best planted in the dormant season before the weather worsens and the soil conditions become unsuitably wet or cold. 'Balled' evergreens (field-grown plants, dug with soil around their roots and wrapped in polythene or hessian), should be planted while the soil is still warm in early autumn, or in late spring.

When transplanting a plant from one part of the garden to another, try to dig it up when the soil is sufficiently moist to stick to the roots; ideally, enough soil should be dug out around the roots for the main roots to be drawn out of the ground intact. Use a trowel or hand fork to dig out small plants and a spade for shrubs and small trees. I strongly advise you against moving trees over 3m (10ft) tall, for they will most likely not survive the transplanting, nor you the effort of doing so.

Apart from some notable exceptions, with which I shall deal later (see page 55), all plants should go in the ground at the same level as they were planted before in soil or pot. (The soil-mark is particularly obvious on trees and shrubs.) Of

the two undesirable alternatives, planting too deeply is more harmful than too shallowly. Plant too deeply, and the roots will suffocate and the stem rot at the 'collar'; plant too shallowly, and the surface roots may suffer from drought, while on grafted plants suckers will be encouraged to grow in forceful competition.

Container-grown plants and 'balled' plants are the easiest to plant (see illustrations, page 54). A well-grown container plant will suffer no check when planted in suitable conditions, whereas a bare-rooted plant will, because some roots are inevitably torn. Fleshy-rooted plants, like daphnes and magnolias, resent with a sullen passion having their roots disturbed, so container plants of these are to be preferred.

Water the pot and let it stand a while, so that the plant comes out easily when you turn the pot upside down (holding the stem, or stems, of the plant firmly between the fingers the while)

Here, a mixed bag of plants is waiting to be planted out in a garden. In the meantime, the terracotta pots, in which they are contained, mean that they make an attractive display.

and knock the edge of the pot against an immovable object. Soft black polythene containers or stiff 'whalehide' pots can be cut open with the sharp knife which you will have in your pocket, of course. At the risk of appearing bossy, ON NO ACCOUNT pull the plant from its pot – you may be lucky and the plant may come away with its neat rootball intact but, there again, it may not.

Dig a hole slightly wider and deeper than the circumference and depth of the pot, put in a planting mixture – either bought ready-mixed or made up of half soil, half moist peat or peat substitute, and 100g (4oz) of bonemeal per bucket – and place the plant upright in the

Water well before attempting to 'knock out' a container plant. Plants need to go into the ground at the same level as they were before. Note the mulch.

hole. If the plant is 'pot-bound', try to tease out the roots away from the pot-shape they have acquired. A planting mixture is not necessary if you have already dug in some well-rotted organic material some days or weeks before but it certainly is helpful if you have not, and will allow your plant's smallest new roots to establish quickly in a congenial medium. If you need to support your plant, put a stake in place before planting, not afterwards, in order to avoid harming the roots.

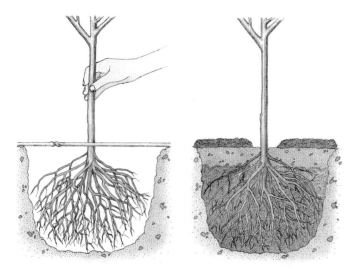

Plant a tree to the same depth it was in the nursery with the help of a cane laid across the hole. Fill in with soil, adding compost if the soil is poor.

The roots of bare-rooted plants are regrettably prone to drying out. However carefully you have wrapped them in polythene or newspaper, it is wise to submerge the roots for a while in a bucket of water before planting. Dig the hole wide enough to take all the roots comfortably (this is something about which the most punctilious of gardeners is inclined to be lazy) and deeper than the plant's roots will go, put in about 5cm (2in) of the planting mixture, tread it lightly (or not at all in soils that easily compact), and place the plant in the hole (see illustrations below), turning it round until its best 'face' is prominent. Many plants, especially trees and shrubs, definitely have a 'front' and a 'back'. Spread the roots out as evenly as possible; fill in with soil or planting mixture, holding on to the plant so that it remains at the right depth and shaking it slightly to ensure the mixture surrounds the roots; and gradually, and carefully, tread the soil down around and over the roots. If you are planting a tree, try to get a friend to hold the stem at the right level while you fill in the soil. Alternatively, place a hoe or bamboo cane across the hole, and lean the plant against it so that you can keep an eye on the level at which you are planting it.

Recent research has pointed to the advantages of mulching substantially after planting. It is drought and competition from weeds that stunt the potential development of newly planted plants; a generous mulch (see pages 35-7) solves both these problems.

Plant small bare-rooted plants with a trowel at a depth that will leave the crown of the plant (where stem meets the roots) at or just below surface level. The roots should be spread out as you would do for shrubs or trees. Bedding plants such as sweet Williams can be put into the ground at speed, provided they are watered afterwards to settle them in and make up for any shortcomings in the planting. Whatever you do, do not allow any root to remain exposed on the soil after planting, for it will surely die, and, whatever the size of plant, make sure the roots are not squashed into the planting hole. I do not recommend that the soil be tamped down afterwards with the handle of the trowel; fingers can do a more delicate and precise job.

Incidentally, the best way of removing summer bedding plants from seed trays is to knock one end of the tray against the grass at the edge of the flower bed where you are working. The soil will be pushed together at that end, and a gap at the other end of the tray will allow you to tease the plants apart and plant them one by one. Those in 'modules' are best removed by pushing with a finger from the bottom; the plant and root ball will pop out easily, provided they are moist.

Leeks are planted by making a hole with your dibber and dropping them in, watering them lightly so that a little soil drops from the sides of the hole (see illustration right). The point of this is to ensure that the leek stem can expand easily. Members of the cabbage family, which appreciate firm planting, are planted by

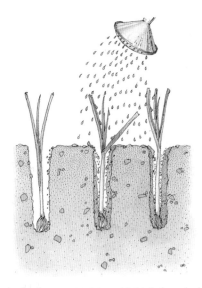

Drop the leeks into 15-20cm (6-8in) deep holes, 15cm (6in) apart. Water gently so that soil from the sides of the holes falls lightly around them.

dibbing a hole, putting in the plant, stabbing the dibber into the ground about 5cm (2in) from the plant stem, and pulling it towards the stem, so that the hole closes off tightly round the stem.

If you plant in the late autumn or winter, it is unlikely that you will have to water after planting, but if the soil is dry below the surface, it is always a wise precaution. Indeed, it is foolhardy not to. Plants must make all their new roots in a short space of time; if the soil is dry, any fertilizer in the ground may scorch them; and watering also helps settle the soil around the roots so that you have a better idea if you have the level right. Set down on paper, all this looks very complicated but indeed it is not. I feel sure you will wish to concentrate on good planting techniques to ensure that your plants 'get away' well, but of course you can often make do with a method of planting that falls short of this.

There are exceptions to the rule about planting depths: peonies may not flower if the crown (from which the buds can be seen poking) is planted more than 2.5cm (1in) below the surface; roses not grown on their own roots will sucker if planted too shallowly, so the union between 'stock' and 'scion' (just above the point from where the roots issue) should be just below the soil surface.

These summer bedding plants have been individually potted up, so will suffer no check to growth when planted out.

Heeling-in

Heeling-in is the expression given to that most useful of techniques, namely, giving plants a temporary home when you cannot think at that precise moment what to do with them. It is almost inevitable that the day a parcel of highly perishable plants arrives, you will be frantically clearing your desk before leaving on a lengthy business trip. The plants must be put somewhere safe quickly, if you are not to lose them.

Dig a trench for bare-rooted trees and shrubs, preferably in a sheltered place, put the roots in, and cover them with soil. Lean them at an acute angle, so that the wind will not push them over, but do not let them touch the ground in case the tips are burned if there are heavy frosts (see illustration left). Container-grown plants are also safest if 'plunged' in the ground until you get home.

Heeling-in is a temporary measure; be careful not to leave plants too long, for they will grow roots, and a rather lop-sided root system may result. When I was once asked by importunate builders to move plants out of a house border one snowy day in winter, and heeled them in in the vegetable garden, I found that, even nine months later when the ground was ready to receive them once more, none had taken any hurt from being rudely transplanted for the duration; indeed, they had developed some lovely little fine roots. Plants can be very tolerant when it comes to that sort of thing.

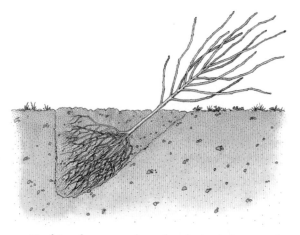

Heel-in a bare-rooted tree by placing it in a trench at an acute angle and covering with soil. Make sure that the stems do not touch the ground.

Protecting

Well up on my list of jobs to do to avoid work in the future comes the protection of my less hardy plants in winter. It is not so much the money that I begrudge when I have regularly to replace *Fremontodendron* and *Agapanthus*, *Ceanothus* and *Abutilon*, but I do dislike taking time and trouble to make a plant happy so that it will flower freely, only to find that a few really cold east winds in late winter have dispatched it to 'its long home'.

In some gardens, frost is the force to be feared, but in others, such as mine, cold, drying winds are the real enemy. Many of my tenderish

The same level of protection offered by this charming old glass cloche, much prized by collectors, can be achieved with cheaper polycarbonate cloches.

Polypropylene netting has been stretched around four wooden stakes to create the ideal protection from windblast in the winter for a young conifer.

cistuses have seemed fine after a harsh winter, only to go suddenly brown and die in a matter of days after bitter winds in early spring. In order to be on the safe side, I advise you to protect half-hardy plants just before winter sets in.

Having said that, it sometimes surprises me how tolerant plants from more temperate regions can be of our climate. Like humans, it is the young and the very old that feel it the worst and particularly need the vegetable equivalent of a fortnight in the Canaries to set them up (see chart, page 59).

Newly planted shrubs and trees, like newly born babies, are the most vulnerable, so they should receive most attention. Start with the evergreens, because of the resistance they present to the wind and because of the potential damage to their long-lasting leaves. If you planted conifers in the autumn, rig up a screen in early winter (see illustration above). It will not look very beautiful, be assured of that, but you can award yourself points for effort. The material to use is the light, green, polypropylene netting which looks rather like the sacking in which onions arrive at the greengrocer's. This is very flexible, lets only 50 per cent of

wind through (which is paradoxically not harmful), and can be used to stretch around stout stakes on the outside of a vulnerable plant. Straw or bubble polythene can be placed inside the structure for additional protection, although holes should be made in the polythene to prevent 'sweating'. The other advantage of these screens is that they let through some light, which is a consideration if the winter is long, and do not encourage too humid an atmosphere inside, which would assist the growth of fungal diseases like *Botrytis* (grey mould). Large tender plants grown as specimens in the open, rather than against a warm wall (which always increases the chance of their surviving the winter) will need the same treatment. The netting can also be stretched over light timber frames (which even I am capable of putting together) to make excellent protective screens when leaned against a wall for tender wall plants.

Some plants must be protected from frost without fail, and certainly it is an optimistic gardener who does not lay something over her *Agapanthus* in the early winter. These South African bulbs are relatively hardy, but they are inclined to rot if their crowns do not have some protection from winter and rough weather. Straw and bracken are the materials most often suggested, most cleverly in a sandwich of chicken wire, but composted bark or peat substitutes are more readily available alternatives (see illustration below), and will provide a warm,

Plants, such as this Agapanthus, *which would rot if buried in snow or waterlogged, need their crowns protecting with some fibrous, porous material.*

protective blanket. Because the removal of tomato plants from their growing bags in the cold greenhouse coincides, more or less, with the urge to protect plants in the garden, I often use the spent peat compost for this purpose. Potash is the main ingredient of tomato fertilizers, and since potash is what I sprinkle around tender shrubs to strengthen their wood before winter sets in, this material is highly suitable for putting around half-hardy plants.

Those gardening on heavy soils, or those growing alpines and other drought-tolerant plants, or both (if any there be), need to do something to protect susceptible plants from the wet. In the case of alpines, this is far more important than protecting them from cold and wind. Alpines, being dwarf, are not affected by wind, for even on an excessively windy day, there is rarely excessive turbulence at or near ground level. Wet, on the other hand, kills them stone dead, for it gets amongst their woolly leaves and rots them; hence the emphasis laid on putting grit around the collars of alpine plants. Of course you will be growing these plants in a well-drained medium, but it is advisable to put additional protection over them in the winter. Glass is the material most usually advocated but is no good for gardeners with

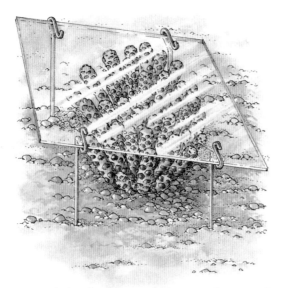

A simple homemade support for a small square of Perspex sheeting is all that is required to protect woolly-leaved alpines from winter wet.

small children. Preferable is the less aesthetically pleasing plastic cloche. I place whole cloches, without end pieces to aid ventilation, over my raised alpine bed which, quite fortuitously, they fit quite well. When the plants begin to show signs of flowering, I take them off. What I have achieved is a miniature alpine house. It is not beautiful but it serves the purpose. If you have only one or two plants to protect, a sheet of clear Perspex, secured by four pieces of wire clipped to the sheet and then pushed into the soil, will do the trick (see illustration below left).

Cloches are used both to protect plants and warm the soil, and are demonstrably a good thing. They can be used either for individual plants or for plants in quantity, and come in many different forms, from two panes of glass or plastic clipped together, to polythene tunnels and even 'floating' polythene cloches or 'horticultural fleece'. Used to warm the soil in the spring, they enable the gardener with foresight to steal a march on her fellows; in colder areas where there may be a risk of frost for eleven months of the year, they are vital if most vegetables are to be grown at all. They are especially helpful for those crops, like parsnips, that are prone to rot during the long time the seed takes to germinate if the soil is wet and cold.

Cloches magnify the sun's rays, which helps to dry out and warm the soil, and offer protection against wind and heavy spring rains. I am all for cloches, and use them extensively, but I do not expect them to be a universal panacea. There are even times when their presence can become positively counter-productive. For example, with the exception of floating cloches or horticultural fleece, they must either be removed in early summer, or have shading painted on the surface, if seedlings are not to be burned by the magnifying-glass effect of the sun on cloche.

The floating cloche is a good idea in theory, and a fiddle in practice. It consists of thin polythene with evenly spaced slits cut in it. As the seedlings grow, they push up the polythene, push against and through the slits, and as these open, they let in air and water. This kind of cloche is not suitable for anything which grows with a pointed head, like cabbage 'Hispi', or for onions, but otherwise can be helpful. If you are *extremely* far-sighted, you can bury one edge in soil, anchor the other side with a wooden batten and, when the crop no longer needs protection, lift up the polythene on the batten side and roll it over to do the same job for the adjacent plot, anchoring it once more on the other side.

As with all creators of damp, warm conditions at ground level, this cloche will greatly encourage slugs to flock to your lettuces, so slug pellets are unfortunately necessary. Weeds grow, well, like weeds, which is why one side should be battened so that it can be picked up relatively easily, in order to weed amongst the seedlings. I cannot deny that this undermines the attractiveness of the floating cloche for me.

Better by far is the horticultural fleece now available; this is a lightweight blanket which is permeable both to water and light, is easy to use, and can be laid over the ground to help warm it, or over new seed beds. It will 'give' as the seedlings grow. It is easier to manage than the floating polythene cloche, and does not cause the crop to 'sweat' in humid conditions. As an additional benefit, it will also prevent attack by unwelcome pests such as the carrot root fly.

Whichever cloche you decide to use, the most important decision is when to put it on to achieve the greatest benefit. The idea is to put the cloche in place a week or two before you intend to sow your seed so that the sun will, amplified by the glass or clear plastic, warm up the soil still further and also dry it out somewhat. Curiously, I use cloches as much in autumn as I do in spring: to hurry on a few late-sown lamb's lettuce or tardy Chinese cabbage. It is remarkable how much growth these salad crops will make in fine, sunny autumns. You can also use cloches to ripen a few late tomatoes outside, should your kitchen window-sill be full. Provided the soil is dry, you can also use cloches to shelter harvested onions that need ripening and drying off.

The best modern invention for protecting tender plants is horticultural fleece. As well as allowing rain through, it also acts as a light blanket.

Some people use cloches to protect the flowers of certain winter-flowering plants, particularly *Helleborus niger*, the Christmas rose, which has the innocent whiteness of its flowers easily besmirched by mud splashes. Cloches are also a good idea on the raised bed or rock garden where you know, with a bleak certainty, that your woolly-leaved *Androsace* will not survive the winter outside without protection from the rain.

Plants needing winter protection

The following need protection during the winter months in all but the mildest districts

Abutilon × *megapotamicum*	*Crinum*
Agapanthus	*Dahlia* (if left *in situ*)
Androsace	*Draba*
Callistemon	*Hebe speciosa*
Camellia (some)	*Magnolia* (some)
Ceanothus (some)	*Nerine*
Cistus (some)	*Olearia*
Cordyline australis	*Phormium*
Crinodendron hookerianum	*Saxifraga* (some)

Staking

Staking young trees appears, on the face of it, eminently desirable, and was in the past much advocated. Recently, however, the desirability of staking has been thrown into question. Research has shown that the majority of trees are better off not being staked at all (except in very exposed places like the seaside). The principle is that of the man who, recovering from a temporary illness (in this case transplanting), gets so used to walking with a stick that he is weaker when he throws it away than if he had never had it. Instead of a sturdy, independent tree, there is a weakling dependent on a crutch.

It would appear that an unstaked tree develops not only a more extensive root system, but also a tapered stem which, thicker at the bottom, aids stability in the face of the 'wind sway' that it encounters. If there is little or no 'wind sway' and tapering cannot develop properly, trees are extremely vulnerable to being blown over once the stake is removed. It is as simple as that. If the idea of not supporting your trees, like not supporting your family, offends your sense of right and wrong, continue to stake, but use short stakes only, or less than, a third the height of the trunk to where the branches begin (see illustration right). Heavy staking is appropriate, according to the scientists, only when large trees are to be planted in exposed coastal positions, or places where vandalism is a problem (which will not be an overriding anxiety in the average private garden). Eucalyptus trees, which grow rapidly and are famous for 'windblow', may need more than one stake, but even these should only be short ones. Of course, if you buy a container-grown tree which has been staked in its pot, it may well need to remain staked, at least for a while, but the length of the stake and the duration for which the plant remains staked should be kept to the minimum. The only commonly encountered occasion when a tall stake will be necessary, that I can think of, is if you plant a grafted plant, especially the weeping form of an upright tree like a birch, which has been supported while it was in the nursery.

If you feel anxious for the fate of your conifer hedge in a windy position, thin out some of the branches when transplanting the trees, in order to cut down on the wind resistance. The branches will soon be renewed naturally.

The advice not to stake has a positive side-effect. A great deal of damage can be done to a tree by tree ties biting into the bark of the stem as it grows and expands in girth. Even in a small private garden, it is possible to forget to examine trees regularly – at least twice a year – and in really bad cases a tree may die as the result of the tie constricting it so tightly that the thin layer of food cells under the bark is destroyed.

Bought tree ties are all much of a muchness but come in different sizes. In cold weather, the

Trees planted in normal conditions require a short stake for no more than 18 months. Note the buffer between the tree tie and stake.

plastic ones are difficult to manipulate, and most are difficult to adjust once they have been in place for some time. A pair of laddered tights will serve the purpose as well, and also have a little 'give', but they are hardly decorative.

Although it may be possible to avoid staking trees, one can hardly get out of supporting many of the larger and more vigorous herbaceous perennials. Even here, there is a great difference between the individual species in their capacity to hold up their heads. (In this respect, plants resemble humanity.) Some of the largest perennials, for example, like *Macleaya cordata* or *Eupatorium purpureum*, have tough, sturdy stems, whereas the far shorter michaelmas daisies lean, if unsupported, like seaside holidaymakers in a gale. The worst offenders are undoubtedly the daisy family, particularly noticeable because there are so many of them, like the tall asters, echinaceas, gaillardias, heleniums and rudbeckias, but tall campanulas, delphiniums, *Echinops*, *Galega officinalis*, *Geranium psilostemon*, hollyhocks, Oriental poppies, peonies, phloxes, *Physalis*, *Polemonium*, tall salvias, *Saponaria*, *Sidalcea* and *Thalictrum* all need a hand as well.

Staking herbaceous perennials is rather a pleasant task, once you have assembled twine and canes around you. The secret is to do it early, but not too early. I prefer to do it when the growth is about 30cm (12in) high, for I do not much care for bamboo canes sticking skywards like a frontier stockade.

A normal herbaceous clump will require three or four canes pushed in the ground at equal distances, just in from the outermost leaves. They should be shorter than the ultimate height of the flower heads. (Avoid using only one cane for a clump; the plant stems will look very bunched and squashed if you do, and the object is defeated if the result is unpleasing to the eye.) Encircle the canes with the string, doubling it tightly around each cane as you go, so that the plant is in its own enclosure. As the leaves grow they will hide the twine and eventually the top of the canes as well (see illustration above right).

The staking of perennials should, ideally, always be unobtrusive. The obvious canes and string in this picture are for the purpose of illustration.

Less obtrusive, for smaller plants at least, are what are known as pea sticks. For years, I had no idea what these were as peas did not appear to make sticks, but the expression actually refers to those twiggy sticks that you can cut from birch, hazel or other small trees with which to prop up pea growths. Their availability is decidedly limited, however. If you cannot get them, use bamboo canes or those green-painted thin sticks which would be perfect were it not for their extraordinary capacity for insinuating splinters into one's fingers.

Circular wire frames on tripods of different heights, with several compartments to the circle, are widely used today, because they are so easy to set up. Even better, to my mind, are the linking metal stakes which, like the tripods, come in different heights and will make any size of squarish circle, depending how many you join together.

Provided the tall plants are adequately, and discreetly, staked, most other perennials, if planted close together, hold each other up quite

well. You can help by including a good number of strong-stemmed plants amongst the wobblers, and by siting the border in as sunny but sheltered a place as is possible.

Chrysanthemums, large-flowered dahlias and delphiniums need and deserve a sturdy single stake for support. In the case of the larger dahlias, you will need a proper 2.5cm (1in) square one. These plants make a lot of leaf, and are very heavy, especially when wet.

The traditional method of employing stout 2.5m (8ft) bamboo canes, 23cm (9in) apart, and tied together with garden string, still gives the best support for vigorous, twining sweet peas.

The unobtrusiveness of the staking is a matter of much less moment in the vegetable garden, unless you are gardening *au potager*. However, the line must be drawn at the virulently green plastic netting which is available for the taller

'Wigwams' of three stout poles, put in place before planting or sowing, are one method of supporting twining plants, such as runner beans.

peas and beans to grow up. As this netting also needs stakes to support it, it is, to my mind, no great improvement on the other method, which consists of four stakes, two at each end for a double row, with two or three lines of unobtrusive thick garden twine stretched between the stakes. The peas or beans will need support for no more than a few weeks anyway, and it is a fiddle to disentangle the stems from the netting at the beginning of each season. Somehow, the size of netting one gets never quite runs to the length of row one wants.

If you are growing runner or climbing French beans, you will need to erect either a 'wigwam' of three stout poles, tied together at the top (see illustraton above); or one pole in the middle with radiating strings pegged to the soil, using tent pegs or similar; or netting attached to stakes at the ends of the row; or a double row of 2.2m (7ft) or 2.5m (8ft) canes or poles which lean towards each other and are tied at the top.

Most people gradually evolve a method that suits them, depending on how much room they have, how many canes, and to what lengths they wish to go.

There are some roses that also need support. The most obvious are the standard roses which, though unattractively stiff in my opinion, may nevertheless be suitable for planting in formal situations (see illustration below). A stake is also helpful for those with heavy heads on slender stems. Some of the large old shrub roses have stems that trail on the ground when in flower. This rather undermines the purity of the bloom which is plainly the point of them. An elaborate wooden square can be erected for the branches to lean out against, but it is easier, it has to be admitted, to hold them up with canes more or less hidden in the foliage. In a perfect world, cast-iron supports would be affordable, as they once were.

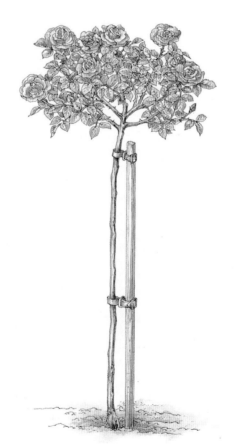

A standard rose, with so much top-heavy growth, requires two rose ties and a stout stake. Be sure to loosen the ties as the stem girth increases.

Deadheading & cutting back

Cutting overblown roses in summer and trimming the stalks of spent flowers in the autumn find favour with gardeners, perhaps because these activities combine little effort with considerable effect, and please our tidy-minded souls. Never wishing to have my own pleasure spoiled, I am slow to spoil anyone else's, but I have to say that most of us do too much of both.

Summer deadheading is advisable for some plants, it is true. Roses immediately spring to mind, though only repeat-flowering roses benefit; deadheading them is one of those golden jobs where you can see the result (see illustration below). It is done when the first flush of flowers is just about over, and has the effect of encouraging the rose to flower once more. As we know, flowers do not flower for our benefit specifically, but rather to reproduce themselves, so cutting off their heads before they can set seed means they have to start all over again. It is, of course, a waste of time with roses that have only one flush of flower; nothing will encourage a single-flowerer to have another go. Apart from the Bourbons, which do have a kind

Deadhead repeat-flowering roses, or single-flowerers if the hips are not required, by cutting back the stems. Do not cut off much leaf.

of autumn flush, and the modern shrub roses, like the Hybrid Musks, which are 'recurrent', no 'Old Rose' warrants being trimmed back. If you wish to make potpourri, simply pull the flower from its calyx.

Other plants, like *Dianthus*, delphiniums and herbaceous geraniums, respond in the same way to having their old flowers cut or trimmed, using either shears or secateurs. They rarely flower with the same exuberance the second time round, but such a capacity is still well worth promoting.

Just as there are some obdurate single-flowerers amongst the roses, so many shrubs will not flower again if deadheaded, except in unusual climatic circumstances. Some plants, like the species lilac, *Syringa microphylla*, have a little second flutter in some years when they feel like it and the weather is favourable, so should be cut back after the first flowering.

Herbs, and other strictly 'foliage' plants, should be deadheaded before flowering, unless you wish to save the seed, because the leaves are inclined to deteriorate when plants are channelling all their energies into flower and fruit production.

It may seem unnecessarily perverse to question whether cutting plants back in the autumn is always necessary; it is, after all, one of those tasks hallowed by long tradition. However, more than a hundred years ago, William Robinson was questioning its value in a conspicuously rhetorical manner. Let us consider why we do it.

The argument runs that if we do not cut back perennials after flowering, they will look untidy. Strictly speaking, that is so, but do they look better when reduced to a mounded crown of clean-cut short sticks than as brown and sere flags waving in the wind or brightened by a winter sun shining from behind them? I know which I prefer, although I recognize that some plants die more gracefully than others. I certainly do not cut my ornamental grasses in the

autumn any more; I leave my peonies alone because they bronze rather prettily, and I am slow to remove the flat seed heads of achillea. I will admit, reluctantly, that some soft plants such as hosta are improved by being cut down and cleaned up.

Even if they might look better left, the argument continues, do not they harbour insects in the winter? Well, they do, or certainly may, although it makes precious little difference in the scheme of things, for it is the weather that has most influence on the size of pest infestations. I would suggest, however, that any herbaceous perennial attacked by fungus, such as mildewed michaelmas daisies, should be cut hard back and the trimmings burned.

Well then, goes the argument, promiscuous plants must certainly be prevented from seeding. This, on the face of it, seems persuasive; yet, there are few things I am really sorry to see

If you stay your hand in autumn and do not shear or cut off the seed heads, this can be the attractive result. It will probably last through the winter, especially if the weather is frosty rather than damp.

seed all over the place. Most plants are introduced deliberately, and you will probably be delighted to see them multiply without any effort. If the seedling is not true to type, as happens in the case of the progeny of fertile hybrids, and if there is no improvement in the next generation, you will simply dig it up. Any unwanted seedlings are easy to pull out in the spring during the first good 'weed'. True gardeners set much store by the finding of interesting seedlings, and many of the most beautiful of our garden plants have been introduced by sharp-eyed and diligent gardeners who have turned their faces resolutely against cutting their plants back in autumn.

Cultivating the soil

Digging

It is, as we established in chapter 2 on soil, sometimes necessary to dig. If you know what the main objectives in digging are, how to do it becomes plainer. Firstly, it is done for the purpose of incorporating bulky organic material into the top-soil (which can have a quicker effect on soil fertility than simply putting it onto the surface). Secondly, it is done to break up heavy and compacted ground, so that the action of the weather, by freezing and thawing the soil water, will succeed in bursting apart the soil particles, making it far easier to rake a heavy soil into a workable 'tilth' in the spring. Thirdly, it is done to break up a compacted 'pan' (see page 28). Most importantly of all, it is exercise to keep you warm on cold winter days. If digging did not exist, we should have to invent it, for it combines, in more or less the

right quantities, hard, unpalatable labour with tangible, beneficial results.

In brief: the length of a spade's blade is called a 'spit' (this is just one of those picturesque old words with which the true gardener protects his occupation from the incursions of novices, 'haulm', the leaves and stems of potatoes, is another). Digging down to a spit's depth is called 'single digging' (see illustration below). Digging down to a spit's depth, then forking over the spit below and incorporating organic material into that second spit, is called 'double digging' (see illustration, page 67). It is more than double the work, let me assure you, but it may be necessary in the following three instances and these three only, namely: if the soil has not been cultivated or fed for a long time (for example, if you take over a neglected garden whose fertility is in doubt); if you

Single digging

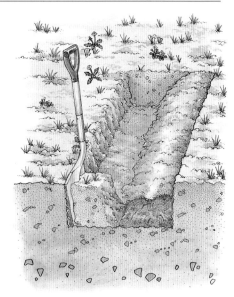

Dig out a trench a spit deep and about 38cm (15in) wide. Put the soil in a barrow and take to the end of the ground you intend to dig. It is used to fill the final trench. Don't be too ambitious; digging is best done in small doses.

Fork over the bottom of the trench to help aeration. Add one bucket of organic material (homemade compost or well-rotted manure) per square metre (yard) to the trench. Proprietary concentrated manures must be used sparingly.

Working backwards, skim any weeds into the trench, then dig another spit's depth and width and place the earth on top of the organic matter in the trench in front. Try to keep it level and only a little proud of the surrounding soil.

garden on heavy soil and you wish to make a new bed or border; if you wish to establish a 'deep bed' for growing vegetables (see page 154). There is such a thing as 'trenching', which is cultivating ground to the depth of three spits, but we will draw a veil quickly over that.

Digging is worse than a waste of time if the soil is waterlogged, or even so wet that it sticks heavily to your boots (walking on it in those conditions squeezes out the air, so undermining the soil structure); if there is snow on the ground; if the soil is frosted (if you bury frozen soil it may stay frozen into the spring, long after the top part has warmed up).

Digging is enjoyable only if you have a good spade which comes to hand well, you push the spade down vertically so that it gets down to the required depth, and you take little spadefuls which will not exhaust you quickly. The point is to keep going steadily and reasonably effortlessly, which means abandoning it when you are tired. A half-hour stint will be quite long enough at first. If you have a weak or painful back, buy a spade that does the lifting and turning when you pull a lever; alternatively, use a small, easy-to-manage rotovator.

Not digging at all (the so-called 'no-dig' method) is possible, at least in the vegetable garden, if you spread large quantities of compost on the top of the soil. The organic material will be drawn down in time by earthworms who will do much of the soil aerating for you. Because the process is slow, you will find it best to plant young plants out of trays rather than sow seed straight into the decaying organic matter. On a clay soil, digging is so difficult and the risk of compacting the soil by walking on it so great, that this is a real alternative.

I write with real feeling when I say that rings should be removed from your fingers before you begin digging. The first dig of the year will almost certainly come as an unpleasant shock to your hands, causing them to blister like old paintwork in the summer sun.

Double digging

Dig a 60cm (2ft) wide trench initially, and barrow its contents away to where the final trench will be dug. This requires digging in 'bites' so it is helpful to stretch garden lines, at right angles to each other, to keep the trench straight.

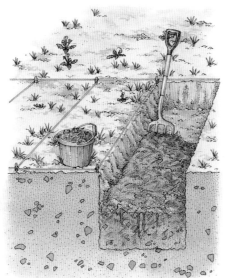

Fork the second spit up and then lay organic material on top. Do not incorporate this into the second spit, as is sometimes advised, for it will be out of reach of all but the most vigorous and questing roots.

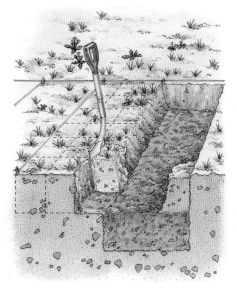

Put soil dug from the second trench to the back of the first, adding more organic material if you want. This is hard work and difficult to do neatly at first, so don't despair! Fill the last trench that you make with the soil from the barrow.

Gardeners tend to acquire a variety of hoes. All of these can be used for weeding but the middle one, a draw hoe, is also invaluable for taking out drills.

Hoeing

Hoeing is surprisingly difficult to do well. So lethal am I with a hoe that I have been forced to abandon hoeing in my crowded old borders. Because of my lamentable memory as to where exactly I have planted a new treasure, I have too often shorn off promising shoots. The usefulness of the hoe is limited, in any event, for it is the weeds interspersed closely among your cultivated plants that take the most food and water, and these you must weed by hand.

In the vegetable garden, however, a hoe is very useful, except where deep beds are used, in which case you might as well use a hand fork. If you do like hoeing, sharpen the end of the hoe with a file; not so much so that you can cut the head off a globe artichoke with a single deft stab, but so that it will glide easily over the soil, wreaking destruction quietly and efficiently. The point of hoeing is not to uproot perennial weeds (this is best done with a fork) but to weaken them, while leaving annual weeds to die

in the sun. People hoe too deeply; it is harder work and not necessary.

Raking

Raking the soil is another task, like hoeing, that looks simple enough but may be done incorrectly. In one sense, this does not matter very much, except when making a new lawn or vegetable seed bed; then avoiding bumps and depressions is a laudable aim. But it can be overdone: too much, and light soil will become dusty; if heavy, it will cake together; and deep rakers will bring up a lot of unwanted stones to the surface, which will disturb the level.

Initially, the back of the rake should be used to break down any lumps that have remained after digging and weathering, and the rake then used lightly, in long movements to and fro, first one way and then at right angles, so that the level is maintained (see illustration below).

Any fool can rake up leaves from the lawn with a spring-tined rake or besom. Raking thatch on a lawn, however, is the most awful job it is possible to imagine, with the possible exception of chemical spraying. It is almost unbelievably hard work, unless you have shoulder muscles as strong as iron bands and an extremely high boredom threshold. If you cannot afford an electric lawn rake, hire one.

After breaking down any lumps in the soil with the back of the rake, rake lightly, to and fro, in one direction, and then at right angles.

Other useful techniques

Blanching, earthing up & forcing

Blanching – the process whereby green leaves or stems are made white by excluding light, without which the green pigment chlorophyll cannot be manufactured – is a technique used on several kinds of vegetables to make them less coarse in texture or to banish the bitter taste the vegetable naturally possesses. Blanching, which is generally less popular today because it entails quite a bit of work, is done in a number of ways, although the chances are that you will really only need to know about how to achieve white-stemmed leeks.

Earthing-up is a way of blanching, and is used to prevent potatoes, celery, carrots and leeks from turning green. Potatoes, especially, must have the earth mounded up well on both sides of the row, for green potatoes are quite poisonous. Carrots require a little soil drawn up over the crowns of the roots as these expand, to prevent them from going green on exposure to light.

Leeks are planted in deep holes, but will have longer white stems if earth is drawn up around them as they grow; endive has its leaves tied together, and a clay or plastic pot inverted over them; and celery (apart from the 'self-blanching' type) is usually earthed up in a trench (many gardeners also tie the celery shoots together, and even wrap the shoots in cardboard so that no earth can get between them to rot the heart). Seakale, now coming back into fashion, is blanched (and can also be forced) in the spring by being covered with large pots. Special seakale pots are available. Chicory, too, is not only blanched but forced as well, by transplanting the roots (called 'chicons') in autumn into a pot, upturning a similar pot on top, and keeping the pot in a minimum temperature of 10°C (50°F). They will be ready in about a month.

Forcing means bringing plants on faster than they would otherwise grow, and often involves giving plants artificial warmth. Bulbs such as

Earthing-up

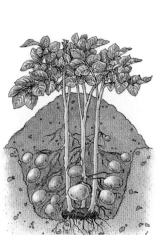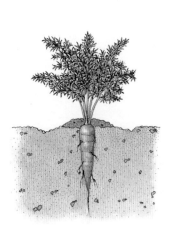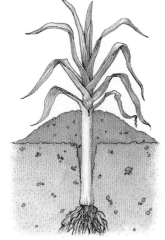

There are several vegetables that benefit from being blanched, that is, having the light denied them so that they cannot make the green pigment chlorophyll. Potatoes, celery, carrots and leeks are blanched by having soil earthed up round them to varying heights, as illustrated above. The draw hoe is the most useful implement for earthing-up, and there is the added bonus that weeds are discouraged in the process.

Seakale is blanched and slightly forced in spring, by having a large light-excluding pot put over the new shoots. Note the colour of the unblanched shoots.

hyacinths are forced into flower by being brought indoors in late winter; winter-flowering herbaceous plants like hellebores can be dug up, potted up, and brought inside to flower earlier than they would outside, and with less chance of their petals being chewed to shreds by slugs or splashed with mud. Even strawberry plants can be potted up and brought into a cool greenhouse in mid-winter, to flower and fruit earlier than is possible outdoors. Forcing rhubarb in heat is for the real devotee. The most I will ever do is to put an old dustbin over the roots outside in the early spring, which is a far cry from digging up the crowns and bringing them into a heated greenhouse

Thinning

Thinning is the technique used to achieve fewer, but larger, fruit. It is necessary for

peaches and grapes, neither of which will produce good-sized fruit otherwise. You may also be advised to thin the fruit of gooseberries or fruit trees. If you are really short of anything to do, thin gooseberries in early summer, and apples and pears after what is known as the 'June Drop'. Unless I have a tree whose branches I suspect will break under the weight of fruit, I leave thinning entirely to Nature.

Thinning is also what you do to seedlings, especially vegetable ones, once germination has taken place (see illustration below). Inevitably, one sows too many seeds in the mistaken belief that germination will be nowhere near 100 per cent. However, this is now a rather old-fashioned view, because vegetable seed germination is so dependable (usually at least 80 per cent). Exceptions to this general proposition are broad beans, which germinate adequately but make delicious meals for mice, and parsnips, which sometimes rot early in the season before they have a chance to germinate. Thin seedlings to the width apart you would like the mature plants to grow, or a half-way stage towards that, if this is a job you enjoy. You can eat lettuce and spring cabbage thinnings. It is worth making the effort to sow carrot seed very thinly, for removing seedlings inevitably means you crush the leaves, and the strong scent will attract the carrot fly (whose grubs tunnel into the incipient roots and make them inedible).

Thin out lettuce seedlings when they are large enough to handle, leaving twice as many as needed. Thin again 2-3 weeks later.

Chitting potatoes

Chitting is the process by which potato tubers are started into growth early in the year indoors. This speeds up the rate at which they grow away and, if the tubers are started off in late winter, in a light, frost-free place, they do produce a better crop. This is particularly true of 'early' potatoes. I put mine in a seed tray, on newspaper, with the 'rose' end uppermost, where most of the 'eyes' (dormant buds) are to be found (see illustration below).

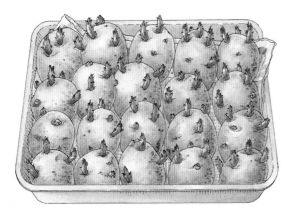

Place potato tubers on newspaper in a seed tray to encourage them into growth before being planted out. Rub off any surplus shoots.

Pinching out

Pinching out is the technique of removing the growing tip of a stem, which will encourage the two lateral buds below to shoot and therefore produce more flowers, or bushier growth. If you pinch out the flower stems of, for example, the houseplant *Coleus*, you will not only encourage it to form a good balanced bushy plant, but you will stop the nondescript flower stalks detracting from the appearance of the multi-coloured leaves. The bushy growth of basil plants is ensured by pinching out the tops of young plants when they are approaching 15cm (6in) in height.

Pinching out is also the method used to 'stop' the growth of some types of tomato plant when sufficient flower trusses have been set; this encourages the plant to divert all its resources into producing large fruit rather than more flowers.

Budding & grafting

If you really want to frighten a gardening beginner, breathe the words 'budding and grafting' in her ear. Even experienced gardeners sway like waterweed in a swollen stream when these words are mentioned. Most people never quite discover what it all entails and are more than happy to remain in ignorance. That is as it should be. Budding and grafting have only a very marginal general application and are not worth the blood that you will inevitably spill in the learning. Not only do these techniques require manual dexterity of an uncommon order (and a very sharp knife) but also patient aftercare. In case you are curious, they are ways of propagation, joining part of one plant (the stock) to another (scion).

Storing

Few of us still possess a special fruit room, with the names of the varieties written on the face of each tray, so we have to make do with wrapping apples in squares of newspaper or greaseproof paper and putting them in a shallow cardboard box, or placing them in deeper boxes (unwrapped) in polystyrene indented trays or cardboard boxes with paper compartments. Pears are stored unwrapped. The essential is to keep the fruit cool, but not frozen, and separate, so that the common disease 'brown rot' does not spread from apple to apple.

Storing apples in wood shavings keeps the fruit dry and ensures that brown rot cannot spread.

Watering

Watering sounds a straightforward gardening task but it should not be done carelessly or haphazardly. Fortunately, more harm is done by incorrect watering in the greenhouse, or in the house, than in the garden, where mistakes are often ironed out by the tolerance of soil and climate, and where disasters can always be blamed on natural rather than on human agency.

When, what, and how much should you water? People are often surprised how early in the growing season they need to water, and many have a touching but erroneous faith in the efficacy of rainfall. 'The soft, refreshing rain' is often wasted, however, either because it falls in

lashing torrents and runs off a dry soil (as a result of the 'cap' that too easily forms and prevents its entry) or because the sun comes out too quickly and evaporates much of it. An average soil in which there are plants growing will lose the equivalent of about 2.5cm (1in) of rain a week in the summer through evaporation.

It is the soil that should chiefly determine how much water to give the garden; that, and the weather, and the kinds of plants you grow. On light, free-draining soil, and in drier areas, watering clearly becomes necessary far earlier in the season than it does on heavier, moisture-retentive soils in wetter areas. Wind, as well as sun, will dry out the top-soil if there is a lack of leaf- or mulch-cover, while plants that enjoy moist places, and have big thirsty leaves, like *Ligularia*, will need watering long before the drought-loving, silver-leaved artemisias. It is, therefore, impossible to be dogmatic about when to water, and what.

You do not, however, have to be an expert to know that a plant requires water if its leaves go limp and it wilts. Unfortunately, leaving it too long before you water may cause cell damage, and the plant may soon reach what is known as its PWP or 'permanent wilting point' – in other words, the point of no return. Even if it does not die as a result of water stress, it will perform less well; irregular or inadequate watering of tomatoes, for example, may cause the fruits to split.

Certain plants are always prone to drought in a period of light or non-existent rainfall. The most obvious are all newly planted plants in the spring after they go in the ground, and trees and shrubs for eighteen months or so after that. Early summer is the time of fastest leaf growth, which means that vegetables, especially those with only shallow roots, are at their most

All these plants are tolerant of drought. The stones ensure a cool root-run for the plants and act as a mulch to help prevent evaporation from below.

vulnerable. Plants put under stress through lack of water feel the urge to flower, which means, in the case of spinach and lettuce, that they 'bolt' (run up to flower) prematurely and become inedible.

Other categories of plants which particularly merit attention include half-hardy annuals (see chapter 10), which need watering throughout their lives in dry summers, but particularly in the first weeks after planting; anything grown in a container or tub, especially if it is in a sunny or windy position; climbing plants grown close to the house or to garden walls; most vegetables, particularly tomatoes, peas and beans, *Cucurbitaceae* (which is a grand name for cucumbers, marrows and melons) except when

Young seedlings, such as the radishes and lettuces in the foreground, will die quickly if the surface moisture dries out. This small rotary sprinkler will provide the necessary water quickly and efficiently.

their fruits are ripening, onions (except when ripening off) and celery; also those plants, like rhododendrons, that have shallow roots and revel in humid conditions. Lawns, which always receive the most attention because they look unattractive when yellow, are much less damaged by drought than any of the plants mentioned above.

In the absence of any visible wilting by shallow rooters, check the soil. Take a trowel and dig down 15cm (6in). If the soil is really dry

Although laborious, the most economical method of watering plants is individually from a watering can. It is important to water each plant thoroughly, so that it is not encouraged to make only shallow roots which are vulnerable to drought.

below about 5cm (2in), you must prepare to water the soil substantially. If you merely sprinkle the surface with water, you will encourage roots to come up to find it, only to die when the soil dries out again; you will also make them dependent on you, so that you will be forced to water more often thereafter.

What constitutes a good watering is a poser. If you have a shrub that is suffering, take the rose off a 9 litre (2 gallon) can and empty the water slowly all round the base of the plant. Trees will need even more water until their roots are well enough established (after about two years) to seek the water further below. A lawn or dry border will need sprinkling with water for an hour in one place before you move the sprinkler on.

Fortunately, watering is no longer the chore it was, although a little money will have to be spent on adequate equipment if the business is to be made less arduous (see also page 81). Watering cans now come in plastic or metal, and hosepipes have improved immeasurably in the last few years; because of the nylon thread

that runs through them, they rarely kink even when pulled round corners, and are now a positive pleasure to use. However, even with a proper nozzle attachment, it is difficult to direct a sufficiently fine spray from a hosepipe not to 'cap' the soil; for this you will need a sprinkler attachment (see illustrations, page 75). If you wish to water a specific plant, the hose mouth can be left on the ground near it and the tap turned on very slowly to direct a slow trickle onto the roots.

Sprinklers not only release you from the burden of standing with a cold hosepipe in one hand for long periods, while water drips down your legs, but the size of droplet is smaller than that from the rose of a watering can, and is more evenly distributed.

My only problem with a sprinkler is remembering to turn off the outside tap. Anyone else with a defective memory may like to consider buying a timer. This fits onto the tap and can be set to turn off the tap when required. A deluxe model is on the market which will turn the tap on as well as off. Of course, these will not deliver a set amount of water because water pressure fluctuates. Fortunately, you can also now get a 'water controller' which fits onto the tap and switches off the water when a specific quantity of water has been delivered.

I personally favour oscillating sprinklers because most work quite well even when the water pressure is low, which it so often is in the evening, and they can be adjusted to avoid an area if you wish. If you water in strong sunshine in the middle of the day, you will have to avoid getting moisture on the leaves, because the water droplets will act as magnifying glasses and the leaves will burn, so it is more sensible to do the job in the evening, even though everyone else is doing it too. After all, it also provides a good reason for being outside at what is undoubtedly the best time of the day for enjoying flower scents. Watering then comes into the category of 'pleasant pottering', and it is very restful to watch a sprinkler, knowing that it is even more effective than if you were doing it by hand.

However, sprinkling is expensive if your water is metered, and, if not, you may well need to buy a sprinkler licence from your local water authority. Never waste water; it is a resource which we all agree should be conserved wherever possible.

A useful and far less wasteful alternative to the sprinkler is the seep hose (see illustration below), which is a flexible tube with many little holes along its length. It can be buried easily under a mulch, and will moisten an area of about 23cm (9in) to each side. It avoids the damage done by large droplets landing on petals and spotting them, and also the risk of caking the top of a heavy soil.

A refinement on the seep hose is the full-blown drip-irrigation system, in which pipes are buried throughout the garden, with nozzles emerging at strategic points. It is expensive to install, but is economical of water and easy to regulate, and I foresee this system becoming very popular. My only reservations are that, if you do not want the whole garden watered at one time, you have to go round removing a branch line or shutting off a drip head; and you

may object, like me, to using it in the flower garden where the pipes cannot easily be buried.

There are alternatives to watering. If you wish to sow vegetable seed when the soil is dry, you can rake moist peat or peat-substitute into the top-soil. Rigging up shading material in particularly sunny parts of the garden will help, as will putting down a mulch. Mulching soil that is dry is, strictly speaking, not a good idea, but if the situation is serious, it will at least prevent further evaporation. In all other circumstances, leave the soil undisturbed (something I am always only too happy to do) because hot sunshine can help a crust to form which effectively prevents any more water from evaporating from below. If this is the case, weeds, which compete for moisture as well as nutrients, will have to be eliminated by hand.

In the vegetable garden you can create a 'dry mulch' by hoeing the surface. This forms a dry layer on the top which slows evaporation.

The last resort is to grow only drought-resistant plants. That is less hardship than you think, for some of the most beautiful of all plant species come from arid regions.

Rotary sprinklers should not be used in hot sunshine, for wet leaves can be scorched. They are most useful for borders with low-growing plants or vegetable gardens.

Oscillating sprinklers produce a much taller arc of water, which makes them useful for shrub borders, fruit gardens and expanses of lawn. They can be wasteful of water.

Seep hoses, laid on top of the soil, are economical, for the slow trickle of water is designed to soak the ground just by the hose. They are most useful for kitchen gardens and flower borders.

5

TOOLS OF THE TRADE

THERE IS NOT MUCH ACHIEVED IN THE GARDEN WITH JUST YOUR BARE HANDS. EVEN SUCH AN OBVIOUSLY MANUAL OCCUPATION AS WEEDING IS HARDLY POSSIBLE WITHOUT AT LEAST A HAND FORK, AND MOST OTHER TASKS REQUIRE ONE OR MORE INTRIGUING TOOLS OR PIECES OF EQUIPMENT. THE CHALLENGE IS FINDING THE RIGHT ONES, WITHOUT SPENDING TOO MUCH MONEY AND CLUTTERING UP THE SHED.

THE BEST TOOLS ARE INHERITED ONES, IT HAS TO BE SAID. LONG-USED, WELL-WORN TOOLS SEEM TO COME TO HAND BEST. BUT, IF YOU CANNOT PERSUADE ANY GARDEN-MINDED MEMBER OF THE FAMILY TO PART WITH THE CONTENTS OF THEIR TOOL SHED, DO NOT DESPAIR. THE FOLLOWING ACCOUNT SHOULD GIVE YOU A FAIR IDEA OF WHAT YOU NEED TO BUY, AND YOU MAY BE SURPRISED HOW QUICKLY NEW TOOLS LOSE THEIR SHINE AND BEGIN TO MOULD THEMSELVES TO YOUR PARTICULAR NEEDS.

No gardener can work without proper tools, and, if only because they are expensive, they deserve respect and care. Looked after properly, they will last many years and become almost like old friends. In this orderly tool shed can be found all the essential large tools that any gardener is likely to need, safely hung up yet easily found. Would that all tool sheds were as large and well-stocked as this one!

Power tools

The world is roughly divided into those who are intoxicated by power machinery, and those for whom it is a constant, mildly unpleasant anxiety. I fall very definitely into the second category, although I do admit that some of the best fun I ever had as a horticultural student came from driving a dumper-truck loaded with soil or compost.

What to do about power-machinery is every gardener's dilemma. It is always a temptation to buy an expensive machine that is too big for the job, but it is possible, though it does require self-restraint, to restrict the number and size of the tools you buy.

If you have a lawn of any size, you will almost certainly need a petrol engine or electric lawn mower, either with cylinder or rotary blades (see page 42). Mini-tractors with rotary blades underneath are for large gardens, or committed power-players.

If you have 0.2 hectares (¼ acre) or more of vegetable garden, you might consider a rotovator, but as the best are the biggest, it is better to hire one. The larger ones (which you may or may not be able to manage) are driven by powered wheels, have a cowl to protect your feet from the blades, and have depth adjusters so that you do not dig at the same depth each time. These are tools for the young and able-bodied, and most people will happily do without them.

A rotary mower, with a box, will pick up a limited quantity of leaves, but you can get a suction leaf sweeper which sucks the leaves into a large bag. Buy a 40cm (16in) electric hedge trimmer if you have a length of hedge which is tiring to clip by hand. The electric strimmer has its place for banks, around trees and along boundaries, but in the smaller garden a pair of hand shears may be sufficient.

For any equipment powered by mains electricity you will need a 'residual current device' which cuts off the power if the cable is cut. This is an essential piece of safety equipment and should be in every toolbox.

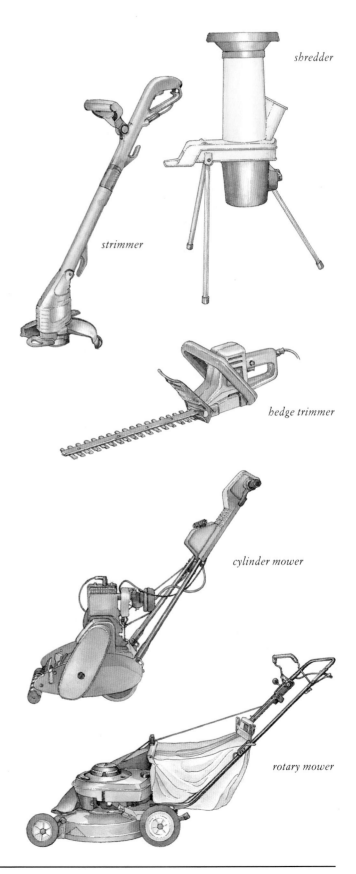

shredder

strimmer

hedge trimmer

cylinder mower

rotary mower

Hand tools

Forks, spades & trowels

There are nearly always two versions of hand tool: one so ridiculously expensive as to be almost out of the question, and the other cheap enough to make one equally hesitant. The most essential garden tools, for example, are made of two strikingly different materials: stainless steel and forged steel. Stainless steel tools are a delight, especially the spade. The blade enters the ground cleanly and with little resistance, and is, in effect, self-cleaning. Forged steel tools, less than half the price, rust if left out in the rain and must be cleaned periodically with a scraper and an oily rag, and coated in oil when not in regular use.

It is now possible to buy tools which will all fit onto a single shaft. If you possess no tools at all, this seems to me an option to consider carefully, provided only that the shaft is the right length for you.

A large garden fork for digging over stony ground and for lifting potatoes (a special potato fork is unnecessary if care is taken with the ordinary one) is a necessity, as is a small border fork for 'titivating', as gardeners call it, a border where there are plants growing that must not be harmed. One spade, for digging and planting, is enough; which variety will depend on the state of your back. The kind with which you lift the soil by pulling a lever is immensely useful if you are troubled in this way. A shovel for shifting compost or soil is helpful but not essential.

A hand fork is vital for grappling at closer quarters with recalcitrant weeds, while a trowel is necessary for planting, and transplanting, smaller plants and bulbs. A half-moon edging iron and a pair of long-handled edging shears are highly desirable if you have a lawn. A pair of thin but sturdy gloves is useful for weeding, distributing fertilizers and measuring out chemical concentrates. You may also find hand shears useful for trimming short lengths of hedge and clipping over soft-stemmed plants.

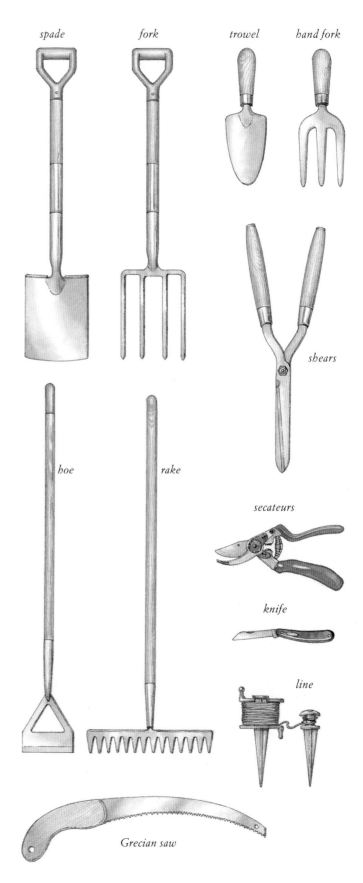

spade   fork   trowel   hand fork

shears

hoe   rake

secateurs

knife

line

Grecian saw

Hoes

Hoes should be restricted to the vegetable garden, unless you grow your bedding plants in straight lines and are happy to see chance seedlings decapitated. I find the Dutch hoe, which you push, infinitely easier to manage than the draw hoe, which you pull and chop with, but you may feel you need a draw hoe for making drills for seed-sowing and for earthing-up potatoes. Some people find a three-pronged cultivator is useful for preventing a crust forming on the soil top, but I find it no better than a hoe for that, or for weeding, so consider it an unnecessary luxury.

Rakes

You will require an ordinary garden rake for breaking down clods of soil in order to make a tilth for seed beds in the spring. It can also (with the head turned upside-down) replace the draw hoe for taking out seed drills, and is essential if you wish to level ground or make a new lawn.

For sweeping leaves or rubbish from the lawn, I prefer the rubber rake to the more picturesque besom. It lasts longer and is easier for the inexperienced to use. You will need one or the other (that is, if you don't want to invest in a garden 'vacuum cleaner' which sucks up any rubbish). A spring-tined rake is also useful, but don't imagine that it is easy to remove thatch with it. Instead, hire an electric lawn rake, which will make your grass look temporarily ravaged, but will do a better job than you can with your paltry spring-tined rake. They are only suitable if you possess a small expanse of lawn, or if you have moss, blackened by lawn sand (see page 44), which needs to be removed.

Other garden equipment

Lines, dibbers & kneelers

You will need a garden 'line' if you grow vegetables or wish to straighten a lawn edge. You can make one, using two stout, short sticks and a length of stout twine, but a brass one can be tightened more easily and effectively. I would advise two sorts of 'dibber' for making holes in soil. The large one is usually made by sharpening the point of a snapped-off wooden tool handle, and is invaluable for making holes for transplanting leeks and brassicas. The small version is slightly better than a pencil for lifting seedlings from a seed tray and pricking them out (see page 89).

A pair of kneelers to fit round your knees is as vital as any other single piece of equipment. There is no point in taking risks with stiff joints, for, as Kipling wrote:

Oh Adam was a gardener, and God who made him sees

That half a proper gardener's work is done upon his knees.

Knives & pruners

Buy, or cause to be given to you, a proper gardener's knife which you can sharpen, rather than making do with a pen knife, for you will use it every time you go into the garden for some small purpose or other. The kind with a straight blade is best (the curved-blade pruning knife has been superseded by the very good modern secateurs). I implore you to treat your new knife with respect and especially be careful if the spring is strong, for it is the work of a millisecond to cut your finger badly. You will need a small, flat oilstone to go with it.

A pair of good-quality scissor-action secateurs and a curved-bladed Grecian saw are very useful. If you have an apple orchard or other large tree, you may wish to buy a long-handled telescopic branch pruner, but far more useful for general use is a pair of 'parrot-billed' long-arm pruners. Everyone has shrubs that cannot always be trimmed with secateurs alone. And don't forget a pair of thorn-proof gloves.

Watering cans, hoses & sprinklers

Everyone needs a watering can, either metal or plastic, which must have a well-fitting rose. The best all-purpose can is the 9 litre (2 gallon) version. It is, however, heavy when full of water, so think about something smaller, if you are not strong. Plastic is obviously lighter than metal. There are different kinds and sizes of 'rose' available; I suggest buying two: one coarse, one fine. You can attach a 'dribble bar' to fit plastic cans. This L-shaped hollow tube, with regular holes, is especially useful for applying weedkiller to paths.

A length of non-kinking flexible hosepipe is highly desirable in gardens of any size, and with it a compatible nozzle. Not essential, but useful, is a drum on which it can be reeled. I strongly advise the purchase of a hose dilutor. This gadget, which can be fitted to a hose and connected by a tube to an ordinary watering can, will make liquid and foliar feeding easy, even pleasant. You can direct it by hand or place it on the ground pointed at the plants to be fed and watered. Because the rate of dilution can be altered, there is little waste of fertilizer.

Unless you feel strongly about water conservation, sprinklers are a boon. There are oscillating ones which can be adjusted to cover a smaller or larger rectangle of ground, and sprinklers which spin round in a circle; the first is best for a lawn, the latter for flower borders (see page 75).

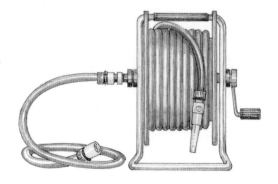

What did we do before the invention of the hose reel? It has made the business of keeping an orderly and unkinked hosepipe easy.

The galvanized watering can is a charming artefact – if only it were as light as the garish plastic variety and not so prone to bark one's shins.

Sprayers

You will need two sprayers, one for pesticides and fungicides and the other for weedkillers – unless, that is, you keep a watering can and dribble bar specifically for the latter. Whatever is used should be kept for that purpose only, and should have its purpose painted on the side. However careful you are, weedkiller residues are difficult to wash away completely, and you will not want to risk defoliating your roses more effectively than blackspot could.

It is tempting to buy a bigger sprayer than you strictly need; you should try to be realistic about the amount of spraying you will do, for it is remarkable how often you will find a reason for not spraying. On the other hand, the larger and more expensive hand sprayers are less likely to leak than the smaller, cheaper ones, and that seems to me an important consideration when dealing with chemicals. I use one with a pump action, and a trigger that stops the flow immediately the pressure is taken off it. Unless you have an orchard, you are unlikely to need a knapsack sprayer which is heavy and therefore off-putting.

Cloches & fleeces

The word 'cloche' comes, like many good things, from the French. It means a bell, and was the word used for the nineteenth-century invention, the bell-glass, which was the earliest form of glass protection for plants.

Nowadays, plastic cloches have almost entirely superseded glass ones, not only because they are easier to erect but also because most people with children do not like the idea of glass in the garden. The most common kinds of cloches are the following: the barn cloche, which is the shape of an American barn with a mansard roof; two pieces of glass, held together by a stout clip; the round corrugated plastic cloche; and the low polythene tunnel stretched over wire hoops (see illustrations below). There are also the so-called 'floating' polythene cloches and, easier to use, horticultural fleece, both of which will warm the soil in the spring, and provide congenial conditions in which seedlings can develop (see also pages 58-9).

Most glass or plastic cloches are only 60-90cm (2-3ft) wide, which makes them useless for fitting over deep-beds (see page 154) in vegetable gardens. The best alternatives are floating cloches and horticultural fleece.

Wheelbarrows & 'donkeys'

You will have to have a wheelbarrow; either one such as those that are used on building sites, or one with a large plastic ball for a tyre. The first is best for wheeling on paths and for heavy loads because it is sturdy, the second for wheeling across the lawn when the going is soft or wet. But life for me would be insupportable without a large polypropylene sheet with four handles. My 'donkey' enables me to traverse the bumpy terrain of my garden to the fire and compost bins far more easily with light and bulky rubbish like leaves, because I can either sling it over my none-too-broad shoulders, or drag it along the ground. The polypropylene bag with rigid sides is also invaluable.

Miscellaneous

There is a group of miscellaneous tools that will hang in your shed in readiness for the rare occasion when you need them very badly indeed. Amongst these I would number the half-moon edging iron, the turfing iron (for removing turves) and the bulb-planter (see page 149). However, since a reasonably sharp spade can be substituted for all of these, they are not high on the list of priorities.

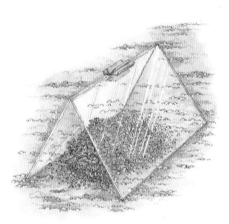

This simple cloche, made with two panes of glass and a metal clip, is useful for protecting a single plant, but, unfortunately, is easily broken.

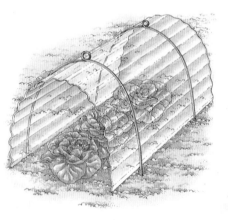

This clear, corrugated polycarbonate cloche comes as a flat piece, which can be joined to others to cover a long vegetable row. End pieces are available.

This type of cloche is easily made from a length of wire and some clear polythene. It is easy to construct but not very sturdy or longlasting.

Tool maintenance

Good garden tools become good friends. Looking after them is important but, fortunately, well within the compass of even the most inexperienced gardener. There is not much excuse for idleness in this respect, although there are occasions when a desire to do just one more thing may keep you out in the garden until it is too dark to see your way to the shed.

Tools should not be left out in the rain, although I know it is a temptation to leave the potato fork in the ground where it will be needed tomorrow. After use, try to find time to clean the mud from tools with a scraper. After scraping, rub the metal with an oily rag and hang the tools up. Several times a year, I rub the wooden handles of my tools with linseed oil, but I appreciate that not everyone does. Buy a file to sharpen your forged steel hoe and spade on the upper side; they work better if you do.

The builder's barrow is the sturdiest one to use; virtually indestructible, the only problem there is likely to be is the occasional flat tyre.

Be careful, however, not to cut your foot with your sharpened spade; it should be no longer blunt, not razor-sharp.

Electric tools need far more looking after. Maintenance ranges from sharpening the cutter bars on a chain-saw to cleaning the sap from hedge trimmers and a lot of things in between about which I know very little. I contribute my fair share to keeping lawn mower maintenance firms in business, and rarely, if ever, even change a spark plug. I say this not to run myself down particularly, but to reassure the thousands of other people who feel that it is only they who cannot understand the instructions for changing the oil in the mower.

6

MAKING NEW PLANTS

E VERY GARDENER PROPAGATES AS A MATTER OF
COURSE, EVEN IF SHE HAS NO IDEA THAT SHE IS
DOING SO. SOWING SEED IS PROPAGATION; TAKING CUT-
TINGS IS PROPAGATION; DIVIDING HARDY PERENNIALS IS
PROPAGATION. PROPAGATING SIMPLY MEANS INCREASING
PLANTS. MOST GARDENERS, ONCE THEY HAVE MASTERED
THE BASIC PRINCIPLES, ENJOY THIS ASPECT OF GARDENING
AS MUCH AS, IF NOT MORE THAN, ANY OTHER; INDEED I
HAVE NEVER MET A KEEN GARDENER WHO WAS NOT
COMMITTED TO INCREASING HER STOCK. IT IS INFINITELY
MORE SATISFYING, MYSTERIOUS, CEREBRAL, INTRIGUING
AND FRUSTRATING THAN GRASS-MOWING COULD EVER BE.
AND, TO BE PROSAIC, IT WILL REDUCE THE NUMBER OF
PLANTS YOU NEED TO BUY.

I SUPPOSE I SHOULD NOT BE SURPRISED THAT WE ALL
ENJOY PROPAGATION, FOR THE INSTINCT TO MAKE NEW
CREATURES, AND TO LOOK AFTER THEM ONCE THEY ARE
MADE, IS MORE DEEPLY EMBEDDED IN US THAN ANY
OTHER. INCREASING PLANTS IS FRAUGHT WITH POTENTIAL
DIFFICULTIES AND DISAPPOINTMENTS, TOO, BUT IT IS ALSO
IMMENSELY SATISFYING.

*This is obviously the home of a keen propagator. The greenhouse
is full of trays and pots planted with little treasures, and there is an
overspill of pots outside. The stool signifies that the house belongs
to someone who wishes to be comfortable when taking cuttings!*

How to propagate

Most propagation is well within the compass of the amateur gardener, and because it is so much easier to propagate than you could ever imagine, you will probably end up with far too many plants. However, there is always the produce stall at the village fête, and since no gardener likes to let a friend leave empty-handed, propagated plants usually find homes in the end.

The only limiting factors on propagation are space, time and money. Nothing that I shall mention requires much expensive equipment, and if you have an airing cupboard, a wide window-sill, a cold greenhouse and/or a cold frame, and not much cash, or time to spare at the right moment, this chapter is for you.

What you will need

Your first requirement will be 'compost', and compost in this context is not garden compost but the medium in which seeds like to germinate and plants to grow in pots, before they go out into the big, wide world of the garden. Composts are composed of a free-draining mixture of ingredients; some include soil and some definitely do not. I hope that is clear. Ordinary garden soil is not a suitable medium to use for growing plants in pots.

Unless you are going to propagate on a large scale, I do not advise you to make your own composts. Buy, ready made-up, what you think you will need. The larger sizes of bags are the cheapest, proportionately, and they are surprisingly quickly used up. For those seeds that I know to be slow to germinate, and also for potting plants in large pots, I prefer John Innes loam composts to loamless or so-called 'universal' or multi-purpose composts, which have some peat or peat-substitute in them. This is because peat (the major constituent of loamless composts) is very difficult to wet once allowed to dry out, so slow-germinating seed may desiccate and die, and the alternative, a peat-substitute such as coir, holds water so well that it is easy to overwater the plants.

That said, I find loamless composts very suitable for quick-germinating seed like half-hardy annuals, for pricking out seedlings and for growing small plants, provided, that is, I water the plants regularly with a liquid feed after a few weeks. Contrary to traditional belief, this is sometimes also necessary for those grown in loam composts. If the leaves of the seedlings begin to yellow, it is time to feed them.

Plastic pots and trays are the most commonly used containers for propagation. They are not entirely ideal because they become brittle when exposed to light, and break when you tread on them, but they are cheap and have a way of multiplying in the garden shed, much as coat-hangers do in the wardrobe. They are, however, of little use unless they have good drainage holes. Plastic pots retain water too well to suit some plants, and I use clay pots, which I have husbanded over the years, for growing alpine plants which hate damp conditions.

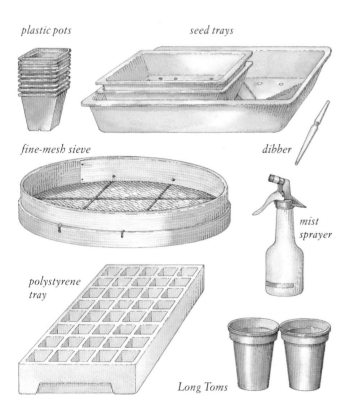

plastic pots

seed trays

fine-mesh sieve

dibber

mist sprayer

polystyrene tray

Long Toms

Half-hardy annuals, reared commercially in polystyrene modules, are easy to extract by pushing them up from below.

I like the expanded polystyrene trays ('modules'), which are divided into individual bottomless compartments, because you can push up and remove the contents of any compartment when it is ready for planting, without disturbing the rest. These are particularly suitable for large seeds, like those of sweet corn, which are traditionally sown in pots rather than in trays, and for 'multiple seeding' (see page 159). These compartments defy the laws of gravity, for when you fill them with compost, hardly anything disappears through the bottom. For sowing seed such as sweet peas, which have long roots, I use long cardboard sweet pea tubes or 'Long Toms' filled with compost.

Horticultural plastic trays come in two sizes: the half-trays are particularly useful, because you will often have too much seed to sow for one pot, and not enough for a whole tray. All seeds require moisture to germinate, and most require darkness. You will therefore require a supply of newspaper to cut out the light, and, if you are not using a 'propagator' with a clear plastic cover, some rectangular pieces of glass to put over the seed trays to prevent evaporation. You can use little squares of flat, rigid, plastic sheeting as an alternative. People who are clever with their hands make wooden pressers with handles to fit the trays and pots, to enable them to press down the compost evenly. I have not got them, so I use the bottom of a larger pot for pots, and the bottom of a half-tray for the trays.

Everyone needs a 'dibber' for planting cuttings or seedlings, and a fine-mesh sieve is useful for producing a fine covering for compost for seed pots and, occasionally, for breaking up lumpy compost.

I find a small hand mist sprayer extremely useful for watering the compost after seed-sowing. It is slower than a watering can, but you will be in no danger of harming the tiny seedlings. A small watering can with a very fine rose will do the job faster, provided you learn the trick of starting to water before passing over the tray, and continuing beyond, so that heavy dribbles do not drop on the compost and dislodge your small seed.

Sowing seed

Beginners should buy seed rather than save it from year to year. Commercial vacuum-sealed packaging ensures that the seed stays viable for years because no air and moisture can enter to begin the ageing process. Bought seed is, therefore, much more reliable, and there is now a wide range available: trees, shrubs and wild flowers, as well as the more conventional vegetables and flowers.

Gardeners setting about seed-sowing for the first time may find it useful to buy 'pre-germinated' or 'primed' seed, which is sold in a state of suspended animation, ready to go the moment it is sown and watered. The little plants will get away to a certain start, removing the likelihood of seedlings (such as those of winter-flowering pansies) being badly affected by high summer temperatures. Begonias and pelargoniums will germinate faster and more uniformly if sown 'primed'.

You can buy seedlings and little plants ('plantlets') of common plants very cheaply from most garden centres, and you can also buy them, slightly less cheaply, from some mail-order seedsmen. If you wish for something you think might be difficult to propagate, or which requires more heat than you can well provide, or you intend to go skiing when you should be sowing, then buy them: as seedlings, as plantlets, or even as two-month-old plants. However, if you want anything unusual, or in a single colour, you will have to sow it yourself (see illustrations below), but, for the unconfident or hard-pressed, there are many instances when more-or-less instant gardening is a great deal better than no gardening at all.

Seed sowing out-of-doors is dealt with in the chapters on vegetable growing and hardy annuals; here, I am concerned with sowing seed inside, or 'in heat' as it is called.

If you wish to grow, rather than buy, half-hardy annuals such as petunias, as well as tomatoes and the modern pelargoniums, you will have to germinate the seeds inside in warm conditions in late winter or early spring. Hardy perennial species (not hybrids) can also, and

How to sow

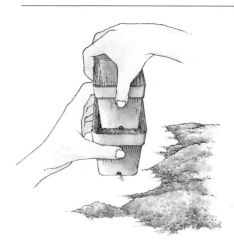 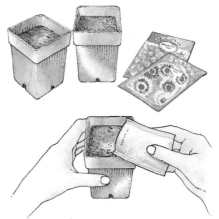 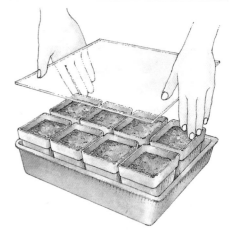

Put the seed compost in the pot and press down lightly with your fingers, and then with the bottom of another pot, until you have a flat and even surface, about 1cm (½in) below the rim.

Mix very small seed in its packet with fine 'silver sand' for an even spread. Tap the packet gently on the pot rim. You can also put the seed in one palm and tap it gently with one finger of the other hand.

Lightly cover seed with vermiculite if it needs light to germinate, or sieved compost if not. Cover with Perspex. Put in a window-sill propagator or other warm place if heat is needed for germination.

often should, be grown from seed, if only because you may not be able to find the plants you want in nurseries and garden centres.

Seeds of alpines usually need a winter outside before they will germinate, so use a clay pot and loam seed compost. Put some grit on top of the seed, so that you can remove any weeds which have the temerity to emerge, prevent damage from rain, and discourage mice from stealing the seed. Then put the pots somewhere cool and sheltered outside, and check them now and then to see if the seeds have germinated.

Seedlings should not be left for long in the seed pot or tray after germination. There is little or no nutrient in seed compost, so they will eventually starve, and there is also the danger of a fungal disease of overcrowded seedlings called 'damping-off'. This is alarming when it occurs, because it causes the seedlings to collapse and die very quickly. You can prevent this by shaking the seed with a fungicidal seed dressing in a paper bag before it is sown, or by watering the newly sown pots with a fungicide.

Once the first seedlings have germinated, they require to be put in the light on the window-sill and, when they have grown their first 'true' leaves, 'pricked out' into a tray or module (see illustrations below), using John Innes loam potting compost No.1, or a loamless compost.

Any plant that has been moved to a new habitat is inclined to be a little vulnerable, so keep the clear plastic casing (if you have one) over the seedlings in the tray for a few days after transplanting. After that, allow the plants to grow in natural light at room temperature, trying to remember to turn the tray round through 90 degrees every few days, to prevent the seedlings leaning too obviously towards the window. You will never get such good, straight, sturdy plants as you will if you grow them in a heated greenhouse, where the light is coming in from all sides, and this may matter to you sufficiently for you to invest in a greenhouse and heating equipment; on the other hand, it may not. After a month, feed the plants every seven days with a weak solution of liquid feed.

After gardeners have had their say about 'damping-off' and 'pricking-out', they turn their attention to 'hardening-off'. This is the process whereby plants are acclimatized to outdoor temperatures, including natural temperature fluctuations, before being planted

Pricking out seedlings

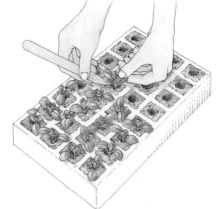

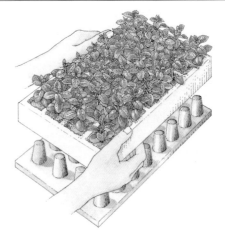

Use a label, pencil or dibber to remove seedlings from their pot when pricking out. Hold onto seedlings by one of their leaves, rather than by the stem, as they are very easily damaged.

If you transplant seedlings into polystyrene or thin plastic 'modules', they will grow on with little competition and will be easy to remove without disturbing the others.

When the seedlings have outgrown the cell modules, roots will start to appear below. Push the seedlings out from beneath with a finger or special remover, and pot on, or plant out, immediately.

Cold frames, which can be as elaborate as this one or of a much simpler construction in polycarbonate, are invaluable for hardening-off plants.

permanently outside. This takes place in late spring, as the days are lengthening and the temperatures are rising, but as nights are, of course, colder than days, the plants should at first be put outside only during the daytime, and continue to be protected at night. If you do not harden off plants gradually, and the nights are cold, they will suffer – and visibly appear to suffer, for their leaves will turn white.

Hardening-off, however, is difficult to do if you not are on the spot all the time. Rather than taking the pots in and out of the cold greenhouse (if you have one) every day, you could put them in a ventilated cold frame, keeping it closed at night, or, even easier, line them up somewhere sheltered and warm in the vegetable garden, put a cloche over them when you come home in the evening, and newspaper over the cloche if frost is forecast. If your plants have been grown on the kitchen window-sill, move them first to the cold spare bedroom, and then, as above, to the vegetable garden.

Do not be hurried by the advice on the backs of seed packets into sowing your half-hardy plants too early, especially if you live in a relatively cold region. There is first the problem of where to put all the trays of pricked-out seedlings until the nights are warm enough to chance them in the unheated greenhouse. Then the plants tend to sit in their pots, not growing much because they are first constricted and then starved. The only half-hardy annuals that really need to be started off in late winter are *Begonia × carrierei*, pelargoniums, lobelias, African marigolds, gazanias and antirrhinums. I have learned not to sow my hardy annuals outside too early, either.

Taking cuttings

Although seed-sowing seed is suitable for annuals and vegetables, it can be rather slow as a method of reproducing perennials. Vegetative, or asexual, propagation is the technique that takes advantage of the extreme amiability of most plants and their consequent willingness to regenerate from portions of themselves.

The capacity of a plant to root from cuttings varies; it depends on factors such as the age of the plant, the season of the year, the species, and the conditions in which it is not only rooted but reared after rooting. Most plants are quite easy, but you must be prepared for some losses, and to try another method if one fails.

The commonest form of cutting is the stem cutting, classified as 'softwood', 'semi-hardwood', and 'hardwood' (see illustration below), depending on the maturity of the stem from which the cutting has come. As is logical, soft-

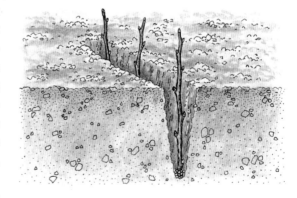

Take hardwood cuttings from deciduous plants just after leaf-fall. Cut 23cm (9in) lengths of this year's wood, and place in a slit-trench, into which has been trickled some sand, about (15cm) 6in apart.

wood cuttings are taken in spring to summer; semi-hardwood cuttings (of, for example, deciduous shrubs) in early autumn; hardwood cuttings (for example, poplar, blackcurrant, rose) in the early dormant season. Semi-hardwood cuttings, especially of evergreens, are often taken with a 'heel', that is, torn from a main stem with a little piece of that stem attached. An 'Irishman's cutting' (don't ask me why) is a small shoot with roots pulled from the crown of, for example, early flowering chrysanthemums. The optimum length of cutting depends on the species; roses are best taken from non-flowering shoots about 23cm (9in) long in autumn, while a softwood cutting of *Philadelphus* would be only 8-10cm (3-4in) long. In general terms, the healthier the wood the more easily it will root, and non-flowering shoots are usually best, though this is not always possible. Good cultivation in the way of pruning and feeding earlier on in the season will encourage the growth of useful cuttings wood.

If you cut a shoot from a plant and let the cut end dry out, it will not root; nor is it much more likely to do so if that end is crushed rather than cleanly cut. This is because the stem has to form a 'callus', from which the roots will grow, and callus formation arises most readily from a clean, moist stem. So, you will need your sharp knife and a plastic bag in which to place the cutting immediately you have cut it, to keep it moist, as well as cuttings compost, a dibber to make a hole in the compost, a tub of hormone rooting powder, and some sort of enclosed, humid environment in which the cutting can survive while it is growing its callus and roots (see illustrations below). As the shoot is very vulnerable to water-loss through its leaves at this time, and it cannot replace that loss until the roots have formed, trim off the larger leaves.

Most of us have tried, at one time or another, to 'strike' cuttings by plonking them in the ground outside and hoping for the best. Survivors, apart from very amenable plants like poplars and willows (which will even grow roots in water), are not numerous, especially if the cuttings are put in full sun. On the other hand, most shrubs will root very readily if cuttings are taken from the right part of the plant, at the right time, and put in the right medium.

There is a lot of talk of the efficacy or otherwise of hormone rooting powder. Most cuttings will root perfectly easily without it, but it does contain auxins which either encourage or hasten the formation of the roots. The cutting should first be dipped in water, and then its

How to take a softwood cutting

Softwood cuttings are taken early in the season, from non-flowering shoots. Cut the shoot just below a node, removing the bottom leaves, and dip the base of the cutting in hormone rooting powder. Make a hole in the cuttings compost with a

dibber and push the cutting down to the bottom of the hole. Cover immediately with a rigid plastic cover or a clear polythene bag, secured with rubber bands, ensuring that it does not touch the cutting.

base (only) put in the powder; all excess should be shaken off, because auxins encourage root initiation but retard root growth.

Cuttings have a regrettable tendency to rot, so cuttings compost is composed of half peat or peat-substitute and half grit or perlite, so that it drains well. There is a theory that the grit in the compost irritates the cuttings into rooting, and that placing them round the edge of the pot will also help. I believe the grit helps as much because it prevents waterlogging as for any other reason. As for placing the cuttings round the edge, this may well have helped in the days of clay pots, because gaseous exchange takes place at the interface between clay pot side and atmosphere, but this is not the case with modern plastic pots.

Cuttings should not dry out; they must be kept in a humid environment, and will root the more readily if the compost is warm as well as moist. Putting them in a pot or tray in a closed case which has soil-warming cables beneath the compost (or in a heated window-sill propagator) does a great deal to speed rooting.

You can usually tell when a cutting has rooted because it starts growing green leaves from the top, but if there is no such sign, and your soul can no longer be contained in patience, remove

Both seedlings and rooted cuttings are best left in their pots until good root systems have formed before planting out.

the covering and pull the cutting gently. If it resists the pull, it is rooted; if not, you will have to replant it, won't you?

Because there is no nutriment in cuttings compost, the cutting, once rooted, will need to be re-potted quite quickly into a loamless potting compost, or into John Innes No.1. Later, it can be planted out, after a period of toughening up, or repotted into a bigger pot. John Innes No.1, incidentally, contains half the amount of fertilizer of John Innes No.2, which is used for rooted shrub cuttings, while John Innes No.3 has twice as much as John Innes No.2, and is only used for large plants that are to be kept in the container for a year or more. A recently rooted cutting is best kept in a pot in the cold frame for a while before being planted out, because it will be feeling a little fragile and, even more to the point, if planted in the garden will all too often become the innocent victim of a clumsy boot. If you grow the cutting on in a pot, feed it regularly with a liquid fertilizer in the growing season; if it is getting root-bound, repot it, or it will slow down in growth or 'suffer a check', in the jargon.

Division

Far and away the most commonly performed propagation technique for herbaceous perennials is division (see illustration right). Division with *most* plants is very easy, and will inevitably result in your having far more viable plant material on your hands than you need.

The herbaceous perennial will, over a period of time in the garden, have grown out from the middle and developed new buds which, if they are detached with roots attached to them, can become independent plants. Most herbaceous perennials will anyway require this process of detachment and replanting every three or four years, or so, if they are to continue to flower their hearts out.

Dividing your plants in this way will involve you in a philosophical dilemma. Do you plant your entire garden with rooted crowns of *Rudbeckia* 'Herbstsonne', and by so doing ensure a sea of waving yellow daisies in autumn;

do you endeavour to pass some on to your neighbour, who probably gave you the plant in the first place; or do you harden your heart and take a trip to the compost heap? Nature can be frugal, desperately frugal, with the seed of, say, tree peonies, but she is recklessly prodigal with divisions of the daisy family.

Division should be done in the autumn, after flowering, and offers a good opportunity for reviving a bed that may not have been touched, except for the odd mulch, for many years. After lifting your clumps of plants, dig the border over and incorporate organic material, taking care (of course!) to cover up the plants with newspaper or polythene; roots dry out quickly on a bright autumn day, and it is a nuisance to have to dip them in a bucket of water before replanting them.

The essence of successful division is to separate a piece that has both root and buds; it is fruitless otherwise. Detaching these pieces can be done in several ways. It would be foolish (and you would not believe me) to assert that it is *all* effortless; there are some plants that resent being parted from their fellows, and

Hostas are long-lived plants which can be divided, but only with strenuous effort. You may have to be ruthless with your knife and cut the solid roots.

resist strenuously any efforts to separate them. The goat's beard, *Aruncus dioicus*, has very wiry roots which cling valiantly together, like the survivors of a shipwreck. Hostas may require a knife, for their roots seem to form a solid block after a couple of years. Oriental poppies often have but a single root, which you will need to

How to divide

Helianthus, *with their fibrous roots, are easy enough to dig up and prise apart with your bare hands. Discard the old centre, and replant only the outer portions.*

When dividing dahlia tubers, make sure that there is at least one crown bud to each division. As the tubers are soft, use a chisel or sharp knife to cut up the stem and prise them apart.

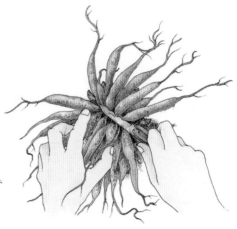

When dividing peony rhizomes, before the buds get too big, cut from below with a sharp knife, and ensure that there is at least one bud to each division, and preferably more.

Anemone japonica, *the Japanese anemone, is one of the plants that will propagate best from root cuttings. Cuttings taken in the dormant season can be planted out the following autumn.*

slice up. This tends to break off regrettably easily at the neck, and since it is essential that your divided plant has both roots and buds, you may be left holding a large tuft of useless leaves. Plants with soft tubers, like dahlias, will need gentle prising apart; a thin cold chisel inserted between the tubers will help to effect this (see illustration page 93). Try to avoid becoming irritated and hacking at the crown with a blunt spade, for it is not only damaging to the plant but rarely works successfully. It is better to dig the plant up and make a cut from the base upwards so that the crown damage is kept to a minimum. Try not to replant into a dry soil (as

is often the case on light soils in warm autumns) but pour the contents of a watering can into the hole first and let it drain, so that the roots will quickly establish themselves again. This, for the insatiably curious amongst you, is called 'puddling-in'. It is a very useful little habit to acquire, especially if you garden on a free-draining soil.

Some plants do not appreciate being disturbed, and should rarely, if ever, be divided. The burning bush, *Dictamnus albus purpureus*, is a well-known example. *Eryngium*, the sea holly, is not mad keen, and hellebores, acanthuses and peonies should also be left alone if possible. Some die; others cease flowering for a year or two. However, if you have bought an established garden, and the peonies are in the wrong place, divide and move them. Do it carefully in late winter, using a sharp knife to cut

Take root cuttings in situ, by removing soil around the roots, or dig up the plant. Cut the root end nearest the crown straight and the other end at an angle. Put in cuttings compost, covered with grit or sand. Thin roots may be lain horizontally in a tray.

through the roots and crown from the bottom, and plant them with the crown, that is where the buds and roots meet, 2.5cm (1in) below the soil (see illustration page 93).

Root cuttings

If I had to choose one gardening operation that coupled ease of execution and high success rate with unpopularity, it would be that of taking root cuttings of herbaceous perennials (see illustrations above). I cannot understand why so few people go in for this, when, as in the case of oriental poppies, for example, it is so much easier and more fruitful than division. It can be done at any time in the dormant season and *can* be done in many cases without even digging up the whole plant. Not every perennial is receptive to this treatment, but it works particularly well with *Phlox, Brunnera,* Japanese anemones (which do not divide easily) and with fleshy-rooted plants which are difficult, such as poppies, *Catananche, Romneya,* and *Verbascum.*

Layering

Layering is another process of propagation It is simple, effective and requires practically no aftercare. It is also painfully slow.

Layering is the process whereby 'cuttings' are rooted without being severed from the mother plant. This appears a paradox; what I mean is that stems can be induced to root without being cut through completely. Shrubs such as rhododendrons and viburnums layer quite readily if a suitable low-growing shoot is pulled to the ground, the underside slit with a knife and a stone positioned to keep it in position (see illustrations below). In place of a stone, you can use flexible wire.

How to layer

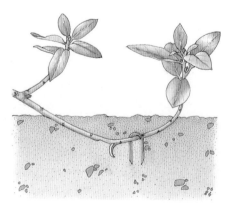
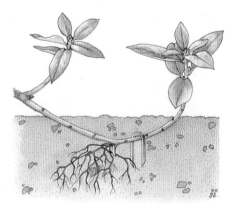

Layering works well for shrubs with low-growing shoots, such as rhododendron. Make a depression in the soil in the dormant season, then cut the stem underside half through, and pull it down.

Hold down the stem with wire or a stone, and cover with soil. A cane can be used to stake the stem upright beyond the layering point, and to mark the layer, but it is not essential.

A good root system will probably take as long as 18 months to form at the cut point. Then you can cut off the layer from the mother plant and pot up or transplant.

7

GETTING PLANTS INTO SHAPE

NOTHING CAUSES MORE CONSTERNATION AND ANXI-
ETY TO THE AMATEUR THAN 'PRUNING'. THIS SIMPLE,
INNOCUOUS-SOUNDING WORD CAN BE CRUSHING IN ITS
AWESOME RAMIFICATIONS, FOR IT OFTEN SEEMS TO
EPITOMIZE THE YAWNING GAP THAT THE AMATEUR FEELS
EXISTS BETWEEN HERSELF AND THE KNOWLEDGEABLE
PROFESSIONAL. IF SHE ONLY KNEW HOW OFTEN THE
PROFESSIONAL HAS RECOURSE TO BOOKS, SHE WOULD FEEL
MORE CHEERFUL FOR, IN TRUTH, THERE ARE FEW PEOPLE
WHO CAN HOLD IN THEIR HEADS THE TIMING AND
METHOD OF PRUNING OF EVERY SINGLE PLANT WITHIN
THEIR DOMINION.

IT SHOULD BE A COMFORT TO KNOW THAT UNDERSTAND-
ING WHAT IS REQUIRED FOR PLANTING (AND TRANSPLANT-
ING) IS FAR MORE IMPORTANT THAN KNOWING HOW TO
TAKE A PAIR OF SECATEURS TO THE FORSYTHIA. IN THE
SHORT TERM, AT LEAST, NOTHING WILL COME TO MUCH
HARM BY NOT BEING PRUNED, WHEREAS IF YOU DO NOT
PLANT YOUR PRECIOUS POSSESSIONS PROPERLY, THEY WILL
QUICKLY INFORM YOU OF THE FACT BY DYING.

This orderly garden owes its appearance in considerable part to
sensible pruning. The low box hedges and battered hornbeam
behind can only feature as they do because they are trimmed to a
level contour, but trimming, of course, stimulates them into new
growth, as can be seen clearly. The central walnut tree will also
have been pruned to achieve a clean stem.

When I took my first faltering steps towards learning how to garden, I became absorbed, to the point of obsession, with how to prune roses. I know now that in my profound ignorance I was approaching the difficulty from the wrong direction. It seemed to me that being an expert pruner was the mark of the real gardener, so I used to wander around the garden trying to find things to prune, instead of first establishing why pruning is done at all, and therefore what really needs doing. I was like the commander of an army going to great lengths to find the right site for a battle which he could actually avoid fighting altogether.

In the event I did more harm than good. I neatly cut the flowering buds from a winter jasmine because I did not realise that it flowered on growth made the previous year; I pruned the Hybrid Tea roses down to three buds, as if exhibition blooms were required for a flower show, when they would have looked far better, and flowered more freely, in my country garden, if they had been less harshly treated; and I wasted energy on the tedious and unrewarding task of cutting the little bits of dead wood from a *Philadelphus*, whose flowering was not much affected either way. I was encouraged in this delusion by what little I read that was comprehensible to me; every description of a plant seemed to include detailed instructions on its pruning. I now realise that I should first have learned the principles on which pruning is based, the better to decide what needed doing.

Old habits die very hard in gardening, and some traditions have tenaciously survived the imperatives of changing garden fashions. The Victorians were great pruners, and nothing made them happier than trimming their shrubs into tight domes of foliage. The development of twentieth-century gardening is a reaction to that desire for dominance, and the idea of the 'Romantic Garden' has in many gardens succeeded in relegating pruning to cursory, half-hearted annual forays which often extend only as far as the removal of an arching rose briar threatening to scratch an unwary eye.

Despite this, pruning still takes up acres of space in practical manuals. This is partly habit and partly because there *are* different ways of doing it. I intend to discuss it at some length, but only with the proviso that you do not assume that pruning is as necessary as breathing (except in the fruit garden), and, where appropriate, I shall tell you when it may be usefully abandoned.

The single most important reason why we prune is to promote the good production of flowers and fruit. We prune as much for our benefit as for the plant's. An unpruned plant will eventually become leggy and crowded with dead and weak wood. This will be shed naturally in time, but it may impede good flowering or look unattractive. In shaping a plant as we would like it to look, we also allow sunlight into the middle of the bush, which will ripen the wood. Many plants, particularly roses, flower better the following year if the summer sunshine has had access to the growing shoots, and the death of woody stems occurs most frequently either as a result of disease or because of a shortage of light, especially in the centre of the bush. Most climbing plants will need some 'formative training' when young, to develop a good shape, so that is the time when most pruning is done. And finally, pruning is done to remove diseased growths and prevent the trouble spreading.

None of this makes much sense unless it is understood that the chopping off of a branch or growth above a dormant bud will stimulate that bud into 'breaking' into growth. This is because plants are often subject to 'apical dominance'. The plant manufactures a hormone which prevents or retards the growth of all but the terminal or apical bud. When the apex is removed, the new top bud assumes apical dominance and breaks into leaf.

With alternate-leaved plants, cutting to an inside bud will often ensure inward-looking

The grey-leaved Mediterranean santolina is best trimmed over in late spring; new shoots will already have broken from further down the stems, but this is not a task to do too early in the year.

new growths; cutting to an outside bud will produce outward-looking buds. Opposite-leaved plants have a bud on either side of the stem, naturally enough, so cutting just above them will encourage two outward-facing shoots.

Pruning is what you do with secateurs, and normally refers to work carried out on specimen woody plants, that is, trees and shrubs. 'Trimming' is done with garden shears, and refers to the clipping of hedges, herbaceous perennials, heathers and rock plants.

Besides a good pair of scissor-action secateurs, which are vital, you should acquire a rounded, large-toothed saw called a Grecian saw, and a pair of 'parrot-bill' long-handled pruners (or 'loppers'), which are helpful for the larger branches of roses or other shrubs; it does secateurs no good at all to be used on large branches. You will only want pole-pruners if you have tall trees or an orchard to tend.

I never use chain-saws because they scare the wits out of me. However, I recognize that as a cowardly weakness and I know that there are plenty of people for whom these saws hold no terrors. I can only say, from a safe distance, that they should be used with circumspection and with proper attention to any instructions on safe use. The cable of any electric machine (and

Shrubs needing pruning after flowering

Abelia × *grandiflora*
Chaenomeles (wall-trained): cut back the recently flowered shoots to three buds
Clematis (spring-flowering)
Cytisus (and the related *Genista*): avoid cutting into old wood
Deutzia
Erica
Helianthemum
Jasminum nudiflorum: cut back the flowered shoots almost to the base
Kerria
Lonicera: cut out older wood after flowering
Philadelphus
Prunus triloba
Pyracantha: cut back unwanted shoots after flowering
Ribes sanguineum
Spiraea × *arguta*
Weigela

Spring-flowering shrubs are usually tackled after the flowers. One or two of the oldest stems, particularly from the centre of the bush, are cut out.

The flowered shoots are also trimmed back. If the shape is not pleasing, you can shorten some of the longer non-flowering shoots as well.

this goes for hedge trimmers, too) should be draped over the operator's shoulder, so that cutting through it takes some ingenuity, and a power-breaker (a 'residual current device' or RCD), fitted to the extension lead, which cuts off the current immediately the wires are severed, is essential with all electric tools. It is good practice to force an accomplice to watch you at work – just in case.

While on the subject of equipment, you will still find wood-sealant paint recommended for use on large pruning cuts (anything over the size of an old sixpence, I was taught) to prevent the ingress of fungal infections. Scientific

the spring-flowering shrubs, should have their flowered shoots cut back after they have finished flowering, giving them plenty of time to make some more before the following flowering season (see illustrations left). Those that flower on the current season's growth, which is most of the summer-flowerers, should be cut back hard in late winter or early spring, so that they have time to grow good long flowering shoots before the summer (see illustrations page 102). Pruning back hard means right back, almost to the main shoots in the case of branching shrubs, and almost to the ground in the case of shrubs with shoots growing from ground level.

Spring-flowering Weigela florida *'Variegata' can be thinned and trimmed after the flowers have finished.*

Ribes sanguineum, *another hardy spring-flowering shrub, can be treated in the same way.*

opinion now holds that this may even inhibit the healing process. More useful is using your sharp knife to trim round the edge of the cut to encourage healing callus formation.

I do not wish to bore you with a wearisome list of plants and their pruning requirements, but rather to state general principles so that you will have a good idea how to approach a plant, even if you do not precisely know its needs. The central point to bear in mind is that there is a difference between those shrubs that, as the terminology goes, flower on the old (or last year's) 'wood' (growth), and those that flower on the new (this year's) wood. Those that flower on last year's growth, which includes most of

This is simple enough, but seems to suggest an enormous amount of work. However, more than half the shrubs encountered in gardens really need nothing doing to them, apart from cutting out dead wood (a job that can be done at any time) or trimming back long shoots if they clearly spoil the shape of the bush. What a cheering thought.

Some shrubs can be trimmed to make formal shapes, if you so desire: for example, holly, box, *Osmanthus* and *Pittosporum*. If you do wish to do this, remember to do it after any flowers or fruit are over. Trimming a shrub to a shape is only worthwhile if you do not lose what else it has to offer, or do not mind that you have lost it.

In an effort to get good flowering, modern practice leans much more towards thinning a shrub by cutting whole shoots out near ground level than trimming all the shoots to a uniform length, which makes an unnatural, and not particularly attractive, shape, and causes a lot of hedgehog growth. Thinning has the advantage of letting light into the bush, which will aid good flowering and discourage fungal diseases, and also gives naturally arching shrubs, like *Buddleja alternifolia*, the chance to show what they can do. You may not always be able to avoid shortening the long shoots, for one reason or another, but if you plant shrubs at their maximum spread apart from each other, you will prevent much of that sort of trouble.

We all learn what needs doing in the garden, as much by close observation of our plants as by reading books. I emphasize taking note of when your shrubs flower, and acting on that knowledge, so that if your enthusiasm is as yet untempered by experience, you do not go out and trim your *Philadelphus* to a tight dome in spring, and then write to the gardening papers asking why the wretched thing will not flower. The concept of plants that flower either on 'new wood' or on 'old wood' seems confusing (because it is not immediately obvious) when you first look at an unknown bush. It will become clearer as the seasons pass, and you will not go far wrong if you trim spring-flowerers after they have done their stuff, and summer-flowerers early the following year. Of these later-flowerers, the sturdier plants, like *Buddleja*, are safe to prune in late winter, but less stout beings from warmer climates, like *Santolina* or lavender, are best left until spring.

As with most gardening activities, it is possible to bend the rules where timing is concerned, but, as a general principle, summer-flowering trees and the larger shrubs are best pruned either when they are dormant, or just coming into growth. A tree, like a walnut or birch, will 'bleed' sap if cut in late winter or spring, which will not stop until the plant comes into leaf, and may cause die-back; smaller plants may lose the growths already made, including the forming flower buds. If you miss the moment, your plant will come to no harm if it is left for a year. The strength of the desire to prune does depend largely on the clemency of the weather, so do not mentally castigate yourself if you are a little slow getting round to this task. Most plants are quite tolerant.

Buddlejas are popular hardy mid-summer-flowering shrubs, which will flower best if trimmed back hard in late winter.

It is best to cut them to clusters of leaves already showing. This shrub will take no harm if a proportion of its oldest stems is also removed.

Shrubs needing pruning in late winter or spring

Actinidia kolomikta: cut back sideshoots to three buds in the dormant season and cut out some of the older wood, replacing and tying in the new

Buddleja

Caryopteris

Ceanothus: deciduous varieties should have their flowered shoots cut back to 8cm (3in) in mid-spring

Cistus, Fuchsia and *Hebe:* cut back the frosted shoots in mid-spring; they will be showing buds 'breaking' further down

Clematis (large-flowered hybrids)

Cornus alba (if grown for its winter bark)

Corylus maxima 'Purpurea'

Elaeagnus pungens 'Maculata' (if any shoots have reverted to green)

Grey-leaved shrubs that 'break' from the bottom like *Lavandula, Helichrysum* and *Santolina*

Hortensia and lace-cap hydrangeas: cut out old flower heads

Hydrangea paniculata 'Grandiflora'

Hypericum calycinum: trim over; other hypericums can have old shoots removed

Leycesteria

Passiflora: cut lateral shoots back to 15cm (6in) from their base in spring

Potentilla: cut out a few older shoots to keep it from getting too crowded; likewise for rosemary if getting straggly

Salix daphnoides (if grown for its winter bark)

Solanum crispum: cut back the previous season's shoots to 8-10cm (3-4in) in mid-spring

Spiraea × bumalda

Tamarix pentandra

Wisteria: cut back the previous year's growth to three buds in late winter and, on vigorous plants, the young growth back to six buds in mid-summer

In an attempt to keep the whole subject as comprehensible as possible, I deal with the specific pruning requirements of different kinds of plants (trees, shrubs, climbing plants, roses, fruit trees) in their own chapters.

Pruning may appear to be the most tremendous grind, but it is in fact one of the most intellectually satisfying of all gardening activities, and has weeding and mowing, of which we all do a great deal, beaten out of sight. To stand in front of a wall from which you have delicately untied all the canes of a climbing rose, deciding which of the growths should be cut out and which retained, then neatly tying them to the wires so that the sun can reach equally each growth to ripen the wood and encourage a good flowering, is a very pleasant activity. To do this with the sun on your back on a clear spring day, will make your happiness complete.

A gardener's motto should be 'Keep shrubs young'. Buddleja davidii, *if pruned annually, has the secret of eternal youth.*

8

BUILDING THE FRAMEWORK

HERE IS NOT A GREAT DEAL OF POINT IN MASTERING A VARIETY OF BASIC GARDENING TECHNIQUES, AND ACQUIRING A RANGE OF TOOLS WITH WHICH TO DO THEM, WITHOUT HAVING THE PLANTS IN THE GARDEN THAT REQUIRE CULTIVATION. PLANTS, AND THEIR BASIC CARE, ARE THE SUBJECT OF THIS AND THE FOLLOWING THREE CHAPTERS. WE BEGIN WITH THOSE PLANTS THAT, INEVITABLY, BECAUSE OF THEIR BULK AND PRESENCE, WILL PROVIDE THE FRAMEWORK, HELPING TO GIVE THE GARDEN ITS PARTICULAR CHARACTER AND PERMANENT STRUCTURE. IF YOU ARE BEGINNING A GARDEN FROM SCRATCH, IT IS AS WELL TO CONCENTRATE INITIALLY ON THE PLANNING AND PLANTING OF TREES AND SHRUBS, ESPECIALLY IF THEY ARE TO BE USED AS HEDGES, BECAUSE THESE ELEMENTS ARE LIKELY TO BE THE SLOWEST TO GROW TO THE SIZE YOU REQUIRE.

Here trees are used collectively as a background and singly, as specimens, to act as eyecatchers. The yellow pinnate-leaved tree is Robinia pseudoacacia *'Frisia', and the small tree in the topiary circle is the tulip tree,* Liriodendron tulipifera.

I hope I shall not be thought impertinent if I assume that not everyone knows that trees and shrubs are both woody plants which endure from year to year, and that a tree has a single stem, while a shrub may have several. There is, however, sometimes an overlap: not all trees are resolutely trees, and can often be persuaded to be shrubs by pruning – either intentionally or by accident. If the central leader dies, for example, when the tree is very young, two branches may come up to take its place, with further branches developing lower down. *Acer davidii,* the snakebark maple is a tree, but if several stems are allowed to develop from near ground level (which is sometimes done to show off the striations that are the glory of this plant), it looks more like a shrub. Shrubs, on the other hand, sometimes overstep the mark we have arbitrarily set down for them and burgeon, if

ABOVE: Magnolia stellata, *the star magnolia, makes a most attractive deciduous large shrub or, occasionally, small tree.*
RIGHT: Acer griseum *is a small tree with pretty three-part leaves to complement the cinnamon-coloured peeling bark; these turn scarlet in autumn.*

allowed, into small trees. The hazel, for example, will, if not 'coppiced' (that is, cut down close to ground level every few years) eventually become a small tree.

Most tree species can be propagated from seed, if you have the patience, and many of the commoner ones are now available from seed suppliers. Shrubs are usually propagated from semi-hardwood cuttings in late summer, although hardwood cuttings in the winter are suitable for easy plants such as gooseberries and willows. Layering is suitable for magnolias, rhododendrons and other shrubs with low-slung branches (see page 95).

We have looked at the planting and staking of trees and shrubs in chapter 4; but I would like to emphasize again that a plant that is to grow in the same spot for many years deserves, at the very least, good soil preparation and planting. I will also remind you that the larger the plant the more desperate its need for water is likely to be until the roots are well established. This is particularly true of climbing shrubs – or, more accurately, of plants grown against walls.

When I plant a young tree, especially a fruit tree, I try to remember to cut the leading shoot back by about half its length to a sideways- or upwards-facing bud. In that way a new shoot

---

Favourite trees *(heights given after 10 years' growth)*

Abies koreana (silver fir): conical evergreen; 5 × 3m (16 × 10ft); green needle-like leaves, silver underneath; blue-violet cones

Acer davidii (snakebark maple): deciduous; 6 × 4.5m (20 × 15ft); ovate leaves; sealing-wax red stems; green-and-white striped bark

Acer griseum (paperbark maple): deciduous; 5 × 3m (16 × 10ft); peeling, orange-brown bark; 3 dark green leaflets, scarlet in autumn

Betula ermanii: deciduous; 6 × 3m (20 × 10ft); peeling, pinkish-white bark; oval green leaves make good autumn colour

Carpinus betulus 'Fastigiata': deciduous; 7 × 4m (23 × 13ft); elegant erect flame-shaped habit; oval leaves turn orange and yellow in autumn

Gleditsia triacanthos 'Sunburst': deciduous; 6 × 4.5m (20 × 15ft); fern-like golden foliage in spring, turns green in summer

Ilex aquifolium 'J C van Tol': evergreen; 4 × 2m (13 × 6½ft); dark green, oval, slightly spiny leaves; bears red berries even when male trees absent

Metasequoia glyptostroboides (dawn redwood): deciduous upright conifer; 10 × 3m (33 × 10ft); red-brown bark; soft green leaves turn golden-yellow in autumn

Sorbus thibetica 'John Mitchell' (Mitchell's whitebeam): deciduous; 7 × 4m (23 × 13ft); conical; dark green leaves, silver below; white flowers in spring

will be stimulated to develop and will grow towards the vertical. I do this because young trees often suffer die-back at the end of the main shoot after planting, and on opposite-leaved trees like maple, two shoots may come up to take the place of the leader. If this occurs, take the opportunity the following dormant season to remove one of those two shoots flush with the trunk, so that a smooth line is made, and the other shoot has the opportunity to grow more vertical. If necessary, insert a long bamboo cane in the ground and tie the shoot to it, to encourage it to grow up. This will not only help the appearance of the tree, but will prevent a V-shaped crotch from developing, which will hold rainwater and almost certainly eventually rot the heartwood of the tree.

Tree surgery is for tree surgeons, and I do not advise cleaning cavities in trees, cutting down and removing the stumps of large trees, or cutting off major branches yourself. However, as tree surgeons do not give their services free, or anything approaching it, you will sometimes wish to do some of the work yourself. I personally restrict my efforts in this direction to cutting off dead branches of less than 30cm

(12in) in diameter, or branches that have sprouted from the trunk, low down, and spoil its clean line. Even such relatively minor work requires thought, because a long branch can be heavy and, if sawn from the top, may fall too quickly and tear the bark down the trunk. The proper way to cut a branch of any size is to saw from the bottom to about a third to a half of the way through the branch, some distance from the trunk, then saw right through a little further away from the trunk. If the weight of the branch does make it fall, it will break at the first saw-cut you made, and you are also far less likely to have a saw pinched in the middle of a large branch. After the bulk of the branch has been removed, you should neatly saw the stub close to the main trunk, but not absolutely flush with it, trimming the wound afterwards with your knife to help the healing process (see illustrations below).

Pests and diseases strike most trees and shrubs at one time or another, although the need to do something about them is rarely felt as strongly as it is with those that attack vegetables or roses (see chapter 13). If you have tree stumps in your garden which you fear will

Removing a branch

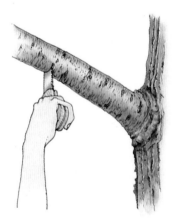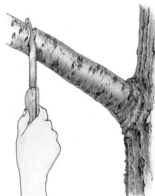

Long, heavy branches have a regrettable tendency to tear off the bark on the trunk as they fall, if they are sawn from the top. The best technique is, therefore, to cut from underneath initially, half-way through the branch, with a Grecian saw. When sawn from above, a little further along, the branch will

fall cleanly. If the branch is more than 2.5cm (1in) in diameter, remove the bulk of the weight by cutting 30cm (12in) away from the trunk, then saw neatly close to the trunk. The wound will heal much more easily if the saw marks are smoothed out by using a sharp knife to trim round the edge of the cut.

harbour honey fungus, and which need to be killed to make extraction easier, put ammonium sulphamate herbicide (which breaks down in time to the fertilizer sulphate of ammonia) into cuts in the bark and heartwood.

Shrubs will need annual feeding with organic matter, at least until well established, and probably until the end of their time. As a general rule, shrubs are long-lived, so deserve some care. If you wish for really good growth, especially if wet weather in spring has washed out the nutrients from the soil, give them a liquid feed using a hose-dilutor. In the growing season, shrubs and trees respond very positively to a foliar feed, and it is easy enough to provide.

I cannot emphasize enough the almost miraculous improvements to the general run of garden shrubs that may be wrought by good feeding. The plants in most people's gardens exist, rather than live, on a meagre diet of a few grass clippings a year, and it is small wonder they are stunted in growth and niggardly in their flowering as a result. Plants with big deciduous leaves particularly benefit. Only the Spartan creatures of Mediterranean countries,

Colourful foliage shrubs, including Berberis thunbergii atropurpurea, Euonymus fortunei *'Variegatus' and* Spiraea japonica *'Goldflame'.*

which consent to grow in our sunniest places in poor soil, will flower less well and grow too much leaf under this regime; but they are very much the exception.

Other routine tasks best not ignored are the protection of tender plants in the winter (see pages 56-9) and weeding, if no weed-suppressant mulch has been applied. Even quite large plants will be adversely affected if they have to compete with the greedy roots of perennial weeds.

I have explained the principles that apply to the pruning of shrubs in chapter 7, but there are many shrubs which are also, and even sometimes exclusively, wall plants, and these, because of the particular and rather artificial situation which they inhabit, require slightly different treatment in the way of pruning, from border shrubs. They are not, naturally, climbers and, generally speaking, make round shapes in the open. If they were left to remain like that, not only would there be no room in the wall

Favourite shrubs

Cistus laurifolius: reasonably hardy evergreen; 2 × 2m (6½ × 6½ft); oval dark green leaves; white flowers with yellow blotch in summer

Daphne × burkwoodii 'Somerset': semi-evergreen; upright bushy shrub; 1.2 × 2m (4 × 6½ft); clusters of scented pink to white flowers in late spring

Lavatera 'Barnsley': deciduous or semi-evergreen; 1.2 × 1.5m (4 × 5ft); masses of white, flushed pink, hollyhock flowers from mid- to early autumn; grey-green leaves

Philadelphus 'Belle Etoile': deciduous; arching shrub; 1.5 × 1.5 m (5 × 5ft); very fragrant white flowers, with purple blotch in centre in mid-summer

Potentilla fruticosa 'Primrose Beauty': deciduous; 90 × 120cm (3 × 4ft); pale yellow cup-shaped flowers all summer; silky grey-green leaves

Rhododendron luteum: deciduous; 1.5 × 1.5m (5 × 5ft); very scented yellow flowers in late spring; colourful autumn foliage

Viburnum farreri: deciduous; 2 × 1.1m (6½ × 3½ft); fragrant pinky-white flowers late autumn to spring; green leaves, bronze when young

grow clematises as wall shrubs. In the wild, most *Clematis* clamber through large shrubs or small trees, as is attested by our own Traveller's Joy (*Clematis vitalba*) – hence their requirement for shade at the roots – so it seems foolish not to follow that idea in the garden. They are much easier to handle if they are allowed to scramble by their leaf-tendrils up old trees in this way, when they hardly need pruning at all (or at least not the spring-flowerers). What turns the species *Clematis* into twiggy muddles, like knitting attacked by the cat, is being forced to hang from one wire attached to a wall. It is *much* better to grow them up open fencing, wire or otherwise. If you grow them with roses around pillars, you will succeed best if you wrap clematis netting loosely round the post. Nor do I like to tie them with string because their shoots are so very delicate and will inevitably be damaged.

Clematises depress me. They are like a clinging friend whom one does not *really* mean to hurt but, somehow in one's impatience, it seems

border for anything else, but one could never avoid being caught up on the thorns of *Chaenomeles* when walking past. Wall shrubs that are not climbers, such as *Abutilon, Buddleja fallowiana, Camellia, Ceanothus, Chaenomeles, Cytisus battandieri* and *Pyracantha,* should have those branches that grow out from the wall removed in spring or summer. As with all shrubs, care must be taken not to cut off the flower buds, so pruning is best done after flowering for spring-flowering shrubs, and in late winter for summer-flowerers. Spring-flowering shrubs like *Pyracantha* and *Chaenomeles* which will later fruit, have their leaf shoots, which grow after flowering, cut back to 8-10cm (3-4in) from their base in mid-summer. This will ensure that the fruit is visible. From these shortened leaf shoots will grow next year's flower buds. Half-hardy plants like *Abutilon* and *Lippia* will require their frosted and dead wood to be cut out after the winter.

Of course, we cannot ever forget clematises, but it seems to me that we should not really

Philadelphus 'Belle Etoile' *is one of the very best of a lovely, highly scented family. Indeed, 'Mock Orange' is* the scent of summer *for me. This one is suitable for a smallish garden.*

Two excellent climbing plants – the pink Clematis *'Nelly Moser' and the self-clinging, yellow-leaved ivy,* Hedera *'Buttercup' – enhance the appearance of this garden shed.*

Favourite climbers & wall shrubs

Ceanothus impressus: evergreen wall shrub; 3 × 3m (10 × 10ft); small leaves; deep blue flowers in early summer

Clematis 'Duchess of Albany': deciduous climber; 2.5m (8ft); small, pink, tulip-shaped flowers in summer

Clematis flammula: deciduous climber; 5m (16ft); dark green, glossy green leaves; tiny white scented stars in late summer and early autumn

Cytisus battandieri (Moroccan broom): slightly tender semi-evergreen wall shrub; 3 × 2 m (10 × 6½ft); open growth; leaves have 3 silver-grey leaflets; cones of pineapple-scented flowers in summer

Lonicera japonica 'Halliana': semi-evergreen twining climber; 5m (16ft); oval, bright green leaves; scented white flowers, fading to yellow, in summer and autumn

Vitis coignetiae (crimson glory vine): deciduous; very vigorous climber; 10m (33ft); large heart-shaped leaves turn scarlet and orange in autumn

Wisteria sinensis: deciduous climber; 8m (26ft); leaves with 11 leaflets; scented pale blue-violet flowers in long racemes in early summer

unavoidable. Whenever I have any dealings with one I feel at my most clumsy and harmful; I always damage the vines, however hard I try to avoid it. However, like the tiresome, but loyal friend, they appear not to mind too much, or are good at concealing it. Clematises are also good subjects for the compulsive potterer, such as I am: they benefit hugely from being encouraged regularly by a gentle twist or twine as they grow, so that they go where you want them to. Indeed, this is necessary work, for once the vines are well established, they are impossible to disentangle from their fellows.

It is not unknown for descriptions of the pruning of clematises to be prefaced with gloomy warnings about how complicated the whole business can be. But, take heart, for the basic principles of pruning have not been abandoned. What causes the (potential) difficulty is that different clematis species and hybrids flower at different times of the year. That is why they need different treatment but, once it is established when they do flower, you can work out how to treat them, even if you have never grown that particular clematis before. You do not even need to know what the name is, just as long as you take note of the time of flowering.

For the purpose of pruning, clematis fall into three main groups. You can prune away the spent flowering growth of winter- and spring-flowerers (*C. armandii, C. macropetala, C. alpina, C. montana,* for example) immediately after flowering. They will then have time to make new long flowering shoots for the following year. The early summer-flowerers (large-flowered hybrids like 'Nelly Moser' and 'Marie Boisselot') flower on this year's wood, so are cut back only as far as new strong buds are showing, in late winter. Late summer-flowerers can all be cut back wholesale in late winter to about 90cm (3ft) from the ground. All clematis, incidentally, perform better for being fed.

All climbing plants, except the few that cling for themselves to walls such as *Hydrangea petiolaris* and Virginia creeper, need to be tied to wires secured to the brick or stonework. Flexible, green plastic-coated wire is probably the most useful, secured to the wall at 45cm (18in) intervals with masonry nails. I still use thick string to tie the shoots to these wires because it 'gives' a little, but there are now proprietary plant ties available which are quicker.

Hedging plants are divided between the handsome and the horrible, of which the few horrible species are much the most commonly planted. Of course, hedges are an essential element of garden design and no one needs to be convinced of their importance and value as internal divisions, as screens and as windbreaks; they are infinitely preferable to wooden fences as far as appearance is concerned, and better than walls for breaking the force of the wind in exposed positions. On the other hand, unlike a fence, there are few climbers that you can grow up them (the exceptions being *Tropaeolum speciosum,* which looks stunning

Pruning late summer-flowering clematis

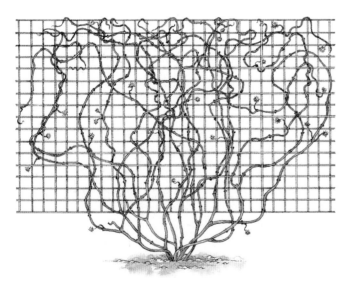

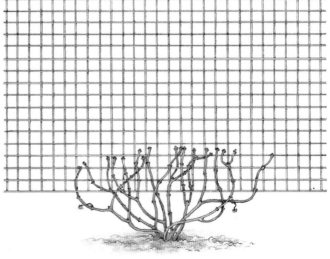

Late summmer-flowering clematis include large-flowered hybrids such as 'Ville de Lyon' and 'Hagley Hybrid' as well as species like C. tangutica *and* C. viticella. *They are classed in group 3.*

Group 3 clematis flower on long stems made in the current season, so last year's wood is cut back hard just before buds start to break in late winter. Pruning could not be simpler.

trailing over a yew hedge, and some of the species *Clematis,* such as *C. flammula,* which will grow through or over a deciduous hedge).

You will have to make a choice between informal hedges which are labour-saving such as rose or tamarix, and formal ones which are labour-intensive such as *Carpinus betulus,* × *Cupressocyparis leylandii, Fagus sylvatica, Ligustrum ovalifolium, Lonicera nitida, Taxus baccata,* but whatever anybody says, the best hedges are formal ones, because symmetry gives substance and credibility to a scheme even if, within that framework, the planting is 'natural' (that is, informal). Formal hedges must be clipped, however, and not only for the sake of appearances. Some kinds are very vigorous, as anyone will know who has let a Leyland cypress (× *Cupressocyparis leylandii*) hedge go for a couple of years and now finds her garden shaded and dwarfed by towering conifers.

Planting hedging plants is virtually the same as planting any other shrub (see pages 52-5);

Here, several types of hedging plant, including the Portugal laurel, make a 'tapestry' effect. Evergreen shrubs make the best clippable hedge and they look ornamental and substantial even in winter.

the difference lies only in preparing a trench instead of a hole. On the whole I advise against staggering the plants in the row; it makes for a hedge that can become too wide and is not as easy to clip. It is better to buy small bare-rooted 'whips'; these will be cheaper and will establish more quickly than large container-grown plants from a garden centre.

Hedges are notorious for taking moisture and food out of the ground, so dig in plenty of organic matter initially, and try to remember to mulch the young hedge in the spring to increase the plants' chances of survival. Give the ground around the base a quick hoe when you remember, although hedge-bottoms tend to be so dry and shady that even weeds lose heart in summer. A spring fertilizer does not come amiss.

Plants for informal hedges

Corylus avellana (hazel): deciduous; broad, toothed leaves; purple form available

Escallonia macrantha 'Crimson Spire': evergreen; oval, green leaves; tubular red flowers; good by the sea

Forsythia × intermedia 'Spectabilis': deciduous; deep yellow flowers early spring, before green leaves

Fuchsia magellanica: deciduous; pendulous flowers, scarlet and purple in summer; good in mild districts and by the sea

Helichrysum splendidum: evergreen; slightly tender; woolly, silvery leaves; yellow flowers summer to late autumn

Lavandula angustifolia (lavender): evergreen; slightly tender; grey-green narrow leaves; fragrant tubular blue flowers mid- to late summer

Potentilla fruticosa: deciduous; several varieties available; flowers from white to deep orange

Rosa rugosa: deciduous; several cultivars available; leathery, wrinkled, disease-resistant foliage; flowers from white to purple, single or double, cup-shaped

Formative pruning for hedging plants depends on what sort of hedge you are growing. After planting, the quick growers like privet and tamarisk should be cut back to 15cm (6in), the others to a half to a third of their height. They will not need any more clipping until the following year when the hedge will benefit from being trimmed several times to encourage it to thicken out. Every year the leaders should be 'tipped' (cut) back a little, even though the hedge will not have reached its full height; except, that is, for conifers including yew, where the leader should be left to grow on. Once the hedge has reached the required height, allow an increase of about 5mm (^{1}/4in) a year. If you do not keep tight control in this way, you risk creating those towering conifers.

It is important to prune hedging plants well, because a hedge rather loses its point if it goes bare and open at the bottom. Horticulturists invented (as long ago as 1647) the word 'batter' to describe the way a hedge is cut so that the top is slightly narrower than the bottom. Creating a batter seems self-evident once you know about it, but I certainly did not latch onto

the reason for it immediately: if you want sunlight and moisture to reach the hedge-bottom, and you wish to prevent the lower branches from defoliating for lack of those two vital commodities. This matters especially with evergreen hedges such as yew.

Hedge-clipping, of the back-breaking, time-consuming variety, has been gratefully abandoned by most people since the advent of electric trimmers. These are lighter and infinitely preferable to the older, diesel-driven sort, and are most suitable for hedges with small leaves. However, although easier and quicker than using garden shears, electric trimmers are not unalloyed pleasure. For one thing, they need to be cleaned quite carefully after use, because the sap of leaves, especially those of resinous conifers, gums up the blades which work with a scissor action. It is also quite possible (even if you are a careful person) to cut through the cable, although the chances are reduced if you keep the cable over the shoulder of the arm that holds the trimmer. Never stretch further than is comfortable and balanced, and never forget to attach the plug of the extension lead to a residual current device (RCD). A cordless, rechargeable hedge-trimmer is now available if you cannot trust yourself in this matter.

However you do it, hedge-trimming is hard work on the arms and shoulders, especially if you are standing on a ladder. Because the best blades are two-edged, the most effective

The hedge-trimmer has supplanted the pair of garden shears for any gardener with a long hedge to cut. Put the cable over your shoulder for safety.

energy-conserving way of using hedge-trimmers is to cut in short sweeps, first one way and then the other. The real purists do not believe that trimmers do such a good job as hand-shears, but they are the sort who will not drink post-phylloxera wine, or wear anything on their feet but 100 per cent woollen socks. The rest of us use hedge-trimmers without qualms. However, shears, though much slower, are the appropriate tool if you have not got very much to cut: just a stretch of privet, say, in front of a terraced house.

The leaves of *Aucuba* and Portugal laurel (*Prunus lusitanica*) should be cut with sharp secateurs. This is a tiresome chore, I know, but shears are inclined to tear such tough, large leaves (see photograph on page 113).

Trimming is difficult to do well at first; but with practice you can get very proficient. It sounds fussy but a bamboo cane (the height of the hedge) placed at each of the four corners and joined with string, will help to give you an idea of the shape you require (see illustrations above right). The eye is easily deceived and mistakes are quickly made, especially when you are cutting into the hedge to make it thinner. And mistakes, when they do occur, are regrettably rather public.

How often you have to cut a hedge depends on the species, and is usually an important consideration when deciding what to plant.

In the perfect world inhabited by gardening writers, privet needs three trims a year. This is two too many for most of us, so let me add another factor to the equation. Instead of pruning, you could use a chemical growth retardant (active ingredient dikegulac) which you dilute and spray on. It is not used nearly as much as it might be, and makes all the difference if you have received the poisoned chalice of a privet hedge which you have not quite the energy to remove in favour of something more interesting. Admittedly, there are some hedging plants for which it is not suitable, such as yew, box, roses (except *R. rugosa*), viburnums and myrobalan plum. You will have to give the hedge an initial trim in the spring, and the

String stretched between bamboo canes is well-nigh essential, if you want to get the top of a hedge level and the sides straight. They need to be removed before you slope the sides to form the 'batter'.

growth retardant should be sprayed on a little while after the hedge has been clipped. Growth retardants are non-specific, so you will have to be careful to avoid spray drift or you may have a lot of stunted border plants. One spray a year is all that is required, however, so this does represent a saving in labour.

Plants for formal hedges

Buxus sempervirens 'Suffruticosa' (box): evergreen; dark glossy green oblong leaves

Carpinus betulus (hornbeam): deciduous; oval, veined, beech-like leaves

Fagus sylvatica (beech): deciduous; oval, veined leaves; several coloured forms available

Ilex aquifolium (holly): evergreen; spined, wavy, dark green glossy leaves; several variegated and spineless forms available

Pittosporum tenuifolium: evergreen; not reliably hardy; oval, wavy-edged mid-green leaves; good for seaside planting; coloured-leaved forms available

Taxus baccata (English yew): evergreen; needle-like dark green leaves; yellow-leaved form available

Thuja plicata 'Atrovirens' (Western red cedar): evergreen; dark green flat sprays of leaves; coloured forms available

9

COMING UP ROSES

THE MODERN ROSE IS A CREATURE OF THE BREEDER'S IMAGINATION. IT IS THE HEIR TO AS COMPLEX A COMBINATION OF BLOOD LINES AS A MODERN RACEHORSE, AND BEARS AS LITTLE RESEMBLANCE TO THE WILD SPECIES AS THE MODERN RACEHORSE DOES TO A WELSH MOUNTAIN PONY. A GREAT DEAL OF CROSSING HAS GONE ON TO PRODUCE PLANTS THAT WILL PROVIDE US WITH THE IDEALS FOR WHICH WE STRIVE: LARGE, COLOURFUL BLOOMS, DISEASE-RESISTANCE, PERPETUAL (THAT IS, REPEAT) FLOWERING, AND STOUT HABIT WHICH REQUIRES NO STAKING. IN THE PAST, MUCH OF THE CHARM AND SCENT HAVE BEEN SACRIFICED TO THESE IDEALS, BUT EFFORTS ARE NOW BEING MADE TO BRING THEM BACK.

The rose is the shrub par excellence *for the mid-summer garden. These roses flower only once, however, but that should not disqualify them from the garden. That is true, after all, of a number of other shrubs, such as* Philadelphus. *We are fussy about this, because there are many roses that either have a few blooms later on or a full-scale second flowering.*

Considered by many the most highly scented of all roses, 'Madame Isaac Pereire' is a Bourbon, so repeats to a certain extent.

'Buff Beauty' is a Hybrid Musk, so it is perpetual-flowering and scented, and makes a large shapely shrub.

The species roses are those that are found in the wild and include *R. rubiginosa*, the sweetbriar rose, *R. pimpinellifolia*, the Scottish rose, and *R. rugosa*, the Japanese rose with the corrugated leaves. Species roses are now, strictly speaking, known as Wild Roses.

Species roses, especially *R. alba, R. gallica, R. moschata* and *R. rubiginosa*, have over the centuries been used in breeding, or have given rise to chance crosses. Roses from China added their particular characteristics, the most especially valued being their perpetual flowering nature. Their offspring, now known as Old Garden Roses, are the Gallicas, Damasks, Albas, Moss Roses, Centifolias, Bourbons, Portlands, Chinas, Teas and Hybrid Perpetuals. At the end of the nineteenth century, the Hybrid Tea roses were developed, and in the early twentieth century the Floribundas (which we are now asked to call Large-Flowered Bush Roses, and Cluster-Flowered Bush Roses); these are the ones predominantly grown in gardens today as 'bedding roses'.

Hybrid Teas and Floribundas are perpetual-flowering (all summer long, in two main flushes) and have a much wider range of colour than the Old Roses, which were stuck in the groove of purple, red, pink and white. However, the Old Roses are making a comeback in the form of Modern Shrub Roses such as the Hybrid Musks and the new 'English' roses, both of which are perpetual. These last often combine the best qualities of Modern and Old: the free-flowering, lax-petalled flowers and flowering shrub habit of the Old Roses, with the perpetual nature and wide range of colour, excluding flame and orange, which are the hallmarks of the Hybrid Teas and Floribundas. It seems to me that the centuries of rose-breeding have finally succeeded in developing some truly garden-worthy plants.

The other classifications into which roses can be roughly divided are: Climbers (which may, or may not be perpetual, depending on parentage); Ramblers (not perpetual); Polyanthas; Patio Roses; Ground-cover Roses and

Miniatures. This alarmingly fast gallop through what is a very complex subject is simply to give you an idea of the diversity of roses, and their origins and uses, so that what follows about their cultivation may make some sense.

Everybody grows roses, mostly with a fair degree of success. Roses are easy to cultivate and hard to kill. I should be being a little economical with the truth, however, as well as doing myself out of a job, if I were to say that all was plain sailing, for they do respond handsomely to a little extra care.

If you do not plant a rose quite properly (see page 55), no very terrible thing will happen to you; indeed, you will probably get away with it. Or would, except for one consequence which will go on irritating you until you can stand it no longer and dig the plant up to plant it again – properly this time. That consequence is suckering, the weakness of all budded roses.

Suckers are not lollipops, nor are they fools; they are vigorous green shoots emanating from the roots, and they are undesirable because they are genetically of the same material as the rootstock, onto which a bud of the sort of rose required has been grafted. This bud is called the scion and it lends its genetic characteristics

Removing suckers from a rose is not a pleasant task, but must be done, if the rose is not to be undermined. Pull the sucker away from the root with both hands. If you value your skin, use gloves.

to the rose bush. The rootstock is restrained by the bud-scion but wishes periodically to break out, especially if it is near the surface of the soil. If it does so, and is given an inch, it will go on to take a furlong, and the suckers will eventually smother the scion and sap its vigour. The result, in place of your named rose, will probably be a thorny briar rose with pretty but short-lived flowers. (Suckers are bad news for lilacs and for lime trees as well.) Suckers need to be discouraged from arising and eliminated when they do arise. Discouraging them means planting your rose sufficiently deeply so that it does not attempt to throw up these shoots. If you cut these suckers off at ground level, which it is extremely tempting to do, the dormant buds below the cuts will be stimulated into growth. It is far better to get down on your kneelers, scrape away the soil around the sucker until you can see where it arises from the root, and, with both hands, pull the sucker away (see illustration below left). There is quite a helpful de-suckerer available, which consists of a handle attached to a long steel stick with a bifurcated end. The idea is that you should stab the sucker underground, near to its *fons et origo.* It works quite well and is invaluable for the addict of one-use gadgets, like myself.

The only sure way of avoiding suckers on non-species roses is to buy those on their own roots. The sale of these is becoming popular with small specialist nurseries who do not deal in large quantities, but is unlikely to appeal to the owners of big concerns. In the future the problem will be solved by widespread micro-propagation of roses. It is agreeable to think that this advice concerning suckers may one day become redundant; I look forward to that.

The important point, therefore, is not to plant roses too shallowly. Otherwise, the advice is much the same as for planting anything, except that roses are particularly particular about not being put in precisely the same place where some other rose has been before. If you do, they may suffer from the condition called 'rose-sickness' or, more properly, 'rose replant disease'. The only way to get round this, if you

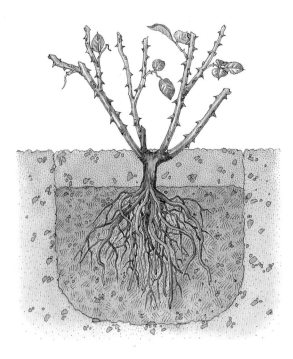

This shows at what level a bare-rooted rose should be planted. A planting mixture is especially helpful if there is a chance of 'rose sickness'.

insist on planting in the same spot, is to dig out a large hole, at the very least 45 x 45cm (18 x 18in), transfer the soil to the vegetable garden and replace it with some to fill the hole (see illustration above). If you have no spare soil, buy a bag of planting mixture from the garden centre. I wish I could say that this procedure was unnecessary, but I cannot. The alternative is to avoid planting roses where roses have been before, but I recognize that this may be easier said than done, especially if you have a passion for roses and garden in a restricted space.

It is worth noting that standard roses must be planted at the soil-mark, if you can discern it, once you have first banged in a large, ugly stake to a level just below the head of twigs where stock meets scion. The plant will require three plastic ties to hold it to the stake and make the artificial appearance complete.

Climbing roses are planted in the same way as other roses, except that, like other wall plants and climbers, they may have to compete for available water with two or three storeys of thirsty brick or stone. Not only, therefore, must they be planted well away from the wall, with

their roots stretched out away from it and into the moister soil beyond, but they must not be planted under the eaves of a house or they will get no water at all. Fortunately, climbing roses are quite amenable to the suggestion that they be leaned against a wall from a distance of 45cm (18in) or so. This all seems so self-evident that one feels an idiot not to have thought of it, but sometimes things need dinning in until they become second-nature.

Is there another subject in the whole of the horticultural canon that provokes as much anxiety, energy, discussion, even controversy, as the pruning of roses? If there is, I do not know it. Pruning has put off more would-be gardeners than any other, for it appears so troublesome. I urge you not to worry, however. The only thing you must never do (and this applies to all flowering shrubs that flower on the current season's wood) is to cut off the shoots, which are to flower, too late in the spring.

Roses in the wild are not pruned; they simply shed dead wood, gradually and piecemeal, and, in spite of not being pruned, they continue to flower. It is just that they tend to make a lot of dense growth, with flowers on the top nearest the sun, and in the garden we require something rather different: we wish our plants (whose environment and upbringing is anyway highly artificial) to produce the maximum amount – or size – of flower, displayed to its best advantage.

Let us imagine a typical scene. You have finally moved to a house and garden; no more living in a flat, three floors up, with not so much as a window-box to look after. The estate agent may have measured the garden in square feet rather than fractions of an acre, but at least it is yours, with which to do as you please.

One day in late winter, you go out into the garden, pick your way delicately over the rubble, and come across some spindly green and

Rosa 'Seagull' looks wonderful cascading from the top of this Prunus serrula*, whose own flowers come earlier in the year. The mulch ground-cover is* Lamium maculatum *'Beacon Silver'.*

brown twigs, which you are pretty certain are roses. Your first reaction is to prune them, because that seems to be the preoccupation of any keen gardener you have ever met. But how?

You probably do what you did when you first moved into a flat and needed to learn to cook: you buy a book and read all about it, imagining that soon, like Celia Johnson in *Hay Fever*, you will be floating through the French windows on summer evenings with a trug basket of long-stemmed, fragrant roses on your arm.

The book you buy, let us call it *The What's What of Gardening*, is severely practical but makes various assumptions. For a start, it takes for granted that you understand the language in which it is written (which sounds to you as complicated and unguessable as a computer manual), and that you know the name of your

'Graham Thomas' is one of the best and most popular 'English' roses. It combines perpetual flowering with good scent and disease-resistance.

unknown rose and, even more problematic, what sort it is: 'Hybrid Tea, Floribunda, Modern Shrub, English Rose . . .' You sternly suppress your rising panic; the bundle of shiny green stems, for which no label has survived, could be any of these; you suspect only that it is not a climber or rambler. Oh dear. But before you throw in the towel, I have some reassuring news: it is not essential at this stage to know exactly what your rose is. Provided that you cut it about no later than early spring, you will get some kind of flowering, whatever happens.

Now for the instructions in your book: 'Cut out the dead and diseased wood.' That is easy:

dead is brown and brittle, live is green, or pur-ply-red in the spring; diseased has brown lesions on green. 'Cut out the overcrowded, weak and spindly wood.' That also is simple, although the advice is now considered rather old-fashioned. By all means cut out shoots that are jostling each other, but retain the weak growths as far as possible. Although it goes against the grain to retain all these little, seem-ingly useless, foliage-bearing, twiggy bits which are supposed to clutter up the plant and divert the plant's food supply from making flowers, they are in fact vital to retain because they pro-duce the leaves that feed the plant. If they are left intact, the flowering will improve.

Trickier is this enigmatic sentence in your book: 'Cut the laterals of climbing roses back to two buds.' Has 'lateral' got something to do with 'side', you wonder? You decide, quite rightly, that the book means those thin side shoots emanating from the slightly thicker main ones. And what about 'buds'? Bud seems to be a key word, whatever kind of rose is being writ-ten about. You know what buds are – green, pointed things that burst into leaf in spring – but you cannot see any; all you can see are smooth green shoots. Well, you are nearly there, in fact; a bud on a rose is the curved line,

Rosa 'Aloha' is an excellent short climbing rose, suitable for a pillar, or a large shrub. Its healthy foliage and free-flowering habit make it most desirable.

Favourite roses

'Aloha': Modern Shrub Climber or Shrub; 2.5m (8ft); repeat-flowering; fragrant, double pink with apricot centre; disease-resistant

'Elizabeth Harkness': Hybrid Tea; 75 × 60cm (2½ × 2ft); repeat-flowering; fragrant; double creamy-pink

'Frühlingsmorgen': Modern Shrub; 2 × 1.5m (6½ × 5ft); grey-green leaves; scented; single, pink with yellow centre in early summer

'Golden Showers': Climber or Shrub; 2 × 3m (6½ × 10ft); fragrant; double, bright yellow flowers in summer and autumn

'Graham Thomas': English Rose; 1.2 × 1.2m (4 × 4ft); double, yellow flowers; repeat-flowering; disease-resistant

'Heritage': English Rose; 1.2 x 1.2m (4 x 4ft); very fragrant; repeat-flowering; cupped, double, soft pink

'Madame Isaac Pereire': Old Rose (Bourbon); 2 × 2m (6½ × 6½ft); very scented; repeat-flowering; very double, deep purple-pink

'Margaret Merril': Floribunda; 90 × 60cm (3 × 2ft); very scented; double blush-white in summer

moyesii: 'Geranium' Species; 3 × 2.5m (10 × 8ft); arching shrub; single, deep scarlet flowers with yellow stamens in summer; red hips in autumn

'Sweet Dream': Miniature Floribunda/Patio; 40 × 35cm (16 × 14in); repeat-flowering; double, apricot-peach

about 1cm (^{1}/$_2$in) long, on the shoot. So, for a climbing rose you should, ideally, count '1, 2 buds' from the junction with the stem 'from which it sprang. In reality, an easier way is to measure about 2.5cm (1in) away from the stem, and then cut above one of those curved lines.

The book will also tell you, when dealing with free-standing roses, 'to cut to an outward-facing bud' – this is because, you are told, die-back in the middle of the bush and insufficient 'ripening' of the wood by the sun will result from too many growths pointing into the centre of the bush and crowding the space. I shouldn't bother. If you study roses carefully, you will see that several buds on a stem may break into leaf, not just the one immediately below the pruning cut. So, roses naturally acquire crossing stems in the middle of the bush, whatever you do. You are also told to cut slantwise about 5mm (^{1}/$_4$in) above the bud, the same way that the bud is facing, to prevent rainwater settling in the bud and rotting it. However, recent research and trials have shown it really does not matter where you cut, provided the plant is well fed and growing strongly. No other shrub is offered such gold star treatment, after all.

Indeed, you can simply cut straight across all the shoots if you want to. Floribundas and Hybrid Teas will both benefit from a laxer pruning regime (see illustrations below). The only roses you need to take a certain amount of care with are those on pillars or growing up walls, and here it is the training, rather than the pruning, that matters the most.

When I was a young gardener, I was told that the second week in March was *the* time for pruning bush roses in southern Britain; there did not appear to be any argument about it. This sort of dogmatic information is rather lowering to the gardener who is keen but who has to work all week, and looks out of the sitting-room windows in dismay on the second Saturday in March to see rain teeming down the windows. Forget the dates. Mid-spring is normally the time, but take your cue from the development of the buds. If the buds are bursting, you are a little late, and in cutting them off you have wasted vigour (although this will hardly matter on healthy plants). The condition you desire is that of swelling buds. At that stage, you can see where they are and more easily cut to a point just above them.

Pruning a Floribunda/Hybrid Tea

Floribunda roses tend to be more vigorous in growth than Hybrid Tea roses, so the pruning regime is less severe.

Prune to make a nicely shaped bush, not overcrowded by old stems, but retain twiggy growths. Mulch with well-rotted manure, if possible.

Shrub and English roses need no pruning for the first year; after that cut out any dead or diseased wood, thin out the oldest stems if the bush is very crowded and cut back good shoots by about a third. Do this in late winter.

Ramblers, which flower only once in a season, are best pruned in late summer or autumn. If the rose is tied to a support, cut away the ties and prune back a few of the flowered shoots almost to ground level, or to where a strong shoot is growing, to encourage more to come. These new shoots tend to flower profusely the following season. After pruning, tie the canes back to the support.

The best time for pruning climbers is when they are dormant, but when *exactly* is a matter of choice. Roses trained on sheltered walls can certainly be done in autumn. My attitude to this is governed by the fact that pruning climbers involves being up a ladder, without gloves while tying in, and keeping very still. Pruning consists of cutting out the dead wood, cutting back the flowered laterals to two buds, and, occasionally, cutting out old stems if you have new ones to replace them with, or you would like new ones to be produced (see illustrations below).

The hips of some roses, such as Rosa 'Complicata', *are well-worth preserving. Routine feeding should prevent any noticeable loss of flower power.*

After the main flowering, the flowered shoots of Shrub, Hybrid Tea and Floribunda roses (and climbers, if you can reach them) can be deadheaded (see page 64), except for those

Pruning a climbing rose

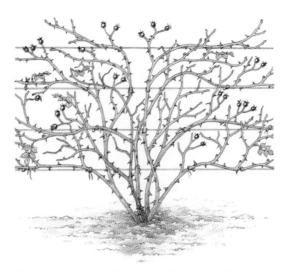

Climbing roses usually need to be taken off the wires before they can be pruned. Remove dead stems, flowered sideshoots and the tips of long stems.

Tie the stems firmly to the wires so they do not chafe each other. Training the stems horizontally encourages good flowering.

roses like *R. moyesii*, whose hips you wish to enjoy, and those which will not flower again anyway, whatever you do. I am not fussy about deadheading once-flowering roses, but I am about the Bourbons like 'Madame Isaac Pereire' and 'Souvenir de la Malmaison', or the Hybrid Musks like 'Penelope' and 'Buff Beauty', which will give me more flowers if I cut off their flowered shoots.

Many gardeners, when they move house, have the task of renovating old rose bushes thrust upon them. Most neglected roses are easily rescued with a mixture of simple pruning, removal of dead and diseased wood, sucker removal, and feeding. After years of neglect, a really hard prune to restore a bush to health will be a shock, and it is best to do the job over two seasons, feeding the plant in spring to encourage what growth there is (see illustrations below).

The larger the bush, the more resistance there will be to the wind. A bush with long shoots, will rock about in the ground and a hole may open up around the base of the stem. If this happens in winter, rain and snow must enter, and the action of frost expanding the soil water

will probably do damage to the roots. Cut back the long stems of roses growing in an exposed position, by half in autumn, or a little later in the case of still-flowering Modern Roses, and prune them as usual in the spring. Tread the soil down firmly round the stem bases.

However, before embarking on a major resuscitation job, my advice is to wait until your bushes have flowered once. You can then dig up any that are not breathtakingly pretty in flower, and strong in constitution, and plant named varieties, whose colours and habits appeal to you, somewhere else in the garden.

You may have in summer, on some of your roses, problems with greenfly (aphids), leaf-rolling sawfly, powdery mildew, blackspot and rusts. Use a combined pesticide and fungicide intended for roses – one that does not kill beneficial insects – trying to spray every fortnight or so from late spring until late summer.

This climbing rose has an arching, lax habit, which rebels against too rigid training and tying. After flowering, many of these long stems can be shortened, and the sideshoots cut back to two buds.

Renovating a rose

In the case of really neglected roses, it may be best to renovate them over two seasons. Remove all dead and diseased wood, and also some large stems – a pair of 'loppers' may be necessary for this.

In the second year, leave only the main stems and sideshoots, so that the rose puts maximum effort into regeneration. De-suckering and proper feeding help enormously.

10

PROVIDING THE COLOUR

I T IS NO GOOD RESTING ON YOUR LAURELS, SO TO SPEAK, ONCE THE SKELETON OF THE GARDEN, PROVIDED BY TREES, SHRUBS, ROSES AND HEDGES, HAS BEEN ESTABLISHED. OR RATHER YOU CAN, BUT YOUR GARDEN PICTURE MAY WELL LACK VARIETY, TEXTURE AND, ABOVE ALL, COLOUR IF YOU DO. HARDY AND HALF-HARDY ANNUALS AND BIENNIALS, TOGETHER WITH TENDER AND HARDY PERENNIALS, PROVIDE AN ALMOST INFINITE RANGE OF COLOURS, IN FLOWER, LEAF, STEM AND SEED HEAD. THEY ARE, IF YOU LIKE, THE FLESH ON THE BONES OF THE GARDEN. CULTIVATING THESE PLANTS, BOTH AS INDIVIDUALS AND IN PARTNERSHIP, IS ENDLESSLY INTERESTING, FOR EACH SEASON WILL GIVE YOU THE OPPORTUNITY TO EXPERIMENT WITH NEW GROUPINGS AND ASSOCIATIONS.

Colour and contrast in form have been achieved as much with perennials, annuals and biennials as with shrubs and climbers. Perennial Achillea, Nepeta, *geraniums and delphiniums are supplemented with biennial white foxgloves and annual orange Welsh poppy (*Meconopsis cambrica*). The bamboo canes are almost certainly to support annual sweet peas.*

Annuals & biennials

This book is written for the gardener who would like, by using easy and efficient methods, to achieve as lovely a garden as possible, in the necessarily limited time that she has to spare. That being the case, she may well wish to grow hardy annuals and biennials which, after herbs, are the least troublesome classes of plants, and a great deal prettier. It is true that annuals and biennials must be sown each year, so that they cannot form the framework of a garden in the way that trees, shrubs and hardy perennials do, but, on the other hand, they ensure that any gaps can be colourfully filled, and any colour scheme (especially one that does not please) changed annually. It would be a dull old garden, looked after by a dull old gardener, that did not alter one jot from year to year.

Hardy annuals

Hardy annuals are those plants whose seed is sown outside in the spring, and which flower, seed and die before the winter. They are almost all extremely easy to germinate, which is hardly

Pansies are perennials, usually treated as annuals or biennials. Forms of Viola x wittrockiana *will flower through summer and in winter and spring.*

surprising, considering that the very survival of their race depends on it.

I have a great deal of time for hardy annuals, and am determined, perhaps perversely, to champion their cause. I rather resent the dismissive tone many gardeners adopt when talking about them. Because they require none of the fuss and bother so necessary for the cultivation of their more tender *confrères*, they cannot be worth striving for, so the reasoning goes. But that is to deny the light and delicate charm (a charm not vouchsafed to the lumpish marigolds and ponderous zinnias) of these cinderellas of the summer border. Hardy annuals are transformed on flowering into princesses which captivate in the way the ugly sisters, *Celosia* and *Amaranthus*, never could. I would not be without the deep-blue *Phacelia campanularia* or *Matthiola bicornis* (for its evening scent of aniseed), and, for me, the charm of *Nigella damascena* is everlasting. Hardy annuals are the answer to mid-summer colour for those gardeners who do not have the advantages of heated glass, and are a necessary counterpoint to tender annuals for those who do.

Hardy annuals will not germinate quickly or completely if the soil is too cold or wet, so ignore the advice printed at the bottom of the page of your gardener's diary – it is only meant to be approximate and general – and sow the seed when the soil is sufficiently dry to be raked into 'a good tilth' (not forgetting to sprinkle a general fertilizer some days before), and when the soil temperature has reached the magic 6°C (43°F). Use a soil thermometer until you feel confident that you can recognize roughly when that is; alternatively, put your hand on the soil and sow when it no longer feels cold or very wet to the touch. Early spring is quite early enough to sow outside, even in favoured districts, and late spring is better in cold areas and on the top of hills. What gardeners say about late sown seed 'catching-up' is quite true; early sown seed will languish in the ground and be vulnerable to

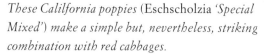

These Calilfornia poppies (Eschscholzia *'Special Mixed') make a simple but, nevertheless, striking combination with red cabbages.*

The 'queen' of annual flowers is the sweet pea (Lathyrus odoratus)*, of which there are dozens of named varieties. Not all are highly scented, alas.*

rot until there is air, warmth and moisture sufficient to trigger germination.

Even the most efficient gardener may, because there is so much to do in the garden in spring, leave the sowing so late that the plants will not have a chance to flower for a long season and so justify their culture. Some years you will be more successful about the timing of seed-sowing than others: *c'est la vie.*

You can sow some very hardy annuals in the ground in the autumn. After all, quite a few, like *Limnanthes douglasii,* will germinate naturally then, if given half a chance. Examples include *Centaurea* (cornflowers), *Clarkia, Echium* and *Calendula* (the pot marigold). The advantage of this is that they will get away well

in the spring but is not worth attempting in very cold districts.

Because the seed of hardy annuals germinates so willingly, it should be sown very thinly; otherwise, there will be much thinning to do, and thinning is a fiddly job, especially on heavy soils. It is easy to pull up too many seedlings inadvertently; the seedlings are also so delicate that they will need to be settled back with a gentle watering afterwards; and seedlings sown too close together are vulnerable to 'damping-off', especially in warm, wet springs.

Hardy annuals sown in straight lines will grow in straight lines, and as no one can be bothered to transplant annuals once they have germinated, and anyway they do not altogether

care for such disturbance, it is best to sow the seed in irregularly shaped blocks or sausage-shaped drifts, and allow the edges to overlap those of other species, in order to avoid that stiffness which is such a hallmark of those orderly, well-behaved, upright citizens, the half-hardy annuals (see illustrations below). The watchword of hardy annuals is prodigality.

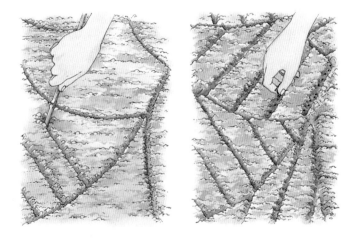

A cane is used to make shallow drills for sowing hardy annuals in irregular blocks. Rake the soil lightly over the seed to cover them.

Cosmos 'Sensation' is a hardy annual, usually sown under glass in spring for an early start.

Sow them, therefore, not in little patches but in large drifts, to the very limit of the seed packet, interspersing them here and there amongst shrubs, from the middle of the border to the front, in the cracks of paving, and along the edges of beds.

The fact that I choose what I grow in my garden automatically makes it an artificial environment, I know, yet, at the same time, I do not wish to regiment my border plants, and I particularly do not wish to order the hardy annuals about, for they are often only refined varieties of our own native flowers, like the corn cockle (*Agrostemma githago*), and the field poppy (*Papaver rhoeas*), and are all able to scatter their seed as lavishly as a budgerigar. That said, in order to be certain that one weeds weeds, not tiny seedlings, it is advisable, within your irregular drifts, to sow the annuals in little straight drills. Once the plants have grown to maturity, any hint of formality will have ceased to exist.

Favourite annuals & biennials

Cobaea scandens (cup and saucer plant): hha; climber; long-stalked, bell-shaped flowers start green, becoming purple

Convolvulus tricolor: hha; 30 × 20cm (12 × 8in); flat, trumpet-shaped flowers, blue with white and yellow centres in summer

Cosmos bipinnatus 'Sonata': ha; 60 × 30cm (2 × 1ft); single flowers, from white to dark pink, with yellow centres all summer; ferny foliage

Dianthus barbatus (sweet William): hb; 45 × 30cm (18 × 12in); clusters of scented single flowers, single- or bi-coloured, from white to deep red

Eschscholzia californica: ha; 30 × 10cm (12 × 4in); ferny blue-green leaves; single or semi-double flowers, pink through yellow and oranges to red

Lathyrus odoratus (sweet pea): ha; climber; 2.5m (8ft); succession of scented, keeled flowers, in colours from white through pink, blue and purple to red

Nicotiana: hha; up to 60 × 30cm (2 × 1ft), depending on variety; long-tubed, star-like flowers; scented in evening

Petunia: hha; 30 × 30cm (12 × 12in); trailing or upright; wide trumpet flowers in variety of colours all summer

Salvia farinacea 'Victoria': hha; 45 × 30cm (18 × 12in); oval leaves; spikes of tubular, intense violet-blue flowers in summer

Viola × *wittrockiana* (pansy): hb; 20 × 20cm (8 × 8in); flat, five-petalled flowers in many colours, often with 'faces', in summer; 'Universal' strain flowers in winter and spring

Key
ha: hardy annual
hha: half-hardy annual
hb: hardy biennial

Sowing is quite the easiest task that could be devised. It is simply a matter of raking over the soil to be sown, to create a 'tilth', scratching the outline of the drifts for the different flowers, using a bamboo cane, drawing very shallow drills within these areas with the cane, and sowing the seed thinly in the drills by rolling it between finger and thumb and moving the hand slowly along the drill all the while. A very light rake afterwards, just to cover the seed with a little soil, will aid germination in most cases, and discourage the birds. Be careful not to rake too fiercely, or you will displace the carefully sited seed. If the soil surface is dry, it is best to water it before sowing, leaving time for it to drain and dry out slightly. Watering after sowing is an excellent way of dislodging the seed. Each patch can be labelled, if you wish, using a waterproof pencil and pressing the label down so far in the ground as to be almost invisible.

Once the seed has germinated, you must watch (in a light soil at least) that the soil does not dry out while the seedlings are small. If you need to thin, it is best done initially when the seedlings have grown their first set of 'true

Sweet Williams are sown in summer outdoors in rows, transplanted after germination and planted out in early autumn, to flower in late spring.

leaves' (those that bear a more obvious resemblance to the mature leaf than the 'seed' leaves do). You may have to thin once more, depending on the ultimate size of the annual being grown. Most seed packets give instructions on spacing. Some annuals like larkspur and the tall *Lavatera* 'Loveliness' need staking with twigs.

After that, there is only weeding and dead-heading to consider. Deadheading affects the flowering of annuals to a marked degree: if the flower head is removed on an annual plant, whose only means of reproduction is by setting seed, it will be forced to go through the whole business of flowering and seeding once more; if you leave it, the plant will settle back complacently and not bother to flower again. This is a good example of where the interests of gardener and plant conspicuously diverge, but do not let this paralyse your will; pinch out the flower heads punctiliously, or trim them with shears, and your hardy annuals will prove some of the best and most rewarding plants you can possibly grow. Hardy annuals should be pulled up in autumn if you wish to prevent an explosion of seedlings the following year.

Biennials

Next to the hardy annuals in ease of cultivation come the hardy biennials. Strictly speaking, a biennial is a plant that germinates and makes a rosette of leaves in the first year, and flowers, sets seeds and dies in the second summer. An example of a true biennial is the Canterbury bell (*Campanula medium*). Biennials make up the staple of what we refer to as 'spring bedding', that is, plants grown in association with spring bulbs. The process is simple: in early summer you sow a packet of the seed of, say, sweet Williams, wallflowers, Canterbury bells or Brompton stocks, in little rows in a sheltered place in the vegetable garden, or in the flower garden if they are well labelled. When they are 'up', you must dig them up gently with a trowel, and replant them singly in rows nearby, usually at a spacing of about 15cm (6in). In the autumn, before the soil cools down completely, lightly fork over the ground where you wish the plants to grow, rake in some bonemeal, and transplant the plants to their final resting places, where they will flower in the spring.

Digitalis purpurea, *the foxglove, is a biennial which will seed itself about freely.*

There are plants which are, strictly speaking, perennials, but which we often treat as biennials, especially if they are part of a bedding scheme. Amongst these I would number polyanthus, primroses and pansies. The first two will last for many years, although they soon cease flowering if not divided nearly every year after flowering; the last, though perennial, have a habit of suddenly dying out, especially under the onslaught of aphids. Anyway, they seed so freely that they should be dug up and replaced if you are not to have a garden littered with odd-looking half-castes.

Half-hardy annuals

Half-hardy (frost-tender) annuals are the staple (although not the whole sum) of summer bedding-out schemes. I personally do not plant large-scale bedding schemes, but I do plant 'bedding plants' thickly in all the gaps there are in my borders. Who does not have a plant die inconveniently on them in early spring, or need to grow something for the summer in a renovated border before permanent occupants can once more be admitted in the autumn, or while waiting in vain for ordered plants to be delivered? Herbaceous borders can become battlegrounds for land-hungry daisies in late summer, so a buffer zone of stout, well-behaved annuals can keep the warring factions apart. In the shimmer of a hot summer's day, shrubs will fade into insignificance in comparison with full-blooded and exciting bedding.

Most half-hardy annuals are drought-resistant, flower continuously (especially if deadheaded), and will not seed everywhere for they fall to the scythe of the first frost. Since, however, this may not arrive until late autumn, frost-tender annuals often have a long flowering season. As with hardy annuals, half-hardy bedding will only work successfully if it is generously and whole-heartedly attempted; it is imperative, therefore, that beds are thickly planted, for few plantings look worse than a meagre scattering of puny lobelias that have been interspersed with stick-like, starved French marigolds.

I suggest you grow your favourite half-hardy annuals from seed, so that you have enough for really thick planting. These frost-tender plants must be sown indoors (see page 88). If sown outside in late spring, they do not have a sufficiently long growing season to flower consistently well. If, however, you forget (and it is not unknown for one to find forgotten packets of seed in a pocket later in the summer), it is certainly worth sowing them outside in the same way as you would hardy annuals (see page 132). How well they develop will rather depend on the summer and cannot be predicted.

Once inside-reared annuals are hardened-off (see page 89), and there is no longer a risk of frost, they can be planted out where they are to flower. Use an ordinary hand trowel to dig the hole, plant with the fingers of both hands, and water the plant in well afterwards with a watering can, soaking the ground all round. A handful of general fertilizer per square metre (yard), scattered a few days before, or even at the same time, will be taken up quickly by the plants and will help them to a positive start. Most people find that summer annuals benefit from liquid feeds watered on in mid- and late summer; this gives them a fillip to continue to flower well, especially if the dead flowers are removed at the same time.

Half-hardy annuals should be pulled up in the autumn, but if inconvenient bad weather puts paid to your best-laid plans, you need not worry, for the first bad frost will kill your *Nicotiana*, and there will be nothing left of their corpses by the spring.

If you are buying plants to put in your garden, be wary of those that are flowering in the tray or module. They are extremely useful if you are designing the scheme 'on the hoof', so to speak, but they flower early because they are under stress, caused by lack of water or nutrient. If you buy these plants, pinch out the flower heads before you plant them and water and feed well. It is wise, if you buy half-hardy annuals from garden centres, to harden them off for a few days before planting out, even if the danger of frost is past.

Perennials

You will almost certainly find that you are growing herbaceous perennials in your garden – provided that Fate has chosen for you an established garden containing something more nutritious than builder's rubble and yellow sub-soil. Perennials are as ubiquitous as weeds but a great deal more desirable, yet the ease with which they are grown undermines their attractiveness in many people's eyes. I suppose this must be because their cultivation contains nothing to put the experienced gardener on her mettle. They are, however, as welcome as manna from Heaven to the new gardener.

The word 'herbaceous' simply means that these plants die down to a 'crown' (or 'perennating bud', to give it its more correct, though less picturesque, botanical name) in the late autumn; from this crown new shoots emerge in the spring. The word 'perennial' is therefore,

Lady's mantle (Alchemilla mollis) *and oriental poppies* (Papaver orientale) *are vital herbaceous perennial components of the early summer garden.*

strictly speaking, unnecessary, as these plants clearly survive from year to year. Some herbaceous perennials ('hardy perennials') live far longer than others; those that turn up their toes after two or three years are called, naturally enough, 'short-lived perennials'. It is as well to know which ones these are, for it is disappointing, having spent time or money or both on a plant, to find that it mysteriously dies out despite all your best efforts to give it the conditions the books say it needs. Amongst the best-known short-lived perennials are the perennial flax (*Linum narbonense*), *Anchusa*, columbine (*Aquilegia*), *Meconopsis*, *Primula* and the hybrid verbascums.

There are also some plants that are clearly not shrubs or subshrubs, yet which do not die away to nothing above ground in the winter. These are referred to, rather loosely, as evergreen perennials, and are invaluable for lending muted colour to the winter border, and solidity to the summer one. Amongst these I would number lambs' ears (*Stachys byzantina*); catmint (*Nepeta × faassenii*); hellebores (*Helleborus* species), *Heuchera* and *Lamium*.

Herbaceous perennials have always been the victims of mutable fashion. Since World War II, the herbaceous border has lost favour and been supplanted by the 'mixed border' of shrubs, perennials and bulbs. There is still, therefore, enormous demand for these hardy perennials, but they must now take their place alongside the other groups of plants competing for our attention, and the invention of the 'island bed' has given rise to a demand for herbaceous perennials short or sturdy enough not to need staking. It seems unlikely that the supremacy of the mixed border will be challenged in the foreseeable future, unless most of the population undergoes a radical change in circumstances.

The vast majority of herbaceous perennials are ridiculously easy to grow. Most are now sold in containers, which means that they can be planted at any time of the year although, like all container plants put in the ground in summer, they can easily dry out. Container planting in autumn or early spring is, however, even safer than planting field-grown plants, because there is little or no possibility of root damage or desiccation occurring in the process.

However, before Hubris brings Nemesis in its train, let me reassure the reader that everything here is not entirely for the best, in the best of all possible worlds.

Firstly, many perennials will stop flowering after a few years because they have taken up their allotted space and nutrient, become overcrowded, and need to be divided or 'split up' (see page 92). That is not in itself a problem, but, while most can be divided in either autumn or spring, there are a few which are really only happy if they are split up or planted in the

FAR LEFT: A late summer mixed border, including Lavatera *'Barnsley',* Achillea *'Coronation Gold' and* Salvia × superba, *shows something of the vast range of colour and texture of perennials.*
ABOVE: A handsome combination of purple campanula and sea holly (Eryngium).

spring, and remembering which is a bore. No herbaceous plants will in fact come to any harm by being divided in the spring, so why mention the autumn at all? Simply because the autumn is a good time (before the soil cools down) for wholesale renovation, especially in warm districts and on light soils, and there is always a great deal else to do in spring. Moreover, roots develop well in autumn.

Secondly, quite a few perennials are decidedly unperennial in a climate with harsh, or even wet, winters. These, which include such beauties as *Salvia guaranitica, S. uliginosa, S. patens,* verbenas, penstemons, argyranthemums, *Felicia amelloides, Osteospermum ecklonis* and *Lobelia cardinalis,* should either have cuttings taken of them in the late summer, or be covered by an open cloche or other protective material for the winter. This really is rather taxing to remember. You may well forget until the first sharp frosts turn the leaves of *Salvia patens* into brown, sagging rags overnight, reminding you painfully, but too late, of your dilatoriness.

If you do not want this bother, or you do not live in a very favoured district, do not grow these plants; and watch out when you are in a plant-buying mood, for nurseries and garden centres are often rather coy about mentioning the tender constitutions of any of their plants: 'not absolutely bone-hardy in all districts' or 'succeeds with us' are coded messages you should learn to decipher. However, if you are a person who enjoys gambling on plants, as others gamble on the speed of raindrops running down a pane of glass, you will enjoy cultivating these more tender, half-hardy perennials.

There are other perennials that should be propagated by cuttings: named varieties of delphiniums, for example, are more successfully propagated by taking cuttings of basal shoots in

This very choice perennial, the Himalayan blue poppy (Meconopsis betonicifolia), *will thrive only in acidic, moist soils and in semi-shade.*

early spring than by division. (Do this early because if the shoot becomes hollow it will not strike easily.)

A few isolated herbaceous perennials are victims of specific pests and diseases, but in general most are reasonably healthy and resistant to disease if they are growing strongly. They are also easy to propagate, as we have seen, and although the pundits insist strongly that you should always plant in groups of three or five plants, I find that if I plant one plant, I can almost always divide it after a year and save myself some money. Also, if I do not like what I have bought or it is not what I asked for, I can throw it out and not feel too badly.

There will always be differences of opinion about cutting back the stems of herbaceous perennials in the autumn. For me there is a quiet beauty in the sere stems of perennials in winter. Some, like peonies, acquire a particular autumn colouring, while others gradually become ragged yellow sticks, but, pretty or not, they undoubtedly add height to the garden. However, although I like the dead heads of the achilleas and *Macleaya cordata*, and the orange

lanterns of *Physalis alkekengi*, I can do without the excessive seeding of *Agrostemma coronaria* or *Helleborus foetidus*.

Summer deadheading to promote flowering, is, of course, another matter (see page 64). Any gardener can see the point of that. Roses are not the only plants that will be encouraged to produce another flower to replace the one so cruelly cut off; there are plenty of annuals and herbaceous plants that react in the same way. The herbaceous geraniums and border pinks are good examples.

There are some lovely forms of the late winter-flowering Lenten rose, Helleborus orientalis, *in gardens. The self-set seedlings are thus worth saving.*

Primula beesiana *is a hardy perennial which thrives best in moist, boggy, slightly acidic conditions. It flowers in early summer.*

Favourite hardy perennials

Alchemilla mollis (lady's mantle): 45 × 45cm (18 × 18in); clusters of tiny green-yellow flowers in early summer; grey-green, rounded leaves

Anthemis punctata cupaniana: 30 × 30cm (12 × 12in); single, white, yellow-centred daisy flowers in early summer; grey dissected leaves

Argyranthemum 'Jamaica Primrose': 90 × 90cm (3 × 3ft); tender, woody; soft yellow, single, daisy flowers in summer and autumn; ferny, light green leaves

Aster × frikartii 'Mönch': 90 × 45cm (3 × 1½ft); single, lavender-blue, yellow-centred flowers continuously from mid-summer to late autumn

Euphorbia characias wulfenii: 120 × 90cm (4 × 3ft); grey-green narrow leaves; yellow-green flowers in broad heads in late spring and early summer

Geranium macrorrhizum 'Ingwersen's Variety': 30 × 60cm (1 × 2ft); rose-pink flowers in early summer; five-lobed leaves turn red in autumn

Helleborus orientalis (Lenten rose): 45 × 60cm (1½ × 2ft); flower colour from cream to deep purple, often spotted, in late winter; five-fingered toothed leaves

Hosta sieboldiana 'Frances Williams': 75 × 75cm (2½ × 2½ft); very broad heart-shaped grey-green leaves, with green-yellow margins; pale lilac flowers in summer

Nepeta 'Six Hills Giant': 90 × 90cm (3 × 3ft); oval, grey-green leaves; tubular lavender-blue spikes of flowers late spring to early autumn

Stipa gigantea: ornamental grass 200 × 90cm (6½ × 3ft); arching stems; silver-purple flower heads in summer turn golden in autumn

11

SMALL BUT
BEAUTIFUL

THERE ARE MANY ASPECTS OF GARDENING THAT CAN INTIMIDATE THE BEGINNER, BUT NONE PROVES MORE UNNERVING – AND YET WITH LESS REASON – THAN THE CULTIVATION OF ALPINES. A GLANCE THROUGH THE EXCELLENT *ALPINE GARDEN SOCIETY BULLETIN* PROVIDES AMPLE REASON FOR FEELING INADEQUATE. EVEN THE TRAINED GARDENER CANNOT BUT BE IMPRESSED BY THE BREADTH OF KNOWLEDGE AND EXPERIENCE APPARENTLY REQUIRED TO READ THE JOURNAL, LET ALONE RECOGNIZE AND GROW SUCCESSFULLY THE PLANTS DESCRIBED. YOU SHOULD NOT LOSE HEART, HOWEVER, FOR THERE ARE MANY THAT ARE EASY ENOUGH TO GROW.

ON THE OTHER HAND, THE CULTIVATION OF BULBS, ANOTHER WONDERFUL GROUP OF PLANTS, LOOKS VERY EASY, AND IS SO, IN THE SHORT TERM. HOWEVER, THERE ARE A NUMBER OF HIDDEN DIFFICULTIES OF BULB-GROWING THAT CANNOT BE RESOLVED UNLESS YOU KNOW SOMETHING OF HOW THESE PLANTS WORK.

These 'pheasant-eye' narcissus, N. poeticus, are some of the loveliest bulbs for naturalizing in grass. They are scented, flower when most other daffodils have finished, and make excellent cut flowers. Partly because they flower so late, and partly because it looks best, the ideal is to plant them in generous drifts on their own. They will multiply in time. The grass can be mown when the leaves start to yellow.

Alpines

This book is not intended to turn you into an alpine expert (there are plenty of fine specialist accounts which will do that) but it would be sad if you did not have a crack at the easier rock plants, for easy many of them are.

You might think that all alpines and rock plants would hanker after their native rocks and fade away in an excess of homesickness, but there are plenty that will thrive, and even more that will survive, in warmer, more humid climates. This is partly because many alpine plants do not cling with the rugged determination of an Everest expedition to sheer cliffs and ledges, but are bog plants, which revel in a peaty, moisture-retentive mixture, or woodland plants which like shade and leafmould. Certainly, there are plenty of alpines as hard to

please as a spoiled child, but there are enough easy ones for the learner to practise on, and there is much we can do to ensure their good health and longevity.

Rock gardens were popular from about 1865 until World War II. Now they are hardly ever built, partly because their requirement for large chunks of natural stone makes them prohibitively expensive; partly because the removal of bedrock from the landscape is ecologically suspect; and partly because they are extremely labour-intensive. It has also been proved empirically that most alpines will thrive just as well, if

Clay pots, stone sinks and raised beds made from second-hand railway sleepers make a suitable, and cheaper, modern alternative to the rock garden.

not better, in a trough or a raised bed, and this is how I advise you to grow them.

Now that the supply of natural stone horse troughs has run out, gardeners today are obliged to make their own substitutes, either by sticking a mixture of 1 part sand, 2 parts peat, and 1 part cement to the sides of glazed butler's sinks with a strong adhesive, or by pouring this mixture, named 'hypertufa', into cardboard box moulds. The results, in the absence of the real thing, are perfectly acceptable. These modern sinks have plug holes which are sufficient to ensure good drainage, provided that, if real rock-hugging plants are grown, a layer of broken-up rubble is laid in the bottom, followed by gravel and then a free-draining compost. (Troughs, incidentally, are best put on stone plinths, or similar, so that any excess moisture can run away freely.) It is now possible to buy special composts for alpines but you can make up a suitable one yourself, by using 2 parts (by weight) soil, 1 part peat, and 1 part small grit. Troughs also give you the opportunity to grow acid bog alpines if your garden soil is alkaline, in which case plant them in a proprietary ericaceous compost.

Once the trough is planted up, it should be top-dressed with small horticultural grit. This not only looks pleasing, but keeps the collars of these damp-sensitive plants dry; weeds are easy to pull out of it and the grit acts as a mulch to conserve moisture in dry weather. However, even with grit, these troughs do dry out in the summer, and should be well watered at intervals. It is the price that you have to pay for growing plants that must not remain too wet in the winter.

An alternative, or supplement, to the trough is a raised bed for the easier alpines and rock plants (see illustration above right). If you live in a stone area, you should be able to track down an amenable builder who will build you suitable walls (dry or cemented), using ropy but adequate old stone. Like the trough, it should not be expected to look 'natural'. These beds need not be more than a few courses high, and holes can be left for plants to grow out of the sides. If you

Raised beds drain more freely than flat ones but, even so, a layer of broken-up rubble in the bottom is desirable, together with a soil mixture which is lightened with grit. Alpines enjoy a cool root-run under rocks, so flattish stones lain on the top of the soil will be appreciated. There are some alpines that will grow in shade, so there is no reason why the wall should not be covered on all sides. Try not to plant anything that will grow out of scale.

have no access to stone, brick will do. The point of raising the bed is so that the soil drains freely and rock plants like *Helianthemum* naturally trail if given the opportunity, so they look well in a raised bed. However, if your soil is very light, this is unnecessary. Either way, a base of broken-up rubble and gravel is topped up with garden soil, which should have grit and some well-rotted peat added to it to make a suitable growing medium for rock plants.

Alpine plants are usually bought these days in small pots, and will almost certainly be pot-bound. Water them well before knocking them out and planting them, using either your hand or a trowel. Alpines usually have extremely long roots, but they will take a while to establish themselves in their new home so will require to be watered regularly in their first summer. This is important, especially as alpines are (it is generally agreed) best planted in spring or summer, rather than in the dormant season. If planted in the autumn, they will sit disconsolately through the winter, and be liable to rot before they have had a chance to make themselves at home.

Waldsteinia ternata is a wonderfully fresh-looking plant, like a yellow strawberry plant, which makes good ground-cover, even in shade.

Most alpines require a sunny position, the exceptions being bog-lovers and woodland plants, which like it shadier.

If they are planted in the right position, cultivation will consist merely of a sprinkling of organic fertilizer in the spring, just before so many of them flower. Generally speaking, they do more than survive in poor soil, they positively thrive; indeed, a rich soil will encourage their leaves at the expense of the flowers, and make them more vulnerable to attack by aphids.

You should provide an annual top-dressing of grit (and bonemeal around the dwarf bulbs) in the autumn, and, in the case of the less hardy species, protection against winter wet (it is unnecessary to protect them against the cold – see page 58). The shrubbier kinds of rock plant, like *Helianthemum*, benefit enormously from being trimmed with secateurs after flowering.

Some alpine plants have the good sense and judgement to propagate themselves. *Sempervivum* and *Saxifraga*, for example, will produce offsets with roots which can be severed from the 'mother' plant and potted up. Others, such as *Helianthemum* or *Thymus*, strike readily from cuttings taken in the summer. Most alpines can be reproduced by seed (see page 89), either collected by you, or bought from a mail-order seed firm. Alpines have not entirely escaped the fate of mixed colours, but it is easier to obtain single colours than it is with the half-hardy annuals.

That is as far as their good fortune goes. Alpines and rock plants are often prey to the unscrupulous and damaging attentions of birds, slugs, aphids and mice (see page 181).

Favourite alpines

Campanula 'Birch Hybrid': 10 × 30cm (4 × 12in); prostrate evergreen; deep violet-blue bellflowers in mid-summer

Dianthus deltoides 'Leuchtfunk' ('Flashing Light'): 20 × 20cm (8 × 8in); dark green needle-like leaves; cherry red flowers in summer

Diascia 'Ruby Field': 8 × 15cm (3 × 6in); heart-shaped leaves; wide-lipped salmon-pink flowers in summer

Erinus alpinus: 8 × 8cm (3 × 3in); evergreen rosettes; short clusters of pink, starry flowers in summer

Geranium cinereum 'Ballerina': 10 × 30cm (4 × 12in); lilac-pink, veined purple, cupped flowers with dark centres from late spring to early autumn

Gypsophila repens: 5 × 30cm (2 × 12in); clusters of small white or lilac-pink flowers in summer; blue-green leaves

Helianthemum 'Wisley Primrose': 20 × 45cm (8 × 18in); subshrub; grey-green narrow leaves; single, yellow flowers in summer

Phlox 'Chattahoochee': 20 × 30cm (8 × 12in); narrow pointed leaves, purple when young; lavender flowers with bright pink eyes in summer and autumn

Viola riviniana Purpurea Group (syn. *V. labradorica* 'Purpurea'): 13 × 30cm (5 × 12in); evergreen; heart-shaped, green-purple leaves; self-seeds; mauve-pink flowers in late spring

Waldsteinia ternata: semi-evergreen; 10 × 30cm (4 × 12in); mats of three-part leaves; yellow flowers in late spring and early summer

Bulbs

You will know roughly, I am sure, what a bulb is. Even if you have never been a gardener, the chances are that you have forced hyacinth bulbs in a pot in a cupboard for Christmas (with which the flowers will, to your annoyance, have just failed to coincide). Bulbs are food-storage organs, and the flower grows up from a bud deep inside. Bulbs include corms (for example *Crocus*), root tubers (for example *Dahlia* and *Cyclamen*) and true bulbs (for example *Narcissus*). Storage organs of this kind also include rhizomes (for example *Iris*). (I do not wish to confuse you, but there is also a group of bulbous irises, which includes the indispensable spring-flowering *Iris reticulata*.) For the purposes of cultivation, however, the exact nomenclature is a matter of the greatest indifference.

Bulbs (or, if you will, bulbs, corms, tubers and rhizomes) are extremely versatile. In such a large group of flowering plants, there are individual species for almost every situation. Most tulips and crocuses come from the Near East and appreciate a 'baking' from the sun when they are dormant in summer; sunny conditions

also please the South African *Gladiolus callianthus* (*Acidanthera bicolor*). Dahlias from Mexico are not hardy and their tubers will not survive a severe winter spent underground outside. There are dwarf narcissi from alpine meadows, and lilies from Chinese woodlands.

Some bulbs will consent merely to exist in our gardens, and will thrive only in exceptional years. Fortunately, many bulbs have been bred to tolerate conditions that their forebears never experienced, so we can find bulbs to flourish in window boxes, urns, tubs, long grass, short grass, shrub borders, woodlands, raised beds and rock gardens; there is no part of the garden where some 'bulb' will not grow.

When you plant a bulb, it will (you hope) be dormant, that is, without roots or green shoots. It will first grow roots, then either leaves and flowers; or, sometimes, flowers before the leaves (as in the case of some autumn crocuses),

These splendid bearded irises are rhizomes, while the ornamental onions (Allium christophii) *are bulbs. Both enjoy a sunny position.*

or even leaves the following spring (as in the case of *Colchicum*). Spring-flowering bulbs are usually bought and planted in late summer or early autumn, at a time when rain is likely. Most flower in the spring, and use up the food that has been stored from the previous year; after this the leaves photosynthesize diligently to make more food to swell the bulb. This is the reason why gardeners make such a thing of not cutting the leaves of flowering bulbs until they begin to yellow – or knotting them, which has much the same effect as cutting them, and

Coincidences are rarely delightful; in my experience, they are usually exasperating and can be disastrous. When I pierce the heart of a particularly favourite lily with a garden fork, I feel sympathy for Rick's predicament in *Casablanca*: 'Of all the gin-joints in all the towns in all the world and she has to come into mine.'

The timing of your planting is actually quite important in order to achieve the best flowering, although you can get away with planting later than recommended if you can live with an element of risk. Tulips are planted later than

The yellow of this dwarf narcissus is enhanced by the acid-green of Helleborus foetidus, *here both grown in a gravelly soil.*

Tulipa 'Spring Green' associates with bulbous bluebells. The tulip bulbs can be left in the ground but may not flower so well the following year.

anyway looks ridiculous. It is generally established that daffodils may be cut when the leaves have started to yellow, that is, about six weeks after flowering. This is an important fact to know if you are growing them in grass and wish to mow the moment it is safe to do so.

I have never found planting bulbs particularly enjoyable. I think that is because there is an awful certainty that your spade or bulb-planter will neatly, and most probably fatally, slice a bulb already growing in that exact spot.

narcissi, crocuses and other spring-flowerers, because the shoots are more affected by frost in the spring. *Colchicum* are planted in late summer. Snowdrops, bless them, thrive when planted, or divided, 'in the green', that is, just after flowering. That is a great joy because they are so easily seen then. The only disadvantage of bulbs, after all, is that they disappear, like the magician's assistant in the cupboard, falsely but completely.

The tender bulbs – *Tigridia*, tuberous begonias, *Gladiolus callianthus*, dahlias and cannas –

should be planted in mid- to late spring, so that they can make their roots and then begin to shoot as soon as the last frosts are over. They have to be dug up when they still have leaves, but only after these have started to yellow or, in the case of dahlias, become blackened by frost.

Bulbs will not flower unless they are a good size, a fact which is more obvious with the large daffodils than with snowdrops; but then it matters more with daffodils. Offset or 'daughter' bulbs, which will not flower in their first year, are concave, not rounded.

How you plant bulbs depends on how many you have and what tools are at your disposal. In well-dug soil, it is as easy as anything to take a spade and dig a shallowish, flat-bottomed hole, in which you can place several. Otherwise, planting in borders has to be done with a hand trowel because a bulb-planter will only work for making holes in grass. Bulb-planters, for 'naturalizing' bulbs in grass, are essentially open-ended cylinders (slightly wider at the top than bottom) with a sharpish bottom rim to cut through grass; they work by removing a plug of grass and soil which, after the bulb is put in, can be replaced and stamped down into place. The best (and most expensive and hardest to find) are the long-handled sort with a foot-rest. A spade can be used to lift the turf and dig out the soil to the right depth but a bulb-planter makes the job much easier.

When planting, it is important to establish which is the top and which the bottom of the bulb. That is not as idiotic as it appears; in the case of flat 'bulbs' like cyclamens and begonias, for example, it is often difficult to tell from where the new roots will emerge. If you are unsure, plant such 'bulbs' on their sides – the roots will pull them the right way up in due course. Daffodils, tulips and bulbous irises have pointed tops so they are easy. Even if they are planted upside down, most bulbs will eventually produce shoots, but larger bulbs will expend energy growing leaves which will have to grow round the bulb before they can grow up, and this will have the effect of making the flower late.

How to space the bulbs depends on their diameter and whether they grow many leaves. I plant small bulbs with thin leaves, like *Crocus* species or *Ipheion*, as near together as I can decently afford, only taking account of the fact that in time the bulbs will spawn babies and become crowded. That does take time, however, and anyway, when you see bulbs appearing on the surface as a result of a subterranean population explosion, or you fancy the flowering is less good than last year, you can easily dig them up, divide them and replant.

Bulbs like to be planted deep, and as a general rule the *top* of the bulb should be planted at a depth equal to two to three times the bulb's width at its widest point – one of those hard-to-compute measurements which affords ample opportunity for cheating (see illustrations below). Many bulbs (sorry, corms) like *Crocus* have contractile roots which will pull them down to what they consider to be the appropriate level, but it is obvious that this wastes energy. More important, if a bulb is planted too shallowly in a light soil, it will dry out too much, which may cause it to come up 'blind', and, as there is nothing more pointless than green daffodil leaves on their own, it is worth making the effort to plant deeply enough. *Iris danfordiae* (one of those bulbous irises I mentioned) splits up all too readily into little bulblets if planted too shallowly, and subsequently refuses to flower for years. *Fritillaria*

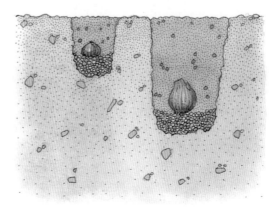

These bulbs have been planted with their noses at a depth equal to twice the width of the bulb. This is a handy rule of thumb, but it is a minimum, really.

The glorious Lilium regale *is a stem-rooting lily, which means it should be planted deeply, ideally two-and-a-half times the depth of the bulb.*

imperialis, the crown imperial, should be planted deeply, and in this instance the corms do best if planted on their sides. The corm also has an unpleasant foxy smell, which is all too obvious if it is near the surface.

If you cannot plant your bulbs because the soil conditions are wrong, or you simply do not have the time, put them into trays of moist peat or peat-substitute (the bulb's version of 'heeling in'). Otherwise, fritillaries and lilies will soon shrivel. In a perfect world, you will soak these for a day and a night before planting, so that they are thoroughly damp, but that presupposes forethought and confounds those of us who have to snatch opportunities to garden out of the jaws of Other Commitments. Bulbs, once they begin to grow moulds, which they invariably do if left for any length of time in a plastic bag, should be dipped in a solution of fungicide before planting. There is no harm, and some good, in doing that to all bulbs as a precaution, although it is only a necessity if the bulbs are actually growing fungi. A deft squeeze will tell

you whether the bulb has soft rot; serious cases should be consigned to the flames.

Whether you plant in straight lines or in 'drifts' should really be no concern of this relentlessly practical volume, but I should like to say that, if you decide on drifts, a handful of bulbs should be taken and thrown out with a broad expansive gesture of the arm and planted where they fall. If you are planting tulips, say, with forget-me-nots (*Myosotis*) in a spring bedding display, plant the forget-me-nots first, then interplant them with bulbs. An inadvertent slice or stab will be almost inevitable if you reverse the process.

The conditions in which these various bulbs thrive are diverse, but on the whole you will do no harm and, in most cases, do active good if you choose lightish soil which contains some well-rotted organic matter. Those with heavy soils are wise to dig in some grit. Like alpines, most bulbs which like sunshine and a light soil will run to leaf rather than flower if fed too richly. Tulip species which burst out of the rocks in Iran are hardly likely to be greedy feeders, after all. The hungriest are woodland lilies, large-flowered hybrid gladioli and begonias. I am a believer in bonemeal for bulbs, as it can be applied in autumn when most are making their roots, without the soil being disturbed at all. Summer-flowerers, such as gladioli, will need it when they are planted in late spring.

It is usually advised that large-flowered garden tulips be lifted after flowering. This is because they tend to flower less well in future years unless planted very deeply. Lifting tulips every year, putting them in a shallow trench in the vegetable garden, with their leaves above ground to continue manufacturing food, is not everyone's idea of truly necessary work. If it is not yours, plant only small groups for spring show in ordinary borders, rather than vast expanses which *have* to be removed in early summer, and lift the bulbs only when their health deteriorates or the flowering falters.

Tender 'bulbs' such as *Gladiolus callianthus*, dahlias and cannas need to be dug out of the ground about the time of the first frosts, and stored in moist peat or peat-substitute, in trays in a cool but frost-free place. It is as well to dust them with yellow sulphur to prevent rotting. You may lose some through rot in the winter, but most will simply shrivel and recover if they have a sojourn in water before planting.

There are a number of tricks that make all the difference, especially if you wish to keep bulbs for many years: daffodils need to be watered in dry autumns when they are forming flower buds, if they are to flower well. Most bulbs benefit from (I hesitate to say 'need') water in dry springs, although you will probably never get round to watering then, but if your bulbs do not perform well one year, at least you will know the reason why. Liquid feeding is not strictly necessary – we all know drifts of flowering bulbs that have never smelt a whiff of liquid manure – but it does help the growth of the bulb if applied just after flowering. Summer-flowering bulbs, like lilies, which are often woodland plants in their native lands, like to be moist in summer, so they will need to be mulched, and since most (the exceptions are *Lilium henryi* and *L. candidum*) need a neutral or slightly acid soil, peat is an ideal material.

Most bulbs can be propagated by digging up an overcrowded clump, pulling away the small bulbs (offsets) on the outside, and planting them either in a nursery bed, or nearby if you wish simply to extend a clump. Rhizomatous irises are usually divided after flowering (every three years or so) by digging up the rhizome, pulling apart any branches that have formed, and replanting the youngest pieces, the outside branches, which will come away with a leaf 'fan' attached. They should be replanted with the top of the rhizomes just showing above the soil.

Favourite bulbs

Allium christophii: up to 90cm (3ft); large round 'drumstick' flowers of many lilac-pink stars in early summer; grey-green strap leaves

Anemone blanda: 8cm (3in); blue (also pink or white) daisy flowers with yellow centres late winter to spring

Crocosmia 'Lucifer': 90cm (3ft); sword-shaped green leaves; deep red flowers in branching spikes in mid-summer

Crocus speciosus: 10cm (4in); flowers before leaves; lilac-blue or purple-blue flowers, with darker veins and orange, much-branched stigma in autumn

Cyclamen hederifolium: 10cm (4in); silver-marbled, heart-shaped, pointed leaves; pink twisted flowers in autumn

Erythronium dens-canis: 20cm (8in); two mottled green and brown leaves; drooping pink or purple flowers with reflexed petals in spring

Gladiolus callianthus: 90cm (3ft); tender; spike of several scented flowers, white with deep purple blotch at base

Lilium regale: up to 1.5m (5ft) tall; clusters of very large, fragrant, outward-facing, white (with yellow throat) trumpet flowers in mid-summer

Narcissus 'Actaea': 40cm (16in); fragrant; white petals, and shallow yellow and orange cups

Tulipa sprengeri: 40cm (16in); red flowers; latest tulip to flower

12

THE KITCHEN GARDEN

I SOMETIMES WONDER WHETHER MOST KITCHEN GAR-
DENERS REALLY MIND ABOUT PRODUCING THINGS TO
EAT. I SUSPECT IT IS MORE A DEEP-SEATED DESIRE FOR
ORDER IN THEIR LIVES, A CRAVING FOR SUPREMACY OVER
THE NATURAL WORLD (WHICH IN OUR MODERN POST-WAR
FLOWER GARDENS – ALL PROFUSION AND GENEROSITY – IS
HARDLY POSSIBLE), THAT ENCOURAGES THEM TO GROW
FRUIT AND VEGETABLES. I KNOW THAT I WOULD RATHER
SPEND AN HOUR ON A SUMMER'S EVENING, BRAIN OUT OF
GEAR, THINNING LETTUCES, WHILE ALL THE ANXIETY AND
ADRENALIN GENERATED IN THE DAY GRADUALLY SEEPS
AWAY, THAN WRESTLING WITH SUCH VEXED DECISIONS AS
WHICH SEEDLINGS OF *CAMPANULA RAPUNCULOIDES* TO
SPARE, AND WHICH TO DESTROY, BECAUSE THEY THREATEN
TO SPOIL MY CAREFUL COLOUR SCHEMES. THE TWO KINDS
OF GARDENING ARE NOT ANTAGONISTIC, BUT COMPLE-
MENTARY; THEY ARE BOTH CONTRIBUTORS TO THE SAME
EXCITEMENT, RARELY EXPRESSED BUT DEEPLY FELT, THAT
COMES WITH GROWING ANYTHING WELL.

It may seem like sacrilege to say so, but not all forms of fruit and vegetables are worth growing. These apples and runner beans will repay the time and energy spent on them, but the sweet corn may not. There is much to be said for growing your vegetables mixed with flowers. Not only are many edible plants decorative, but such a stratagem confuses the pests.

Vegetables

We have to decide whether to grow vegetables by conventional methods, by which I mean growing them in long lines at time-honoured optimum spacings between the plants and between the rows, or to grow them by the 'deep bed' system. On the face of it, the deep bed method should appeal strongly to the amateur gardener. This is the system whereby vegetables are grown in short, 1.2m (4ft) wide beds, which are *never* walked on, all the necessary cultivation being done from paths on either side (see illustration below). The bed is initially double dug (see page 67) and heavily manured – this is repeated every four or five years – but otherwise only lightly cultivated with an annual layer of manure spread and forked in during the autumn. Seed is grown in blocks across the bed, not in lines, and when one crop is finished, the soil is simply raked over again and resown. Because of the deep cultivation, root crops do well in the loose soil and it favours the good growing of salad crops. The most obvious advantages are the easier growing of vegetables on very wet and heavy soils (because the beds are raised up somewhat, allowing better

A deep bed should never be more than 1.2m (4ft) wide so it can be worked from all sides. Double dig the soil and manure heavily before sowing the seed in blocks. Retain the soil with wooden planks.

drainage) and the huge increase in productivity, usually at least double the conventional yields for the area, because most plants can be grown closer than is possible with traditional methods.

That all sounds marvellous, but there are a few disadvantages which must be considered. First, the double digging is very tiring (although only in one year out of four); the amount of work involved is rather dismissed by the proponents of the scheme, but it is a major consideration for older people, those with bad backs, or those for whom bumper crops are not of themselves a real selling point. More conscientious planning is also required to keep the beds well filled, and the beds, especially those made on light soils, dry out quickly in spring and need much watering in the early years, until the proportion of organic material is sufficiently high to act as a buffer against drought. Weeds grow in this fertile environment with a ferocity that is alarming, and are difficult to eradicate except by hand; and in the close spacings, pests and diseases have a field day. Some plants, especially large brassicas, do not crop particularly well when planted close together, and others like runner beans do no better than normally.

However, the deep bed system is clearly a substantial improvement on traditional methods (or rather a return to them). It is particularly suitable for those who have small gardens but would like substantial yields from what room they have, do not mind working for those yields, at least initially, and for those who garden on very heavy soil. Anybody else who is attracted to the idea might like to prepare part of their vegetable garden every year for this system, in order to spread the workload and give them a chance to see how it works for them.

Whatever means you adopt to grow your vegetables, you should make a simple crop rotation. This is good in itself, but also has the beneficial spin-off of forcing you out of your indolence and making you do a rough plan of what is to go where, and when. I remember as a student being set the task of making a plan for a productive, and fully used, vegetable garden. To my surprise, it took hours and several pieces of paper to achieve. I am not suggesting anything so detailed, and, anyway, the best laid plans are thoroughly mucked up by the weather, so these succession ideas need not be too exact. But a rough measurement of the space at your disposal, plotted on graph paper, and divided into the three different groups of crops, with some notes on successional sowing and catch-cropping, will ensure that resources (most importantly yours of time and energy) are used to the best advantage.

The theory of crop rotation centres on a commitment not to grow the same crop, time and time again, on the same piece of soil, for you will exhaust the soil of those nutrients the particular plant requires, and encourage the build-up of host-specific pests and diseases (see illustration right).

Crop rotation is not just for fusspots. Vegetable gardening is highly artificial: growing the same plants in rows, at the expense of other vegetation, and not allowing them to rot down into the soil at the end of the season, is hardly a natural way of carrying on. That being so, you must make some concessions to the high degree of artificiality; in particular, you will need to add a great deal of food for vegetables to grow to their optimum.

For a variety of reasons, we divide vegetables into three groups: the root crops, such as turnips, carrots, potatoes; the brassicas, consisting of cabbages, Brussels sprouts, broccoli, Chinese leaves, and so on; and the rest, a ragbag of peas and beans, salad crops, celery, leeks, onions and spinach.

Once you have established what is to be grown, and have bought your seed from mail-order catalogue, garden centre or horticultural sundriesman, the moment comes, towards the end of winter, when you need to think about preparing a seed bed for your vegetables. I am convinced that a soil thermometer is worth the expense. You simply poke it in the soil where you wish to sow, and if it registers 6°C (43°F) or

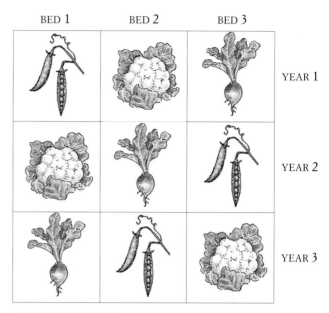

BED 1   BED 2   BED 3

YEAR 1

YEAR 2

YEAR 3

CROP ROTATION KEY

 Root crops such as turnips

 Brassicas such as cauliflowers

 Miscellaneous (peas, beans, salad crops, celery, leeks, onions, spinach)

Manure the soil well for peas and beans. Leave the roots in the soil. The next year, add lime, if necessary, for brassicas. Then follow with root crops which, apart from potatoes, need no manuring but only a spring fertilizer.

more, to a maximum of 22°C (72°)F, the temperature above which germination is inhibited, you sow. I am equally firmly convinced of the effectiveness of cloches or polythene to help warm the soil up and sustain the warmth even if the weather turns foul.

Some crops like lettuce can be sown where they are to grow and thinned out as they grow. Others, like brassicas and leeks, benefit from being transplanted: the first, because they will eventually require a great deal of room and solid planting, but can start life in a seed bed where they take up little room; the second, because transplantation is an opportunity to make holes in the ground in which to drop them, so that a respectable length of the stem will become blanched.

Some people, oddly enough, find harvesting their vegetables far less pleasurable than growing them. Whether it is because the harvesting leaves unwelcome gaps in an otherwise faultlessly symmetrical and aligned row, or because they desire to see their potatoes or beans grow just a little larger, I do not know. Most of us come to terms with eating our produce well enough, even if it is not *strictly* true that consumption is the only reason for all our time-consuming work. (We are slightly ashamed to admit that the sight of a full row of potatoes in flower pleases us as much as that of a bed of roses.)

'There is nothing like the taste of one's own vegetables,' we cry, certain of general approval. But in fact there are some vegetables that are demonstrably no better when pulled from our own soil than when bought in a shop (unless the shop ones are very old). I can see no particular advantage in growing parsnips, onions, celery, maincrop potatoes or swede – but I continue to grow them, thus tacitly admitting that I grow vegetables for more than the satisfaction of simply eating them.

Those examples apart, there are plenty of vegetables for us committed vegetable gardeners to grow without having our motives questioned. Most worthwhile are those that are either grown commercially to too large a size for real enjoyment, such as Brussels sprouts, broad beans, beetroot, carrots and peas, or those that are hard to find or expensive in shops, such as globe artichokes, mangetout peas, stringless runner beans, the more delicious varieties of tomato, celeriac, kohl-rabi, spinach, scorzonera, salsify and the myriad of herbs outside the staples of parsley and mint.

The learner gardener will not waste too much of her time if she begins by growing the vegetables listed in the chart on page 160; they are

I suspect that there are heart-searchings before anything in this highly ornamental kitchen garden (potager) *is pulled up to be eaten. Box edging is a decorative way of retaining soil, built up by the addition of manures, but it needs yearly clipping.*

mostly easy and rewarding. I have not included spacings because they are to be found on every seed packet and make rather tedious reading. The spacings can be reduced if vegetables are to be grown in deep beds.

Whatever you are sowing, you must first dig over the soil (even just a cursory fork over in autumn or spring will be better than nothing), tread down the soil using the heels, as I described earlier for making a new lawn (see page 49), scatter a general fertilizer at a rate of 125g per square metre (4oz per square yard) a week or so before sowing, and rake the soil into a tilth. For salad crops, this should be 60g per square metre (2oz per square yard).

The point of the fertilizer, even in well dug and manured soil, is to provide something immediately available for the seedlings to use. Once the soil is raked, stretch a line between pegs at either end of the row to be sown, as close to the ground as possible. If you are cultivating a deep bed, you will find a board, with

This charming informal vegetable garden most likely belongs to a cottager, where hazel stakes are used to support sweet peas and runner beans.

measurements pencilled or notched on it, more useful. Actually, a board with measurements on it, so that you can plant at the right distance quickly, is one of the few home-made implements I can see the point of having; the alternative is a metal tape measure. Even the idlest gardener will feel the need for something.

Take out a drill, using one edge of your draw hoe, and trying to keep it as close as possible to the line of string or of your board. To keep the line straight, you may want to put your foot on the string as you walk backwards, drawing the hoe towards you. Seed packets tell you how deep to make the drill, and usually how far apart to space the rows and thin the seedlings. There should be no need to water spring seed beds, but occasionally dry, blowy spring weather will make this desirable, in which case, watering the drill and letting it drain before sowing is preferable to watering after sowing, when you risk washing away the seed and caking the surface of the soil.

Sow the seed thinly (especially in the case of carrots, which you will not want to thin later because of the danger of attracting the much-feared carrot root fly), rolling the seed between finger and thumb. Avoid just shaking it out of the packet, for it will come out much too thickly and unevenly. Move the line onto the next row before raking the soil back gently over the drill, and tamping it down lightly with the back of the rake (see illustrations below). Remember to label each row, not only because you may weed up seedlings until you become familiar with the seed leaves of vegetables, but also because you will then be able to hold your head up in the pub because you can remember their varietal names.

Some vegetables do best if they are started off under glass. You may have difficulty enough fitting all your flower seeds in trays on the window-sill, and it is not really necessary to sow celery, onions or leeks under glass; they do almost as well sown directly into the ground. But some vegetables, such as tomatoes (a few seeds in a small pot), sweet corn, ridge cucumbers, and courgettes (two or three seeds to a 8cm/3in pot), do need to be sown inside. You can also try 'multiple-seeding', whereby several seeds of, say, onions, leeks, beetroot or lettuce are sown in a 5 × 5cm (2 × 2in) compartment of a module tray under glass, germinated, and planted out undisturbed in a block. Onions, for example, will push out away from each other and grow well, and the combined weight of the group when harvested will be more than a single onion planted at the same spot. You will get early leeks this way (although no earlier than conventional sowing in a tray) but the blanched stems will be smaller because the leeks are planted as a bunch. This system is useless for root crops.

By whatever means, you will eventually have your seed sown and germinated. This is when vegetable gardening requires that minute attention which it is so hard to give. Weeding should properly be done almost daily, especially if, like me, you do not feel happy using pre-emergent weedkillers, which prevent weeds from germinating, in the vegetable garden. The time-consuming alternative is using the Dutch hoe, or onion hoe for deep beds. The weeds that grow up amongst the plants must be ruthlessly, but gently, pulled regularly, for they are the ones competing most fiercely for food and water. Watering is often necessary earlier in the

Sowing vegetable seed

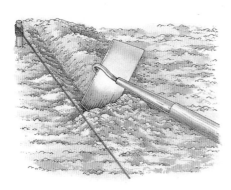

Take out a drill with one side of a draw hoe, using a taut garden line, secured with two short, stout pegs in the soil, to help you steer a straight course.

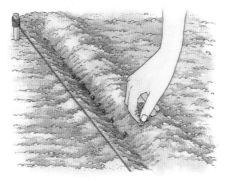

Most seed is best held in the palm of one hand and rolled out between index finger and thumb of the other, while moving your hand slowly along the drill.

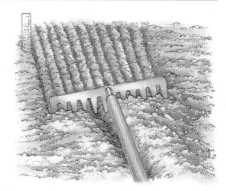

After sowing, rake the soil lightly to cover the seed, leaving it, you hope, at a consistent depth so that it germinates evenly and also fools the birds.

vegetable garden than in the flower garden, because sowing goes on all through the summer. A lawn sprinkler is fine for this, although a pulse-jet sprinkler on a long stem is more use as crops begin to grow upwards. I have mentioned staking in chapter 4, but if you are bored with staking peas, leafless varieties, which were originally developed for the commercial grower,

are excellent. They support each other and are easy to pick as the pods generally grow at the top of the plant.

Vegetables are prey to many pests, diseases and physiological disorders, of which aphids, root flies, caterpillars, birds, slugs, powdery mildew, clubroot and viruses are the most damaging and widespread (see pages 181-3).

This highly decorative rhubarb chard will provide iron-rich 'greens' through the summer and autumn.

The leek 'Autumn Mammoth' is a hardy variety which is best left in the ground until required.

Favourite hardy vegetables

Beetroot: 'Cheltenham Mono'
Broad beans: 'Hylon'
Broccoli: 'Purple Sprouting'
Brussels sprouts: 'Peer Gynt'; 'Fortress'
Cabbage, autumn: 'Winnigstadt'
Cabbage, spring: 'Durham Early'
Carrots: 'Amsterdam Forcing';'Berlicum Berjo'
Cauliflower, autumn: 'Barrier Reef'
Celeriac: 'Tellus'
Chinese cabbage: 'Tip Top'
French beans: 'Purple Teepee'
Kohlrabi: 'Rowel'

Leeks: 'Autumn Mammoth'
Lettuce: 'Little Gem'; 'Dolly'; 'Lollo Rossa'
Onion: 'Stuttgarter Giant'
Parsnips: 'Avonresister'
Peas: 'Hurst Greenshaft; 'Oregon Sugar Pod'
Radishes: 'French Breakfast'
Red chicory: 'Palla Rossa'
Rhubarb: 'Timperley Early'
Runner beans: 'Polestar'
Shallots: 'Longkeeping Yellow'
Spinach: 'Sigmaleaf'
Swiss chard: 'Ruby Chard'

Favourite tender vegetables

Aubergines: 'Black Prince'
Courgettes: 'Ambassador'
Potatoes: 'Maris Bard'; 'Cara'; 'Pink Fir Apple'

Sweet corn: 'Earliking'
Sweet pepper: 'Canape'
Tomatoes: 'Gardener's Delight'; 'Totem'

Herbs

Herbs have a very special place in the hearts of gardeners, because they are, for many, an excellent introduction to gardening. Unlike the rest of horticulture, which depends on a subjective aesthetic about which people hold conflicting views of astonishing intensity, it is impossible to find anyone who does not think herbs a Good Thing. They have memorable English names and are very easy to grow, especially the well-known ones. Most will thrive in any ordinary soil, and their ease of cultivation is gratifying and encouraging. They can be grown in large pots or tubs, or on window sills if you are short of space. You do not even have to propagate them unless you want to; friends are always willing to spare a few runners of mint, or a pot of parsley, and herbs are always a staple of summer plant stalls.

Many herbs are pretty, in an unostentatious way, and can all be grown together to achieve an amiable, if unexciting, effect. Some, however, can also make a valuable contribution to the flower border; there are good forms of some of the drabber species, and these, such as the widely available coloured-leaved kinds of sage and thyme, make good garden subjects.

The majority of herbs come from countries with hotter summers than our own, and so will do best in a hot, sunny, and sheltered spot, in quick-draining, even poor, soil. The exception are the mints. These, including our own native spearmint, are waterside plants and appreciate something moister. Chervil, too, prefers moist roots, and will die if allowed to dry out.

Herbs are herbs because they contain volatile oils which give them culinary, medicinal or cosmetic uses. Which herbs you grow will depend on your particular interests and, to some extent, on your origins. However, if you are very pressed for time and space, I suggest growing only those culinary herbs that are best consumed fresh: sweet basil, parsley, chervil, chives, mint, coriander and dill. These can also be frozen for winter use. Herbs such as thyme, tarragon and sweet marjoram (oregano) are all perfectly acceptable dried, and can be acquired cheaply and easily in that form.

The only thing to remember is that most annual herbs lose flavour in their leaves if their energies are allowed to run to flowering, so it is worth removing the flowers as they appear.

Most of the annual and biennial herbs such as sweet basil, parsley, chervil, dill and summer savory will need to be sown afresh each year, or new young plants acquired. Borage and pot marigold (grown for its dried petals but best avoided) will do the job only too well on their own, and in the process effectively debar themselves from tidy gardens.

Two stalwarts of the herb garden, chives and dill. Chives are a perennial relation of the onion, while dill is a hardy annual.

The annual herb that requires more care than the others, and is probably the most worthwhile, is sweet basil (*Ocimum basilicum*). It is a half-hardy annual which needs to be sown inside in the warm in peat pots in mid-spring, so that it can be simply dropped into the ground once the frosts are over in early summer. It is *completely* tender, so if you want it in the winter (and it loses flavour if dried) then either freeze the leaves or dig up a plant in the autumn and grow it through the winter on the kitchen window-sill. You will achieve a bushier plant, and retain the flavour of the leaves, if you pinch out the flowers. There is also a rather natty purple-leaved form available.

Parsley (*Petroselinum crispum*) is probably the most useful herb of all, and the flat-leaved variety (*P. crispum* 'Neapolitanum') undoubtedly has the better flavour. There are many old wives' tales about this herb, probably because it is a shocker to germinate – unless you know its secret. The old advice about pouring boiling water along the drill after sowing is substantially true, but the same result may be more easily obtained by soaking the seed overnight in water, as you would some sweet peas. This softens the seed coat, allowing water to be more easily taken up and germination to begin. Parsley should be sown 2.5cm (1in) deep in spring; germination takes at least five weeks. Alternatively, sow the parsley in trays inside, and plant outside in late spring. Parsley seedlings will not always succeed if they are just dibbled in anywhere; you may need to dig in some well-rotted manure, and even lime an acid soil. Avoid transplanting parsley once established; it has a taproot which will resent disturbance. Parsley will survive the winter but benefits from a cloche in really bad weather. It is resolutely biennial and will run to seed in its second year, so, once the winter is over, pull the old clumps up and start again.

Chervil (*Anthriscus cerefolium*) is another hardy biennial which, like parsley, may need a cloche in a bad winter. General cultivation outside consists of sowing twice a year, in mid-spring and late summer (for winter use), in rows 30cm (12in) apart, and the plants thinned to 30cm (12in) apart. It is very quick-growing, requiring only two months to attain a useful size. Chervil will quickly die from lack of moisture in hot weather, so water it freely and plant it in a damp spot if possible.

Dill (*Anethum graveolens*) is an underrated herb, although it is easy to cultivate. It dislikes being transplanted, so sow it in rows in a sunny place, thinning the plants to 30cm (12in) apart, and water in dry weather.

Coriander (*Coriandrum sativum*) is a hardy annual, grown for its leaves and seeds. It can be sown either in autumn or early spring.

Another uncommon but useful annual herb is summer savory (*Satureja hortensis*). It should be sown shallowly in spring and thinned to 15cm (6in) apart. It grows to about 30cm (12in) high, and a bush can look quite decorative in the flower border. The leaves should be gathered before the flowers come and, if the flower shoots are cut back, more leaves will appear.

Borage is like one of those naughty but bright-eyed little boys for whom one has more time than for their duller but better-behaved contemporaries. *Borago officinalis* is a confounded nuisance, seeding as freely as the pot marigold but with a flower that has ten times the charm. Once sown, you will never be without it, if you garden on a light soil, at least, and provided you allow the plant to produce its azure-blue flowers. However, the distinctive seedlings can be hoed off easily enough if they turn up in the wrong place. Sow it any time from spring until early autumn.

Now for the perennials. The sweet bay (*Laurus nobilis*) originates from the Mediterranean region, and is not absolutely hardy. In mild and coastal districts it will make a sizeable plant, up to 6m (20ft) or more, but in most gardens it is grown in a tub, and this restricts its growth. It clips well into shapes, and a clipped bay can look lovely. The Dutch have always made a speciality of producing standard and even corkscrew-stemmed bay trees. The bay will vie with your other half-hardy plants for the privilege of a warm corner.

Thyme (*Thymus vulgaris*) is the classic thrifty man's plant, useful both as a culinary herb and as an evergreen in the rock garden. There are many different thymes, some hardier than others, all with a non-invasive creeping habit. Particularly ornamental is the golden thyme (*Thymus vulgaris aureus*), and the lemon-scented thyme (*T. × citriodorus*), of which there are silver- and gold-leaved forms. Another bonus of thyme is that it grows best in poor soil but, since it dislikes cold, wet conditions, it is wise to take cuttings in early summer and put them in a cold frame in case of disaster. They

This herb bed contains several useful but ornamental herbs, such as the yellow-leaved balm, Melissa officinalis *'Aurea', and French lavender,* Lavandula stoechas*, the best lavender for a small garden.*

will root easily. You can also divide and replant thymes every few years. If they have become woody, layer them in spring or autumn. Thyme is resistant to pests, but is attractive to bees.

Chives (*Allium schoenoprasum*) must be the easiest plants in the whole world. They will grow anywhere, inside or out, without care or attention. Even the instruction to divide them

every four years is just to keep you on your toes and hardly necessary. Chives are members of the onion family, and like them enjoy a sunny place and regular watering. Beg a few bulbs from a neighbour in autumn or spring, and plant them in little clumps about 23 cm (9 in) apart and let them be. Discourage them from flowering by cutting off the budding heads unless you wish to grow them in the border, in which case you will still be able to harvest enough leaves while the bees buzz round the pinky-mauve flowers. Chives die right down in the winter, but a cloche will prolong the season. The leaves are best frozen for winter use, or a few bulbs dug up and planted in a pot and brought into the kitchen.

There are two types of fennel: the ordinary *Foeniculum vulgare*, grown for its ferny leaves which smell of aniseed, and used in fish dishes, and the Florence fennel (*Foeniculum vulgare*

Herbs look decorative in their own right, if care is taken with their placing. Here the tall airy fennel contrasts with sturdier rosemary, sage and bay.

dulce) which has stems that swell and can be cooked or eaten raw in salads.

Ordinary fennel grows very tall, at least 1.5 m (5 ft) and often more, so it can be a problem to know where to put it, though the bronzy-leaved variety is now fashionable as a border foliage plant, and can also be used for cooking. When flowering, fennel looks like a giant dill plant that has spontaneously multiplied its chromosomes and is on its way to take over the world.

Fennel self-seeds with abandon, so cut off the flowers if you want to control it. Sow the seed early in spring if you do want it to seed, or later in the spring if you do not (when it will have less time to flower and seed before the end of the summer).

There are three sorts of culinary marjoram (or oregano). *Origanum majorana*, the sweet marjoram, has to be treated as a tender annual in cooler climates, which hardly makes it worth growing when you could grow the hardy perennial common marjoram (*Origanum vulgare*) or the perennial pot marjoram (*Origanum onites*) which, for convenience, can be brought indoors as rooted cuttings in the autumn. There is a yellow version of the common marjoram, 'Aureum', which is quite pretty and can be used in your 'yellow border'. Marjoram leaves are best gathered and dried before the plants flower in late summer.

What of the mints? We must have them but they are a confounded nuisance. They like a shady place in deep, rich, moist soil. The remedy for their roots, which out-creep even Uriah Heep, is to sink bottomless buckets in the soil, or surround them with slate tiles set vertically, so that the roots are confined. You will need to top-dress the soil each year because those roots take a great deal of the nutriment out of the soil. The commonest mint is spearmint (*Mentha spicata*) but I grow *M. × villosa alopecuroides* Bowles' Mint, which is a cross between the round-leaved apple mint and *M. longifolia*, and has a very good flavour.

A herb that can find a place in any border is rosemary (*Rosmarinus officinalis*). There are several ornamental varieties such as 'Miss Jessop's Upright' and 'Severn Sea'. Sooner or later a bad winter will see them off, so be prepared. The easiest way to propagate rosemary is to take 15-23cm (6-9in) cuttings of shoots with heels (see page 91), in early autumn or spring, and plant them straight in the ground where you want them to grow. If you are doubtful about this, put them in a cold frame.

Sage (*Salvia officinalis*) is indispensable, and there are (at least) three coloured-leaved forms which may be useful if you wish to grow your herbs in the flower border. You can take the odd leaf to the pot without the shrub's appearance being in any way affected. Sage, like other salvias, is not guaranteed hardy in a harsh winter. It also grows leggy in time. Grow it in poor soil in full sun, and take cuttings in early autumn, so that old plants can be replaced.

French tarragon (*Artemisia dracunculus*) is useful when cooking fish or chicken, but it is not hardy, and should be planted somewhere warm and free-draining. It will benefit from winter protection in the form of peat, peat-substitute or straw; or you can grow it in a pot and bring it indoors in the winter. Like many other herbs, it needs to have the flowers removed if the leaves are to keep their full flavour, and these leaves can be frozen for winter use. The hardier Russian tarragon (*A. dracunculoides*) is an imposter, with very little flavour in its coarser leaves.

Let no one persuade you that horseradish (*Armoracia rusticana*) is a fit occupant of the vegetable or herb garden. It is ugly in leaf, harbours whitefly, and is impossible to eradicate save by the rigorous use of systemic weed-killers. You may see it suggested that you lift all roots in autumn, store them through the winter and replant selected roots in the spring; but how is such a thing possible? Your own horseradish sauce will be delicious, but is it worth it?

A golden-leaved thyme is decorative enough to earn itself a place in a handsome container. The background is composed of wormwood (Artemisia).

Fruit

It may seem like sacrilege to say so, but not all kinds of fruit are worth growing. If we had nothing else to do, and infinite space, our freezers would, of course, be full of white currants and our larders stocked with home-made sweet cherry jam. However, as this book is not written for full-time gardeners, any grand ideas are best abandoned. Apart from the ground required, a large and efficient fruit cage is a prerequisite, not to mention time to feed, prune, spray, pollinate, pick, store and freeze. Of all aggregated horticultural activities, fruit-growing requires the most time, the most experience, and the most patience. I do not wish to be brutal, but I have been through the outdoor peach stage myself, and have discovered that the work is hard and the rewards limited.

Without a properly constructed fruit cage, I do not give much for the chances of most soft fruit, with the exception of autumn raspberries (which for some reason the birds leave alone, perhaps because of the *embarras de richesses* in berries and insects in early autumn), blackberries, loganberries, tayberries and wineberries. Despite the bullfinches and sparrows eating the buds in winter, gooseberries rarely if ever fail

completely, except in particularly virulent American gooseberry mildew years. Birds usually leave sufficient blackcurrants to harvest, but red- and white currants are non-starters without protection, and cherries suffer badly from bird-damage in winter. Peaches and nectarines almost invariably get the serious disease peach leaf curl, unless you are on the ball with your sprayer twice a year, or can protect them from the wet in winter, and apricots and almonds are hardly better. A regular spraying programme is also important for restricted forms of apples and pears (which anyway require sophisticated and regular pruning and training), but plums, bullaces and damsons survive reasonably well if left alone, and most are self-fertile, which is more than can be said for pears. Medlars and quinces are troublefree.

I have referred here only to those tree and bush fruits that may be grown without much equipment and with a reasonable chance of success. As you become more experienced, you will no doubt wish to grow a wider range of fruits. My advice is to buy or construct a fruit cage (which will be useful for protecting brassicas against pigeons as well), and a specialized book which will take you through the intricacies of pruning particular fruits.

Everybody feels the need to grow apples. Provided that you spray with a tar oil winter wash, you will usually get quite enough apples to satisfy the understandable desire for your own produce; fortunately, the summer spraying programme can be abandoned completely. I have set out below the minimalist's approach.

Apples do not have the sense to be properly self-fertile, which means you will have to grow at least two trees (preferably different cultivars) in close proximity. I suggest growing them on M26 rootstock, which will give you bush trees

Quinces are underrated fruit trees for they are trouble-free and the fruits make an excellent preserve. This variety is 'Vranja'.

of 2.5-3.7m (8-12ft) and be bearing in four years. M26 grows happily on most soils. If you do want a larger tree, ask for one on an MM106 rootstock, which will grow 3.7-5.5m (12-18ft).

Plant with a short stake as you would any small tree, in the dormant season if it is bare-rooted, and try to get hold of a 'feathered maiden' which, despite its name, is not a member of the *corps de ballet* in *Swan Lake* but a two-year-old tree which has laterals (side shoots). To form a bush tree, which will be easy to pick and prune, cut back the main stem to the first good lateral at about 75cm (2½ft) from the ground, after planting.

In later years, how you prune will depend on whether the tree is 'spur-bearing', 'tip-bearing', or 'partially tip bearing'. Most trees, in fact are

Mercifully, the apple tree in the foreground requires no protection from birds, but the raspberries and currant bushes are another matter, hence the attractive home-made fruit cage.

spur-bearing, but a few (most notably 'Bramley's Seedling') bear at the end of the shoots, and 'Discovery', to be awkward, does both. As you know, you should prune lightly if you have a vigorous plant and heavily if it is a weakling, so if the tree, once established, is cropping well, do not prune too hard or you will get leaf buds at the expense of fruit ones. In general terms, in the dormant season cut the leading shoots back by a quarter to a third (they will grow little fruit spurs on the truncated shoots), and the lateral shoots, made in the

previous summer, to about four buds from the place where they originate from the main stem. You can easily tell a fruit bud from a leaf bud: the first is short and fat and the second thin and pointed. If you have a tree like 'Discovery', cut back the long shoots but leave the short shoots alone as they will probably have a fruit bud on the end. Real tip-bearers need little pruning of new wood except to cut back their most vigorous side shoots. Perhaps the lack of attention demanded by 'Bramley's Seedling' is partly the reason why it is such a stalwart of old orchards? Cuts in the wood should be made just above an outward- or upward-facing bud, wherever, in fact, you wish the new branch to point.

All apple trees, especially those that have been neglected for many years, will need their very old and dead wood cut out, particularly that which is cankered. Cankering (which causes lesions in the bark) will kill the whole branch if it has the chance to grow all round it. So cut back any wood to a point past the canker, until it looks clean (that is, not brown) inside. Old trees usually have a lot of wood growing into the middle, and this should be removed to the main branches so that the tree looks more open; branches that cross should also be cut off. An old neglected tree will usually benefit from a mulch of organic matter after pruning, and the removal of the weeds from around the base.

Apples are attacked by sawflies, codling moth, aphids and winter moths. A tar oil winter wash should keep most insect pests under reasonable control, but it is not a treatment that appeals much, for it kills all green growth it touches, and it can also kill beneficial insects. The grass under the trees will also need to be covered with polythene sheeting before you start spraying. Birds are dealt with by netting; wasps by hanging a jam jar of sugar solution nearby. Mildews, scabs and rots are also problems (see page 182-3).

So-called 'step-over' apples are used as a permeable barrier dividing one part of a garden from another. These apples are simple one-tier espaliers, which require only one length of wire to support them.

In some years, the crop of fruits looks to be so heavy that you fear for the intact survival of the branches. Trees naturally drop some fruitlets in early summer, in what is called the June Drop, but if, after that, the crop still looks enormous, pull out a couple of little fruits from the centre of each of the clusters that you can reach. The branches of some fruit trees will need to be propped up with stout stakes in good fruiting years.

There is surely no other spring blossom as pretty as apple blossom. Is it too prosaic to mention that this is the time to put up pheromone traps to catch codling moths and reduce the number of caterpillars?

The apple is ready to be picked when a gentle twist with the hand will bring it away. Apples are notorious for rotting in store (especially if not sprayed against brown rot), so wrap them up individually (the Sunday magazine supplements are the best for this because their moisture content is low), or beg a cardboard box with compartments for fruit, from the greengrocer. No apple should be in contact with any other; not only is there danger of rot spreading, but they ripen too fast if in intimate contact with each other.

The heavy, regular cropper 'Sunset' has an excellent Cox-type taste, but does well in places where 'Cox's Orange Pippin' struggles.

The taste of the distinctive medlar fruits, even when they have rotted, is very sharp and they are best in preserves. Note the lovely autumn colour.

If you wish to grow pears, buy those on Quince A or Quince C rootstocks, the latter being more dwarfing but needing a more fertile soil. Pears must have compatible pollinators, which you will also have to plant, because your neighbours are more likely to have apple trees than pear trees in their gardens. The two most commonly grown pears, because they will cross-pollinate, as they flower at about the same time, are 'William's Bon Chrétien' and 'Conference'. Pears tend to be spur-bearers, so cut the leaders back by about half, and the laterals to four buds in winter. If you remember that basic advice for both apples and pears you will not go too far wrong. 'William's Bon Chrétien', which is an early pear, will need to be picked off the tree before it is truly ripe; 'Conference', on the other hand, can be left until it comes away easily when pulled.

Like apples, pears are beset by brown rot,

scab, birds, aphids, winter moths, caterpillars and wasps (see pages 181-3).

Pears thrive in warm districts, and so do quinces, which are a joy because they require little pruning when grown in the open, and are self-fertile. The fruits have to be gathered in early autumn, because they are a little frost-tender, and stored in a cellar where they will go on ripening for some time.

'Maids are like medlars,
Rotten before they are ripe'

I am not sure that I care for Shakespeare's imputation (though no one who could create Lady Macbeth or Queen Gertrude can have had a high opinion of women), but this is a good way of remembering that the fruits of medlars have to be stored from late autumn for some weeks before they are soft and ripe enough to make into jelly or to eat. The technical term for this is 'bletting'. The Nottingham medlar, which is the tree most usually grown, likes an open sunny place, and rich soil, annually mulched, but it will survive, I have found, in a little shade. Medlars need their laterals cut back in the winter to two buds until they are well-established. They usually also require some staking, as they are inclined to lean and not make a good tree otherwise. The beauty of the medlar is that, apart from the unusual flowers and fruits, the leaves turn a warm russet in the autumn.

Plums, gages, damsons and bullaces are closely related, and are treated similarly. Damsons grow particularly well in the wet west, and gages in warm southern gardens.

The plum needs virtually no pruning once grown up. As a newly planted feathered maiden, it should have its central stem cut back to just above the first lateral, and the laterals cut back by two thirds. Once established, the danger of the silver leaf fungus getting a hold through the wound is so great that it should only be pruned in the spring (certainly no later than late summer, and never in winter) to remove a few dead and very weak growths. Plums become rather scruffy as they grow older but, as that does not affect the fruiting much, they are best left alone. If a heavy crop is in the offing, however, you will have to thin the fruits out (where you can reach them), because the branches break very easily, allowing the ingress of the silver leaf fungus. It is a painful thing to have to do when one so rarely gets two good plum years in succession.

Of the soft fruit, blackcurrants are such reliable croppers and so rarely suffer seriously the depredations of birds, that they are rewarding to grow. They are self-fertile, and fruit on wood that was made the previous year. Blackcurrants are not grown on a leg as you would gooseberries, and it is good practice to plant the new plant slightly lower than it was grown in the nursery, cutting back all shoots almost to ground level, when more will come up from below. Established bushes require their older wood (that which is very dark brown in colour) to be cut out each autumn, to allow the newer, lighter brown growths to flourish. Most old currant bushes have a pest called 'big bud mite' living in the buds. This is easy to see, as the name of the mite suggests; the affected growths should be removed because, not only will the bush fail to prosper, but the mite spreads a virus disease called 'reversion', which alters the size and shape of the leaves, undermining the plant's health and fruitfulness. Blackcurrants like a fertile soil, not too acid, and benefit from a general fertilizer and organic mulch in spring. The ground should be kept clean of weeds, but as they are shallow-rooting, nothing too vigorous in the way of digging over need be contemplated.

Gooseberries are also shallow-rooting and like the same sort of conditions as blackcurrants.

'Victoria' is probably the best-loved of all dessert plums. Helpfully self-compatible, it ripens in very late summer and is a heavy cropper.

I find they are best pruned in early spring because birds will strip them of many buds in a hard winter, so that they will need to be cut back to a live bud to encourage good growth and to improve their appearance. When first planted, gooseberries require their leaders to be shortened by a half, and the low shoots removed, leaving a clear stem for 45cm (18in) or so. This is because gooseberries naturally

pH of the soil, and other variables. It is also, after the strawberry, the blackbird's favourite food. I grow the autumn raspberry, which has not quite got the flavour of the best summer raspberry but is less affected by bird damage, and ripens in early autumn when it is harder to find raspberries in the shops. The autumn raspberry is, in fact, not a late raspberry but a very early one; the growths are pruned back almost

Blackcurrants are self-fertile, benefiting from a fertile soil and annual mulching with manure. 'Ben Sarek' is an excellent large-fruited, late-ripening variety. It is wise to net the fruits against birds.

Gooseberries are rewarding fruit, apart from the unpleasantness of removing them from thorny bushes. 'Whinham's Industry' is a delicious heavy cropper which can be eaten uncooked when ripe.

droop, and will otherwise trail their fruits on the ground. In order to avoid bad scratches while picking, the branches need to be kept from growing into the centre of the bush; for the same reason, any crossing branches or those too close together should be pruned out. Each spring, the laterals should be cut back to about 8cm (3in). Spray against American gooseberry mildew about every fortnight from just before they flower in late spring until about two weeks before picking the fruits. If caterpillars are shredding the leaves, spray with derris or some other non-persistent insecticide (see page 179).

The raspberry, although delicious, is a pernickety fruit, whose cultivation depends on the

to ground level in late winter in order that the new shoots which are stimulated to grow up will flower that same summer and fruit as early as very late summer. They need the same cultivation as for ordinary raspberries (that is, a deep, well-drained, not too alkaline soil, to which organic material has been added before planting, and a spring mulch), and, in addition, a sunny, sheltered place where they can ripen well. However, they will only need a couple of parallel wires, stretched between two posts, because the canes never grow very tall. They do, however, sucker like mad, away from the straight row you have planted, and these growths should be pulled up when they appear.

The other soft fruits worth cultivating are the thornless blackberry, the Japanese wineberry, and hybrid berries such as the loganberry and the tayberry. The loganberry is not only delicious but is less vigorous than the cultivated blackberry, whose taste many people feel is inferior to the hedgerow blackberry. (Can it be the particular mix of petrol fumes and dust that makes the latter's taste unique?) You will need to grow these berries on parallel wires, 30cm (12in) or so apart; the easiest method for the inexperienced is the fan shape. Plant the plants 2.5m (8ft) apart, 3.7m (12ft) apart in the case of the blackberry, and tie in the canes. After they have fruited in the autumn, cut out all old canes, and tie the new ones onto the wires in a fan shape. If you are too mean to buy one of these plants, you can persuade a friend how very easy it is to tip-layer their plant in summer. They should simply pull down a non-fruiting cane, and secure it to the ground with a stone or peg (I find old wooden clothes pegs work quite well); it will soon make roots and can then be detached and transplanted.

The Japanese wineberry may be hard to find, but it is so pretty, with red stems in the winter as well as glistening red and orange berries in late summer, that it should be sought out. The flavour is not overpowering, but pleasant. It can be trained on wires, like the blackberry, or grown against a wall.

'Loch Ness' is a vigorous and quite sweet-tasting blackberry, a good substitute for the hedgerow fruits, if you are in no position to search those out. It is vigorous and should be trained on wires.

Favourite fruits

Apple, culinary: 'Annie Elizabeth', 'Newton Wonder'; 'Reverend W Wilks'
Apple, dessert: 'Cox's Orange Pippin'; 'Discovery'; 'Jupiter'; 'Laxton's Superb'; 'Sunset'
Blackberry: 'Loch Ness'; 'Merton Thornless'
Blackcurrant: 'Ben Lomond'; 'Ben Sarek'
Damson: 'Merryweather'
Gooseberry: 'Invicta'; 'Whinham's Industry'
Japanese wineberry
Loganberry

Medlar: 'Nottingham'
Pear, dessert: 'Beth'; 'Conference'; 'William's Bon Chrétien'; 'Winter Nelis'
Plum, culinary: 'Czar'; 'Marjorie's Seedling'
Plum and gage, dessert: 'Coe's Golden Drop'; 'Laxton's Delight'; 'Victoria'
Quince: 'Vranja'
Raspberry: 'Malling Jewel'; 'Malling Joy'
Raspberry, autumn: 'Autumn Bliss'
Strawberry: 'Aromel'; 'Tamella'
Strawberry, alpine: 'Baron Solemacher'

13

KEEPING THE ENEMY AT BAY

I T WOULD BE MOST AGREEABLE TO PRETEND THAT GAR-
DENING WAS SIMPLY ABOUT MAKING A BEAUTIFUL
GARDEN, BY PLANTING AND MAINTAINING A VARIETY OF
LOVELY PLANTS IN COLOURFUL HARMONY WITH EACH
OTHER. IT IS ALL THIS, OF COURSE, BUT THERE IS AN-
OTHER FACET TO IT WHICH CANNOT BE IGNORED. THIS IS
THE NECESSITY TO KEEP WITHIN TOLERABLE BOUNDS ALL
THOSE ENEMIES OF GOOD PLANT GROWTH AND HEALTH.
THESE ENEMIES TAKE MANY AND VARIOUS FORMS, BUT CAN
BE CORRALLED INTO THE FOLLOWING BROAD CATEGORIES:
PESTS, DISEASES, PHYSIOLOGICAL DISORDERS AND WEEDS.

Daisies may be considered a weed in lawns, but look how
attractive they can be, especially in an informal situation where
there is a generous, attractive planting of blue and white
Viola cornuta *and* Geranium x magnificum *nearby.*

Pests, diseases & physiological disorders

If you are an absolute beginner, you will be in a state of blissful ignorance, a state of nature like Adam and Eve before the Fall. You will know only that there are flowers, vegetables and fruit that you would like to grow. You may, it is true, know about potato blight, but only tangentially from your study of Irish history, and will, therefore, be more interested in the social implications than in the disease's life-cycle. You may know about the relationship between greenfly and ladybirds, know that blackspot is less likely in cities, and that broad beans get blackfly if you do not pinch out the tops. You will, however, lucky thing, be innocently unaware of fruit tree red spider mite, will never have encountered cherry slugworm or tortrix moth, and may even think that damping-off is a way of cleaning clothes.

You will not retain your innocence for long, unfortunately, and will soon be worrying about a whole range of pests and diseases that might

'Companion planting' can be helpful as an alternative to chemical spraying, and certainly looks prettier. Open flowers like these Helichrysum *attract insects such as hoverflies which feed on aphids.*

beset your plants in the garden. Your anxiety will be fuelled by gardening books, especially by the arcane books that specialize on the subject. Such books can often mislead because of their even, unemphatic tone; occasionally an author will describe a pest as serious and widespread or, on the other hand, trivial and uncommon, but on the whole no judgement is made, leaving you worrying as much about strawberry rhynchites, which is rare, as about chrysanthemum leaf miner, which is common.

To read of all these ills is to wonder how anything has a chance to grow at all, but of course there is a fierce balancing battle being waged out there in the garden, and one that does not always result in a victory for pests. It has been estimated that a single blackfly, if left in peace to multiply, will produce 2,000,000,000,000,000 offspring in the course of three months in the summer. If that were the case, we would be wading knee-deep in them every time we went outside. But that is to reckon without the good offices of lacewing, hoverfly, wasp and ladybird.

The matter is complicated because it is not always clear who is on the side of the angels. The wasp, for example, is, from a purely anthropomorphic point of view, a great nuisance to us around fruit trees in late summer. The wasp only gets in our way, however, after the nest is broken up and the workers are no longer preoccupied with feeding the young with a wide variety of (to us) undesirable garden caterpillars and aphids.

In a way, we worry far too much about all the thousand natural ills that the garden is heir to. To know about them is to wish to do something about them, and this is the greatest mistake.

I intend, therefore, to point out clearly which pests, diseases and physiological disorders are ubiquitous, or, at least, common, and to ignore all those that are only very rarely encountered (see pages 181-3). Admittedly, it is not always easy to see where to draw the line, and a good example to illustrate what I mean is the case of clubroot in brassicas. This is a most disabling disease of the cabbage family, so bad in some places that it hardly makes their growing worthwhile, and yet, though I grow brassicas, I have never had clubroot in my garden. The simple reason is that I garden on an alkaline soil and the fungus thrives only on soils with a pH lower than 7. No vegetable gardener with any pretensions to the name who cultivates an acid soil would refrain from liming the soil to prevent, or limit, the spread of this disease, and yet I, and millions of people like me, do not need to know that such a disease exists.

Tolerance is a virtue, and cultivating it is as helpful for the making of a pleasant garden as manuring one's soil; nevertheless, it often depends less on scientific reasoning than emotional irrationality. For example, I do not mind the frog-hopper on rose bushes, and so ignore

the cuckoo-spit which has the frog-hopper inside; but I am driven almost demented by the rose leaf-rolling sawfly, and will go round picking off the disfigured leaves, even though they may have no larvae left inside.

I can put up with a collection of fruit tree pests, which the commercial grower must combat, because, in most years, I harvest a sufficient crop notwithstanding. We are marvellously po-faced about not spraying against, say, leek white tip, either because we do not have it, or it is hardly bothersome, but let those greenfly sap the energy of our favourite roses and we are out with the sprayer once a week, and the devil take the hindmost. We may pretend we can co-exist with plum sawfly, while secretly knowing that what will make the real difference to the crop is not a debilitating insect but a devastating late spring frost.

Weeds

Weeds have a peculiar fascination for us. They are endlessly interesting, like an enemy who occupies our thoughts and schemes so much more than any friend and who (though we would never admit it) we should miss if he suddenly moved away. I know the weeds in my garden better than most of my flowers and, without them, my victories would be insipid affairs. Weeds provide the challenge that most gardeners require. They may sometimes appear to us as ineradicable as sin, but we would be sorry to have to admit that, like sin, we were not conscious of a strong urge to overcome them.

How well we know weeds. Even in childhood, some hard-pressed grown-up, jealous of our idleness on summer days, will send us out to weed the paving with a broken kitchen knife. Throughout our lives they are a recurring theme, and in old age their rankness mocks our failing powers. Even the wild-flower gardener has little time for weeds, and tries to pretend that wild flowers are pretty and timid, like ragged

robin and cowslip, not strapping and aggressive, like creeping buttercup or ground elder.

No gardener can avoid weeding. It is best to learn to enjoy it, for it is a constant which will never go away, unless the scientists invent the infallible, toxic only to weeds, selective weed-killer. Most people grow to savour the way they have to slow down their pace to weed, and the freedom it gives for untrammelled reflection. All that is only possible, however, if we feel we are ultimately getting somewhere, rather than desperately fighting against stacked odds.

Fortunately, there are ways of making weeding more enjoyable. I allot myself a small area, smaller than I am likely to have the energy for, and stake it out in my mind's eye. I have learned not to go out imagining that, if the weather holds, I shall have the whole garden 'done' by teatime. I choose, if I can, that part of the garden in the sun, especially in the late winter when I need to feel the warmth of it on my back. I take out a trug basket and a 'donkey', the one for perennial and flowering or seeding annual weeds, the other for leafy annual weeds. Putting perennial weeds on a compost heap is like sowing tares deliberately amongst wheat; the heat of the compost heap will never kill those roots, so they must be burned on the fire-heap or in the incinerator. I get pleasure from such perfectionism, although I have been known, in a fit of absent-mindedness, to throw the string, secateurs, knife, and all the other contents of the trug onto the fireheap as well. A bucket will do equally as well as a trug.

That is all very well, but how do you tell a perennial weed from an annual weed? After all, are there not two sorts of nettle, annual and perennial? Broadly speaking, you can tell from the roots, until you learn to know your weeds as well as your own children. Annual weeds have no well-developed root systems, whereas the perennial nightmares, like ground elder, couch grass, creeping buttercup, bindweed and nettle, have good roots because they must survive through a succession of winters. Nettle roots are thin, stringy, yellow, and tear quite easily; those of ground elder are thick, fleshy, off-white and hairy, and they lie not far below the surface so can be got at by digging; those of bindweed are grey-white and tubular, grow both along and down towards the earth's core, and snap with distressing ease; couch grass has white 'stolons' with pointed tips; the perennial sowthistle grows enormously fast, plump and juicy. If the earth is mercifully damp after some soft refreshing rain, the sowthistle (like the dandelion) can be drawn up easily, cleanly, and without the dreaded snap that leaves you with sap on your hands, and half a rosette of leaves. All these perennials seed, and they must be prohibited from doing so, as any of their roots can reproduce a new plant (although, if regularly hoed or picked off, they will eventually weaken to the point when they die out).

The annual weeds are legion, but we feel we do not properly have to bother much with them till they start to flower. This may be short-sighted; the cabbage aphid, for example, will live on shepherd's purse. I use a hand-fork and kneelers for removing annual weeds, and sometimes, in idleness, a border fork if I do not feel like bending. I always take away the weeds that I have removed; this is partly because I know that, in moist weather, weeds may root again, and partly because I desire that satisfaction which results from the presence of clean brown earth. I have given up the hoe, except in the vegetable garden where seeds are sown in straight rows, for I consider it now a thoroughly offensive weapon. I have too often hoed off precious self-sown seedlings on the first fine spring day.

I cannot overstate the importance of being able to identify the common weeds. If you have not been brought up to garden, and have not absorbed, their names and the look of them by a kind of horticultural osmosis, then ask a friendly gardener to take you round her garden, and point out to you speedwell, annual and perennial nettle, bindweed and creeping buttercup. (However keen a gardener, she will be able to find some for you!) It is a great disappointment for any new gardener to find that she has nurtured some plant through the spring, and scrupulously avoided hoeing it off, only to find it turn overnight into a rampaging weed which flowers and seeds all over the garden.

Dandelions and speedwell look so attractive, that it seems harsh to eradicate them. This is no time for a soft heart, though, or there will soon be nothing else.

Using controls & chemicals

Many people do not like the idea of using chemicals at all. They would rather be vigilant about manually removing pests, diseased plants or weeds, keeping fungal diseases at bay by scrupulous attention to garden hygiene and developing a tolerant 'live-and-let-live' attitude.

By encouraging the natural enemies of pests, usually parasites, predators or diseases, they hope to establish a rough equilibrium in the garden. So-called biological controls are highly satisfactory because no chemicals are involved and the predators are specific and harm nothing else, but to use them correctly and efficiently requires a certain knowledge and thought about the pest's life cycle and environment. This form of control is now so well established that it is possible to buy or mail-order predators or parasites for several greenhouse pests, as well as controls for outdoor menaces such as vine weevil and slugs. There is a bacterium available to control cabbage caterpillars. There are also traps impregnated with synthetic sexual attractants, for use against codling moths on apples. Biological control is undoubtedly the way that gardeners would like to go in the future.

Certain chemicals are acceptable to 'organic' gardeners; these are usually non-persistent and harmless to mammals, such as insecticidal soap. It is worth remembering, however, that as an amateur gardener, no chemical is available to you which is very toxic to mammals or very persistant so you need not feel too badly about a less purist approach. Chemicals come as concentrates which have to be diluted, as granules, as dusts, and as aerosol sprays.

If you are to spray effectively, the list of chemicals must be small. There are two basic types: contact pesticides, fungicides and herbicides are those that kill pests, diseases and weeds that come in contact with the spray, while systemic ('translocated', in the jargon) ones are absorbed by the plant and go through the system. Systemic pesticides are useful for aphids that suck sap, while systemic weedkillers kill perennial weeds because they travel throughout the plant, killing even the roots.

Spray against potential fungal attack, such as rose mildew, early in the season if you know it will be a problem, but there is little point in spraying against non-existent pests, if you are using a contact pesticide. Systemic pesticides can be sprayed early. You can use non-persistent insecticides based on plant derivatives such as permethrin or bioresmethrin for pest-trouble in the vegetable garden; although their potency is short-lived, you will at least feel confident about using them. The best systemic fungicides which can be used with confidence are penconazole, which is particularly good for rusts, and thiophanate-methyl; the best systemic pesticides and mite-killers are probably pirimiphos-methyl and dimethoate. A combined rose spray containing pirimicarb, bupirimate, and triforine will not harm the beneficial insects. For the vegetable garden, choose only those available that maintain on the label that you can pick the crops within seven days of application.

The invention of glyphosate has quite revolutionized gardening. This non-residual systemic weedkiller works by upsetting the weed's system so that it cannot store food and so dies of starvation. For the first time ever, we can contemplate the eradication of those weeds that turn gardening from a heaven of opportunity to a hell of disappointed expectations. The worst must be ground elder and bindweed, poking through the fence from the next door neighbour's garden, but these can be tackled by carefully painting glyphosate on the leaves. The action is slow; even in late spring, the time of speediest growth, it will be at least two weeks before the leaves blacken. However, it is, I believe, the best solution to perennial weed problems near cultivated plants, and has the beauty of being harmless, when dried, to children and animals. Glyphosate, in liquid form, can be used on derelict or neglected land where a blanket coverage is needed, and the death of the roots of perennial weeds desired. Two applications over a period of some weeks during the growing season will be necessary. Its great advantage over other total weedkillers like ammonium sulphamate is that you can plant immediately the weeds have started to die, for it leaves no residue in the soil. Of course, if you have brambles to contend with, you may have to resort to a special 'brushwood' killer.

As well as glyphosate, the busy gardener should know about weedkillers that can be used for paths, and about those that, with care, can be used amongst cultivated plants. For paths, I suggest you use the contact paraquat or the systemic glyphosate several times a season, or dichlobenil granules in spring to give a season's cover.

For use among cultivated plants there are several options, provided that you have a watering can with a small dribble bar, or a sprayer with a hood so that you can be very careful where you aim the herbicide. For couch and some other grass weeds there is alloxydim-sodium, which hurts only grasses and leaves cultivated, broad-leaved plants (and, it must be said, weeds) alone. In old, neglected rockeries, for instance, it can be very useful. It has little or no persistence, so planting can follow soon afterwards.

For broad-leaved weeds amongst cultivated plants, only paraquat or glyphosate are realistic options in the vegetable garden, and, even then, have to be very carefully applied. I personally do not use herbicides in the vegetable garden at all. I find the hoe just as easy to use and certainly less worrying.

Lawn weedkillers and mosskillers were mentioned in chapter 3. For these, use a watering can with a rose.

Above all, treat the whole business of chemicals seriously and soberly, and, where possible, avoid using them. They are, after all, a source of discontent to the average gardener; she rarely enjoys using them and often feels the need to do so more because they are there than out of an anxiety about the size and quality of her apple harvest or the purity of her lawn.

Safety with chemicals

When using chemicals, always follow the manufacturer's instructions to the letter and use your common sense as well. For example:

Never make up any more spray solution than you think you will need

Wear rubber gloves – concentrated chemicals can be toxic – and take great care not to splash yourself

Use a sprayer with a trigger, so that the flow is instantly cut off when you let go of the trigger

Use a face mask, except on exceptionally still days, because of the risk of wind-drift

Wash your hands and any exposed skin after using chemicals

Spray only in the evening, when bees are less active, because they are easily harmed by insecticides, and for that reason also avoid spraying at open flowers

Do not spray when children and pets are present, and lock up all chemicals in a shed where small, inquisitive hands cannot find them

Keep a special watering can for the purpose of weedkilling alone, preferably with WEEDKILLER painted on the side

Wash the sprayer out thoroughly after use with running water from an outside tap, and pour rinsings onto bare ground. If there is a choice, choose aerosol sprays, dusts or granules as no disposal is necessary. If you have concentrates to dispose of, treat them as 'difficult household waste' and contact your local Waste Regulation Authority for disposal

Never accept chemicals from someone else in an unmarked bottle, and never decant your own

It is not permissible to use products registered for professional use in the home garden

OUTDOOR PESTS	TARGET	DAMAGE	SERIOUSNESS	TREATMENT
Aphids (greenfly, blackfly)	Wide range of plants, especially roses, violas, broad beans, some ornamental shrubs	Suck sap, causing blistering, leaf distortion and yellowing (all aphids secrete honeydew on which black 'sooty mould' grows)	Can be serious when *en masse*, or on young plants. Also spread viruses in their saliva which weaken or kill.	Insecticidal soap. Contact insecticide, preferably one that does not kill beneficial insects like ladybirds and hoverflies. Encourage these beneficial insects. Pinch tops out of broad bean shoots after flowering.
Apple sawfly	Apples	Tunnel into fruitlets, which may drop	Not very serious compared with brown rot or scab	None really practical
Big bud mite	Blackcurrants	Suck sap causing buds to swell. Spreads 'reversion' virus	Affects yield	Remove and burn affected buds in winter.
Birds	Crocus, polyanthus, fruit, vegetable seedlings	Chew buds and/or flowers and seedling leaves	Can be a nuisance	Netting. Repellent sprays
Caterpillars	Ornamentals, brassicas, fruit bushes	Chew pieces out of leaves	Can be serious, especially on edible produce	Hand-pick. Contact insecticide
Celery leaf miner	Celery, chrysanthemums	Visible tunnels in leaves	Serious in large numbers	Burn affected leaves
Codling moth	Apples	As for apple sawfly	Can be off-putting to eat	Hang special pheromone traps in trees from late spring to mid-summer.
Deer	Trees, roses	'Bark' young trees	Yes, locally	Deer fencing, if practicable
Dogs and cats	Any part of garden	Lie on plants. Dig holes. Make messes	Can be a nuisance	Cat and dog repellents
Fly larvae (maggots)				
Cabbage root fly	Brassicas	Tunnel through roots, causing cell collapse	Serious in large numbers	Root collars to prevent eggs being laid near roots
Carrot fly	Carrots	Bronzing of foliage	Serious in large numbers	Protective polythene barriers round carrots (50cm/20in) or horticultural fleece laid over crop. Sow late
Onion fly	Onions	Yellowing of foliage	Serious in large numbers	Remove affected leaves and burn
Leaf-rolling sawfly	Roses	Roll leaves up	Trivial but unsightly	Burn affected leaves
Leatherjackets	Newly established lawns and vegetable gardens	Yellow patches on leaves. Seedlings eaten in warm wet weather	Not a major problem, except in new gardens	Cultivate soil to bring them to surface for birds. Soak lawns and cover with sheeting to bring them to surface, then remove
Mice	Bulbs, pea and bean seeds	Steal or damage seeds	Can be serious	Set traps but secure from birds. Repellents
Moles	Lawns, vegetables	Tunnel and mound	Can be a great nuisance	No really effective remedy
Outdoor whitefly	Brassicas	As for aphids	Can be serious	Contact insecticide. Insecticidal soap
Rabbits	Young trees, roses, garden pinks, other perennials	'Bark' young trees. Eat plants	Can be serious	Fencing round garden. Protective tubes for young trees
Slugs and snails	In spring, any soft green plant but especially delphiniums, hostas, lettuces, campanulas. In autumn, potatoes and carrots	Can eat whole seedlings. Chew leaves. Tunnel into potatoes	Can be very serious, especially as they can climb vertical surfaces	Protect vulnerable plants. Hand-pick. Place sugary solution in container sunk in ground. Surround plants with bark chippings, cocoa shell mulches or plastic bottles. Aluminium sulphate (organic). Parasitic eelworms. For plants in pots, put line of vaseline around pot exterior. As a final resort, use slug pellets but administer them very sparingly.
Squirrels	Fruit and nut trees, bulbs	Steal them	Can be a great nuisance in towns and cities	Netting. Humane traps

OUTDOOR PESTS	TARGET	DAMAGE	SERIOUSNESS	TREATMENT
Vine weevils: larvae	From autumn to spring: shrubs, perennials, strawberries, alpines, plants in pots	Plants wilt and collapse	Serious	Wash all compost off roots of potted plants and repot after purchase. Parasitic eelworm.
adults	From spring to autumn: as above	Eat irregular holes in leaf margins	Not so serious on mature plants	Contact insecticide at dusk. Good hygiene
Wasps	Ripening fruit	Eat pieces of fruit where birds have pecked first	Unpleasant more than serious.	Destroy nests if close to house using contact insecticide. Otherwise, jam jar of sugar solution to drown wasps

DISEASES

Canker	Apples, pears, parsnips	Sunken patches on branches of apple and pear trees which, if they encir- cle, will kill. Brown rot on shoulders of parsnip root	Can be serious in orchards	Cut back branch to healthy wood. Spray with contact fungicide after fruit picked. Lime the soil if acid. Grow resistant varieties
Clubroot	Brassicas, wallflowers	Roots swell and rot	Can be devastating but only on acid soils	Lime soil. Rotate crops in large vegetable gardens. Dip transplants in systemic fungicide dip. Don't grow brassicas in infected soil for up to 20 years!
Coral spot	Trees and shrubs, especially tenderish ones like figs and walnuts	Colonizes dead and alive wood with characteristic orange pustules, weakening plant	Not usually serious unless neglected, when it can kill	Cut out all affected wood and burn
Damping-off	Seedlings	Weakens seedlings causing them to collapse and rot	Can be devastating in trays of seedlings	Avoid sowing thickly. Water sparingly. Spray with fungicide. Good hygiene
Grey mould (*Botrytis*)	Wide range of plants e.g. strawberries, tomatoes in wet autumns. Also trees, shrubs, perennials, bulbs, flowers and other fruit	Grey mould and cell collapse	Can be serious in wet, damp conditions, but worst under glass	Good hygiene. Systemic fungicides. Grow resistant varieties
Honey fungus	Wide range of plants, especially trees and shrubs	Die-back. Deterioration. Death	Can be very serious, especially in old gardens	Good hygiene; remove all dead wood. Grow plants well. Dig up dying plant with stump and replace soil with fresh, uninfected soil
Leaf spots e.g. rose blackspot	A range of plants e.g. broad beans, roses	Unsightly spotting. In the case of roses can result in defoliation	Trivial except for rose blackspot	Systemic fungicide. Remove and burn leaves. Grow resistant varieties
Peach leaf curl	Peaches, almonds, nectarines	Red blistering and distortion of leaves, which fall prematurely	Can be serious on fruit trees	Spray with copper fungicide or contact fungicide at leaf fall and before leaf break. Keep wall plants dry in winter by hanging polythene screen in front of them.
Potato blight	Potatoes, tomatoes	Blotches on leaves, which then collapse. Tomatoes worst hit in wet summers	Can be very serious	Bordeaux mixture (organic) or contact fungicide early summer to early autumn
Powdery mildew	Wide range, especially roses, asters, apples, strawberries, brassicas, gooseberries	White powder on leaves and shoots which saps plant's vigour	Can be serious	Grow resistant varieties. Sulphur. Systemic fungicide
Rots	Variety of fruits and vegetables, especially apples and onions	Disintegration of plant tissue	Often not a serious problem, except in store	Check fruits in store; do not store them touching. Throw out affected fruit and vegetables

DISEASES	TARGET	DAMAGE	SERIOUSNESS	TREATMENT
Rusts	Hollyhocks, hypericums, antirrhinums, mints, roses, pelargoniums	Brown or orange pustules on leaves, which die	Can be seriously disfiguring and weakening	Sulphur or systemic fungicide
Scabs	Apples, pears, potatoes	Corky scars	Can be disfiguring	Pick off affected leaves. Grow resistant varieties
Silver leaf	Plums, including ornamental varieties	Silvering on upper surface of leaves. Inside wood stained brown	Can be serious	Prune out all affected wood in early summer in dry weather. If badly affected, cut down and burn
Viruses	Range of plants e.g. bulbs, vegetables, flowers	Striping of narcissus leaves. Mottling of cucumber, marrow, tomato and petunia leaves. Weak growth on many fruit bushes	Can be serious, even deadly, although many viruses are symptomless, or almost so	Burn affected plants. Buy virus-free (certified stock) fruit bushes
Wilt	Clematis, peonies, asters	Sudden wilting and collapse	Can kill	Do not plant in known affected soil. As a precaution, plant clematis 15cm (6in) deeper than usual so that there is the chance of regeneration if affected. Cut out all wilted shoots. Spray with systemic fungicide

OTHER PROBLEMS				
Chemical damage	Any plant	Can result in death if weedkillers applied to wrong plants, or chemicals to sensitive plants	Not usually serious, but can be	Take care always to read and carry out manufacturer's instructions. Don't spray on windy days. Use the right equipment
Drought	Any plant	Wilting; if to permanent wilting point, leads to death. Scorching of leaves. Premature leaf and fruit fall	Can be very serious, even lethal	Do not let plants wilt, especially those in pots. Water well without waterlogging
Irregular watering	Any plant but especially fruits and flowers	'Bolting' in flowers. Cracking and splitting in fruits and root vegetables	Not serious but irritating	Water consistently or, better still, mulch well in spring so watering is unnecessary in summer
Low temperatures	Particularly young plants	Spring frosts kill blossom and blacken and distort young leaves and plants	Can be serious, especially for fruit harvests	Plant only very hardy plants in frost pockets or cold gardens. Avoid planting tenderish plants where sun will catch them on frosty mornings
Mechanical damage	Any plant	'Barking' of trees from careless lawnmowing or strimming or too tight ties. Careless pruning with blunt tools	Can kill	Take care when using equipment
Snow	Evergreen shrubs and trees	Breaks branches	Not usually serious	Beat off snow before it freezes
Waterlogging	Roots	Death from asphyxiation	Can be serious if not quickly remedied	Drain soil adequately
Wind	Trees, shrubs and tall plants generally, especially evergreens	Can blow plants over, and scorch and desiccate	Can be devastating	Stake vulnerable trees. Protect evergreens, especially when young, with physical barriers, e.g. windbreaks.

14

FINISHING
TOUCHES

A S I DO NOT WISH TO END THIS BOOK ON A DOWN-
BEAT NOTE, I SHALL FINISH WITH A FEW SMALL
GARDENING STRATAGEMS WHICH I FIND USEFUL BUT
WHICH DO NOT REQUIRE MUCH EXPENDITURE OF TIME
AND ENERGY.

WHEN I GO OUT TO WEED I ALWAYS TAKE A RUBBER
RAKE OR BESOM WITH ME, TO SWEEP UP ANY SOIL OR
WEEDS THAT HAVE DROPPED ONTO THE LAWN. IT IS THE
WORK OF A MOMENT, BUT IT IS ONE OF THOSE LITTLE
TASKS THAT MAKE A DISPROPORTIONATELY LARGE IMPACT
ON THE APPEARANCE OF THE GARDEN AND, THEREFORE,
ON ONE'S ATTITUDE TO IT. SIMILARLY EFFECTIVE IS CUT-
TING THE LAWN EDGES AFTER MOWING. THESE LITTLE
THINGS SHOULD NEVER BE NEGLECTED ON THE GROUNDS
THAT THEY ARE SO SMALL THAT ANY TIME (EXCEPT THE
PRESENT) SEEMS THE RIGHT TIME TO DO THEM.

*This is the kind of result that you hope all your labours will bring:
a colourful, yet well-filled and orderly garden, with a strong structure and a few nice touches, like the topiary in a pot. Anyone who
has read these pages attentively will be more than equal to this.*

If you have ever walked round the garden of a keen gardener in very early summer, you will find that the owner makes little dashes to and fro while she talks, nipping off the swelling seed heads from the daffodils. This is a habit worth cultivating. It could not be less strenuous, and it undoubtedly helps the bulbs to concentrate their energies on making offsets rather than setting seed. And since a daffodil takes seven years to develop from seed to flower, but reproduces from offsets in only three, this seems like something to encourage.

It would be foolish to deny that there are some years when things do not go according to plan in the garden; rain in the spring prevents you from making a decent seed bed in the vegetable garden, and you despair of the soil ever warming up. This is not the moment to resolve to give up gardening in disgust; most hardy vegetables can be sown in pots or modules put in a cold greenhouse or light porch, and simply hardened off and planted out later. Not only will the conditions probably have improved by then, but the consistency of the soil will matter far less anyway.

Preventing windrock by trimming long shoots and treading the soil down firmly around shrubs and trees if the plant has been swaying in the wind is another of those little pottering tasks that save work and disappointment. Trees and shrubs are not the only victims; cold weather also encourages alpine primulas to heave themselves out of the ground, and they too should be secured once more. I lost a reasonably hardy (and very uncommon) abutilon one winter because I did not treat this danger seriously enough, and allowed the roots to become frozen.

I try to keep my tools clean, oiled, and, if necessary, sharpened. A scraper can be made from a small piece of metal like aluminium from a hardware shop or DIY store, and hacksawing out two rectangles so that a square piece with a straight handle is left. Using it is a pleasure. Looking after your tools is a congenial task which can be done when it has become too dark to distinguish flower from weed in the border, and demonstrably saves you time, money and irritation. And, moreover, it is a sure sign that you have become a proper gardener!

As the day draws to a close and the shadows lengthen, surely the time has come for a well-earned rest!

I mentioned in the introduction the factors you must consider that make up the time equation. There is one more. However busy and pressed you feel, always leave time for 'pottering'. Amateurs must find out for themselves, for they are unlikely to be told, that the pleasure of gardening lies as much in pottering as in anything else. This is particularly true of that evening hour in the summer, when nothing more energetic seems appropriate than encouraging a few delicate clematis tendrils up their netting, cutting roses for the house, or even seeking out and destroying the devious green caterpillar of the cabbage white butterfly. Pottering is the technique learned more quickly and painlessly

No garden is ever 'finished' – the grass is growing, even as you look, and those flowers in the foreground may soon want deadheading. But I bet the owners enjoy their daily potter round this garden.

than any other in gardening; the technique that enables you to hone your powers of observation by encouraging you to bend down and look at the stigmata on the crocuses in the spring, or examine closely the colours that a rowan tree changes to in autumn. Learning to know your plants is more agreeable and revealing than conscientiously carrying out a succession of tasks, however necessary, and a daily or weekly potter will clarify for you the point of it all.

Index

Page numbers in *italics* refer to illustrations.

Acknowledgments

AUTHOR'S ACKNOWLEDGMENTS TO THE 1987 EDITION
I should like to thank my publisher, who first suggested to me that I write this book. I should also like to express my gratitude to Toby Buchan, Valerie Finnis, Graham Rice, Bill Pridmore and Denise Simmons, who have all helped me in various ways. My thanks go also to Ian Stewart MP, Economic Secretary to the Treasury, for his most useful comments on the making of compost heaps. I am greatly indebted to Graham Stuart Thomas, who kindly and most thoroughly read the typescript and pointed out a number of howlers. Any mistakes which remain are entirely my own responsibility. Finally, I am enormously grateful to my husband, Charles Wide, for his unflagging encouragement and support, as well as his invaluable advice on the correct use of the semicolon.

AUTHOR'S ACKNOWLEDGMENTS TO THIS EDITION
I should like to thank Conran Octopus, for giving me the opportunity to revise and update this book. It has been a pleasure, not least because I could curb my youthful prolixity. I am still grateful to my husband, Charles, for his encouragement and to my children, Emily and Thomas, for showing restraint and understanding beyond their years.

PUBLISHER'S ACKNOWLEDGMENTS
The publisher would like to thank the following photographers and organizations for their kind permission to reproduce the photographs in this book.
1-6 S & O Mathews; 8 Andrew Lawson (Ashtree Cottage, Kilmington); 9 S & O Mathews; 10-11 Jerry Harpur (Designer: Christopher Masson, London); 13 Jerry Harpur (Designer: Christopher Masson, London); 14 right Jon Bouchier/The Garden Picture Library; 14 left Jon Bouchier/The Garden Picture Library; 15 Jon Bouchier/The Garden Picture Library; 16 Jacqui Hurst; 17 Clive Nichols (Coates Manor Garden, Sussex); 20 Andrew Lawson (Gothic House, Charlbury); 21 Andrew Lawson (Gothic House, Charlbury); 22-3 Andrew Lawson; 24 John Glover; 26 Brigitte Thomas; 27 S & O Mathews; 28-9 Jerry Harpur (Gunilla Pickard, Great Waltham, Essex); 31 Michael Howes/The Garden Picture Library; 34 Clive Nichols (White Windows, Hants); 35 right John Glover; 35 left John Glover; 36 left John Glover; 36 right Andrew Lawson; 38 S & O Mathews; 40-1 Andrew Lawson (Gothic House, Charlbury); 43 Stephen Robson; 46 Andrew Lawson (Ashtree Cottge, Kilmington); 47 Andrew Lawson (Ethne Clarke, Yaxham); 50-1 Jacqui Hurst; 53 Jerry Harpur (Peter Wooster & Gary Keim, Connecticut); 55 Stephen Robson/The Garden Picture Library; 56 John Glover; 59 Jacqui Hurst; 62 Andrew Lawson; 65 Brigitte Thomas; 68 Jerry Harpur (Bob Flowerdew); 70 Jacqui Hurst; 71 John Glover; 72 Jerry Pavia/The Garden Picture Library; 73 Brigitte Thomas/The Garden Picture Library; 76-7 S & O Mathews; 81 S & O Mathews; 83 S & O Mathews; 84-5 Juliette Wade (Mrs Susan Brookes, Overstroud Cottage, Bucks); 87 Zara McCalmont/The Garden Picture Library; 90 S & O Mathews; 92 Jacqui Hurst; 93 Andrew Lawson; 94 Andrew Lawson; 96-7 Brigitte Thomas; 99 Andrew Lawson (Ethne Clarke, Yaxham); 101 right Jerry Harpur; 101 left S & O Mathews; 103 Susan Whitney; 104-5 Jerry Harpur (Nick & Pam Coote, Oxford); 106 S & O Mathews; 107 Andrew Lawson (St. John's College, Oxford); 109 S & O Mathews; 110 Andrew Lawson; 111 Andrew Lawson (Docton Mill, Devon); 113 Andrew Lawson; 116-7 Juliette Wade (Hodges); 118 left Jerry Harpur (Deborah Kellaway, Waveney Rising, Norfolk); 118 right Jerry Harpur (Stellenberg, Capetown); 121 Mayer/Le Scanff/The Garden Picture Library; 122 Clive Nichols (Hadspen House Garden & Nursery, Somerset); 123 Andrew Lawson; 125 Andrew Lawson; 127 Jerry Harpur (Park Farm); 128-9 Clive Nichols (Dr & Mrs Brian Glaisher, Mill House, Kent); 130 S & O Mathews; 131 left Marcus Harpur (Design: Rupert Golby, RHS Chelsea 1995); 131 right Andrew Lawson (Hadspen Gardens, Somerset); 132 Andrew Lawson (Gothic House, Charlbury); 133 S & O Mathews; 134-5 S & O Mathews; 137 Clive Nichols (Greenhurst Garden, Sussex); 138 Clive Nichols (Little Bowden, Berkshire); 139 Clive Nichols (Crathes Castle Garden, Scotland); 140 Andrew Lawson (Stobshiel House, Humbie); 141 left S & O Mathews; 141 right S & O Mathews; 142 Jacqui Hurst; 144 Clive Nichols (Turn End Garden, Buckinghamshire); 146 Andrew Lawson; 147 Clive Nichols (Tintinhull Garden, Somerset); 148 left Clive Nichols (Denmans, Fontwell, Sussex); 148 right Marianne Majerus (Turn End, Bucks); 150 S & O Mathews; 152-3 Andrew Lawson (Mrs Coombe, Owslebury); 156-7 Jerry Harpur (Old Rectory, Sudborough); 158 Andrew Lawson; 160 right S & O Mathews; 160 left S & O Mathews; 161 Jacqui Hurst (Joy Larkin's Petit Potager); 163 Jerry Harpur (Gunilla Pickard); 164 Jerry Harpur (Julia Scott); 165 S & O Mathews; 166 Jacqui Hurst; 167 Brigitte Thomas/The Garden Picture Library; 169 Jacqui Hurst; 170 left John Glover; 170 right Marcus Harpur; 171 John Glover; 172 left Michael Howes/The Garden Picture Library; 172 right David Askam/The Garden Picture Library; 173 John Glover; 174-5 Jacqui Hurst; 176 Jerry Harpur; 178 Jacqui Hurst (Tartan House, Wilts); 184-5 Jerry Harpur (Joe Eck & Wayne Winterrowd, Vermont); 186 John Glover/The Garden Picture Library; 187 Steven Wooster/The Garden Picture Library

The publisher also thanks Jackie Matthews.
Index compiled by Indexing Specialists, Hove, East Sussex BN3 2DJ.